ARISTOTLE

Aristotle

Selections from
Nicomachean Ethics
Politics

BARNES & NOBLE BOOKS
NEW YORK

© CRW 2004
Text and Afterword copyright ©
CRW Publishing Limited 2004

M 10 9 8 7 6 5 4 3 2 1

ISBN 0 7607 6240 6

Typeset in Great Britain by Antony Gray
Printed and bound in China by Imago

Contents

POLITICS

Introduction

In the Middle Ages he was often referred to simply as 'the philosopher.' Such was the pre-eminence of Aristotle for Thomas Aquinas and later Christian thinkers that his authority could be regarded as conclusive, even in areas such as astronomy where his understanding was less than trustworthy. By a false association, his modern reputation has been partially tainted, as if the resistance of the medieval Church to the progress of knowledge meant that Aristotle himself was some kind of enemy to science.

In reality, the exact opposite was the case. Aristotle's entire life was spent observing, classifying and analyzing the world around him, and his theoretical speculations were always firmly grounded in how things actually work, or could be made to work, in practice. Any conclusions he came to he compared with the facts, as they appeared to him, as well as popular opinion and common sense – in marked contrast to Plato, whose deductions led him to construct a philosophical world far removed from ordinary experience.

The range of Aristotle's thinking has never been equaled. His work represents a vast, encyclopedic treatment of virtually every field of knowledge: logic, rhetoric, ethics, politics, metaphysics, poetry, biology, zoology, physics, psychology among them. He practically founded many of the areas of enquiry which are today recognizable as separate subjects, and in several cases gave them their special terminology. It is to Aristotle that we owe the first proper analysis of many pairs of concepts that for more than two millennia have played an essential part in philosophical debate – matter and form, potentiality and actuality, substance and accident, universals and particulars.

Above all, the depth and clarity of his understanding are prodigious. Nowhere is this more so than in his treatment of moral and political affairs. If modern science has inevitably left the ancient Greeks far behind, modern behavior has not. At times, certainly, the context of Aristotle's thought will appear alien. We do not any longer live in small self-governing city-states where women are excluded from all communal decisions and ordinary, decent citizens own slaves. But the basic questions of human conduct, both for individuals and societies, remain pretty much the same; and no one has ever illuminated these more precisely, or more constructively, than Aristotle.

Life

Aristotle was born in 384 BCE at Stagira, a small town on the peninsula of Chalcidice in northern Greece. His father Nicomachus was a doctor who spent some years as personal physician to the king of Macedonia at his court in Pella. So it is not unlikely that as a boy Aristotle had already learned something about the exercise of power in an absolute monarchy; no doubt too his father helped to inspire his passion for observing and analyzing every kind of living organism.

In 367, aged seventeen, Aristotle went to Athens. No other Greek city could offer similar opportunities for education: there were teachers of rhetoric and philosophy in abundance, and in Plato's Academy the most dedicated student would find the stimulation of like-minded intellectuals drawn from all over the Greek world. Although there was no organized teaching in the sense of a fixed curriculum, learning was advanced through debate and presumably – at least in mathematics – demonstration. Aristotle found enough to occupy him there for the next twenty years, until the death of Plato in 347. At that point, inexplicably for us, direction of the Academy passed to Speusippus, while its greatest teacher left and went to live at Assos, near Troy (in what is now Turkey), whose ruler Hermeias was a great admirer of Plato's philosophy.

Hermeias had a niece, Pythias, whom he had adopted as his daughter. She married Aristotle and bore him a daughter. Hermeias himself was put to death in 341 on the orders of the king of Persia, after he had refused under torture to betray the plans of his Macedonian allies. Aristotle was powerfully affected by this noble example and wrote a poem in honor of his father-in-law, of which the beginning has been preserved. At this time he was back in Pella, where he had been invited by Philip II, king of Macedonia, to act as tutor to his son Alexander. Plato had taught that good government would only come when philosophers were kings or kings were philosophers, and it seems that Aristotle saw it as his duty to help turn this ideal into reality, as Plato himself had tried to do in Sicily. Alexander the Great, however, when ruling a substantial portion of the known world only a few years later, gave little sign that his teacher had managed to turn him into much of a philosopher.

Aristotle returned to Athens in 335 and set up his own school on a spot of once-consecrated ground called the Lyceum; to this was added a colonnade called the *peripatos*, or walk, which led Aristotle's followers to become known as the Peripatetics. He spent the next twelve years directing studies and research, with particular emphasis on history, biology and zoology. But on the death of Alexander in 323, Athens was engulfed by one of its periodic waves of anti-Macedonian feeling. Aristotle was threatened with prosecution and decided to leave the city, so ensuring that the Athenians (who had put Socrates to death in 399) should not, as he put it, 'sin a second time against philosophy.' He settled in the city of Chalcis, where he died the following year, aged sixty-two.

Writings

The poet Thomas Gray wrote that reading Aristotle is like eating dried hay. Set against the sparkling dialogues of Plato, Aristotle's writing can seem drab and uninspiring. But this probably has more to do with the accidents of literary survival than the nature of the man himself. For hundreds of years after his death, Aristotle was praised as a fluent and elegant stylist, on the basis of the works that were then generally known and easily available. These had been written for a broad public, presented in a form that was easily digestible. But all these so-called 'exoteric' works are now lost, and what we possess are the 'esoteric' ones, those written for the inner circle of Aristotle's own school of pupils. They are densely argued, include technical terms, and lack any kind of polish or ornament. The result is that they can at times seem daunting. Aristotle makes no concessions, nor does he try to hide the fact that philosophy is hard.

These works of Aristotle that still exist have often been described as lecture notes: the bare bones of his philosophy, which would have been fleshed out and expanded when delivered orally. This description takes account of the compressed character of the writing, with its lack of illustrations, anecdotes or jokes. But perhaps we do better to think of them as unfinished drafts, work in progress to which revisions and modifications have been added along the way. This would help to explain why the same material is sometimes repeated, and why connections between topics are often missing. On a number of occasions in the *Politics*, Aristotle says he will deal with a certain question at a later stage, but fails to keep his promise. Moreover, the arrangement of the books in that work, as in others, is uncertain; in whatever order they are placed, we always end up with some arguments assumed before they come to be proved in a later passage.

Despite these difficulties, Aristotle's thought has a marvelous economy and clarity. His procedure is one of analyzing and drawing essential distinctions, within a logical structure that he himself had – for the first time in human history – made properly systematic. Unlike Plato, Aristotle does not resort to bad arguments. Nor is there any trace of mystification or willful obscurity, only a refreshing sense of the acutest of all intellects carefully cutting away the conceptual undergrowth to reveal the underlying patterns of growth beneath. Also refreshing is Aristotle's concern for actual experience, including the things that ordinary people have to say about a subject. On the big questions, especially in the field of morality, he is reassuringly confident that the common view is probably not far from the truth. He may refine such a view and make it more comprehensible, but he will never see it as part of his task to ditch the world we all recognize in order to replace it with his own theoretical fancy.

Nicomachean Ethics

The *Nicomachean Ethics* is the fullest and most authoritative of three Aristotelian treatises on moral philosophy, the others being the *Eudemian Ethics* and *Magna Moralia*. The reason for the name is not certain, but it seems plausible that the work was put together in the form of a book after Aristotle's death by his son Nicomachus.

Although morality might seem to be about values rather than facts, Aristotle begins his *Ethics* almost like a scientific study. According to his general view of the world, every kind of organism always strives to attain some aim or end which nature has assigned to it. We therefore need to consider what is the end to which human life directs itself. The answer, he decides, must be happiness. Everything else – pleasure, honor, intelligence and so on – is valued as a means to some further good, but in the case of happiness it makes no sense to justify it in relation to some higher end. We desire happiness for its own sake.

To some extent, happiness obviously depends on accidents of birth and fortune. But, above all, it is determined by how we act, and Aristotle's purpose is then twofold. First, to establish that it is acting in accordance with goodness that is most productive of happiness; and second, to tease out what this goodness really amounts to in a practical sense. In translation, 'goodness' often ends up being equated with 'virtue,' but this is misleading. Virtue is an old-fashioned and not wholly attractive notion, inseparable from a certain ideal of self-denial; the main issue seems to be avoiding wrong, rather than doing anything that could be viewed as positively fulfilling. But fulfillment is an essential feature of Aristotle's *eudaimonia*, the word normally (and not entirely accurately) rendered into English as 'happiness.' What Aristotle has in mind is something more like well-being, or the kind of state a person is in when they might be said to be flourishing – the human equivalent of a plant that has found good soil with plenty of sun and water.

How someone is to achieve this kind of state is therefore Aristotle's real concern in the *Ethics*. This is a rather different project from most modern moral philosophy, which deals with the principles by which actions can be justified, and frequently occupies itself with imaginary cases testing the farthest boundaries of those principles. So, for instance, if we start from the utilitarian position that good consists in maximizing human happiness, we may wonder whether it would be allowable to cause the death of one innocent person if this would bring great benefit to a large number of others, and if not, why not.

Aristotle is not concerned to answer such questions. What he is interested in is the kind of character required for a person to be happy – to flourish – in the world. As ever, he is eminently realistic. Character, he observes, is produced by habituation: that is, the repeated doing of acts which have a similar quality. Repetition gradually shapes the character in one direction or another. By committing crimes you turn into a hardened criminal, by consistently acting well (however that may be defined) you become a good person. Acting well is easy for the good person, for that is what he or she is used to doing. To Aristotle, the view that goodness somehow depends on waging a constant war against temptation could only be the product of a diseased intelligence.

Politics

At the end of the *Ethics* Aristotle acknowledges that in order to acquire, through habit, the good character that is essential for happiness, training is necessary. And to ensure that this takes place in the right way, there must be good laws. So he must go on to inquire what are the best laws, or to put it another way, what is the best system of government for promoting happiness. This, then, is to be the main subject of his *Politics*, and by introducing it in this way Aristotle makes it quite explicit that the two treatises are meant to be taken together as one integral study of human activity.

If we assume that the Greeks, who invented democracy, were all great admirers of it, we make a great mistake. Almost all the writers we still possess are disparaging or even downright hostile, and Aristotle is no exception. Largely this is because the kind of democracy that took shape in Athens and some other Greek cities was far more radical than anything that goes under the same name in our world. Two features in particular now seem to us quite extraordinary.

First, important offices were held in rotation and distributed at random (by lot); and second, crucial policy decisions were taken by the entire citizen body meeting together. The purpose was to ensure that every (male) citizen had as much influence as every other, and to make it impossible for a single individual, or family, to maintain a dominant position. But there were serious flaws in this arrangement. For one thing, there was always a risk that an eloquent speaker could stir up the emotions of the assembly and induce it to pass measures that would have been rejected in a more rational atmosphere.

There was also the problem that the aim of equal involvement was an impossible one to realize, for the simple reason that the people who found political activity most congenial were those who lived in the center of town and had little else to occupy them. Most farmers and artisans were too busy attending to their livelihood to play a regular part in the business of government, so the affairs of the city could end up being decided by an unrepresentative collection of those for whom serving on juries and attending the assembly had turned into their main employment.

Aristotle's criticisms of democracy need to be read with this in mind. For him, the best constitution is one in which a population of farmers, who cannot afford the time to run the city's affairs themselves, are content to elect to office the most notable citizens, while retaining the power to hold them to account and so prevent them from governing unjustly. Something, in fact, not unlike the modern notion of a representative democracy. For Aristotle, as for most of his contemporaries, the greatest concern was how to achieve stability. No one was likely to forget that at the end of the fifth century BCE, in the thirty-year-long Peloponnesian War, it had been the tightly oligarchic and repressive state of Sparta that had finally triumphed over democratic Athens. Many Greeks drew what seemed the natural conclusion, that it was impossible to impose the necessary discipline on the citizens of a democracy, because they were always bound to be more interested in immediate benefit than long-term advantage.

What none knew, even Aristotle, was that the age of

vigorous political debate was almost over. The scale of the Greek world was changing, and the small, self-governing city was too weak to stand on its own. Large empires had come to stay, and for almost two thousand years the centralized, autocratic rule of a single man became the ideal of human government.

HUGH GRIFFITH

Further reading

Ackrill, J. L. (ed.), *A New Aristotle Reader* (New York, Oxford University Press, 1987)

Barnes, J. (ed.), *The Cambridge Companion to Aristotle* (New York, Cambridge University Press, 1995)

Ross, W. D., *Aristotle*, (New York, Routledge, (6th ed.) 1995)

NICOMACHEAN ETHICS

BOOK ONE

Introduction – nature and definition of happiness

1 Every art, and every science reduced to a teachable form, and in like manner every action and moral choice, aims, it is thought, at some good: for which reason a common and by no means a bad description of the chief good is, 'that which all things aim at.'

Now there plainly is a difference in the ends proposed: for in some cases they are acts of working, and in others certain works or tangible results beyond and beside the acts of working: and where there are certain ends beyond and beside the actions, the works are in their nature better than the acts of working. Again, since actions and arts and sciences are many, the ends likewise come to be many: of the healing art, for instance, health; of the ship-building art, a vessel; of the military art, victory; and of domestic management, wealth; are respectively the ends.

And whatever of such actions, arts, or sciences range under some one faculty (as under that of horsemanship the art of making bridles, and all that are connected with the manufacture of horse-furniture in general; this itself again, and every action connected with war, under the military art; and in the same way others under others), in all such, the ends of the master-arts are more choiceworthy than those ranging under them, because it is with a view to the former that the latter are pursued.

(And in this comparison it makes no difference whether the acts of working are themselves the ends of the actions, or something further beside them, as is the case in the arts and sciences we have been just speaking of.)

2   Since then of all things which may be done there is some one end which we desire for its own sake, and with a view to which we desire everything else; and since we do not choose in all instances with a further end in view (for then men would go on without limit, and so the desire would be unsatisfied and fruitless), this plainly must be the chief good, *i.e.* the best thing of all.

Surely then, even with reference to actual life and conduct, the knowledge of it must have great weight; and like archers, with a mark in view, we shall be more likely to hit upon what is right: and if so, we ought to try to describe, in outline at least, what it is and of which of the sciences and faculties it is the end.

Now one would naturally suppose it to be the end of that which is most commanding and most inclusive: and to this description, *politike* plainly answers: for this it is that determines which of the sciences should be in the communities, and which kind individuals are to learn, and what degree of proficiency is to be required. Again, we see also ranging under this the most highly esteemed faculties, such as the art military, and that of domestic management, and rhetoric. Well then, since this uses all the other practical sciences, and moreover lays down rules as to what men are to do, and from what to abstain, the end of this must include the ends of the rest, and so must be *the good* of Man. And grant that this is the same to the individual and to the community, yet surely that of the latter is plainly greater and more perfect to discover and preserve: for to do this even for a single individual were a matter for contentment; but to do it for a whole nation, and for communities generally, were more noble and godlike.

3   Such then are the objects proposed by our treatise, which is of the nature of *politike*: and I conceive I shall have spoken on them satisfactorily, if they be made as distinctly clear as the nature of the subject-matter will admit: for exactness must not be looked for in all discussions alike, any more than in all works of handicraft. Now the notions of nobleness and justice, with the examination of which *politike* is concerned, admit of variation and error to such a degree, that they are supposed by some to exist conventionally only, and not in the nature of things; but then, again, the things which are allowed to be goods admit of a similar error, because harm comes to many from them: for before now some have perished through wealth, and others through valour.

We must be content then, in speaking of such things and from such data, to set forth the truth roughly and in outline; in other words, since we are speaking of general matter and from general data, to draw also conclusions merely general. And in the same spirit should each person receive what we say: for the man of education will seek exactness so far in each subject as the nature of the thing admits, it being plainly much the same absurdity to put up with a mathematician who tries to persuade instead of proving, and to demand strict demonstrative reasoning of a rhetorician.

Now each man judges well what he knows, and of these things he is a good judge: on each particular matter then he is a good judge who has been instructed in *it*, and in a general way the man of general mental cultivation.

Hence the young man is not a fit student of moral philosophy, for he has no experience in the actions of life, while all that is said presupposes and is concerned with these: and in the next place, since he is apt to follow the impulses of his passions, he will hear as though he heard not, and to no profit, the end in view being practice and not mere knowledge.

And I draw no distinction between young in years, and youthful in temper and disposition: the defect to which I allude being no direct result of the time, but of living at the beck and call of passion, and following each object as it rises. For to them that are such the knowledge comes to be unprofitable, as to those of imperfect self-control: but, to those who form their desires and act in accordance with reason, to have knowledge on these points must be very profitable.

Let thus much suffice by way of preface on these three points, the student, the spirit in which our observations should be received, and the object which we propose.

4   And now, resuming the statement with which we commenced, since all knowledge and moral choice grasps at good of some kind or another, what good is that which we say *politike* aims at? or, in other words, what is the highest of all the goods which are the objects of action?

So far as name goes, there is a pretty general agreement; for *happiness* both the multitude and the refined few call it, and 'living well' and 'doing well' they conceive to be the same with 'being happy'; but about the nature of this happiness, men dispute, and the multitude do not in their account of it agree with the wise. For some say it is some one of those things which are palpable and apparent, as pleasure or wealth or honour; in fact, some one thing, some another; nay, oftentimes the same man gives a different account of it; for when ill, he calls it health; when poor, wealth: and conscious of their own ignorance, men admire those who talk grandly and above their comprehension. Some again hold it to be something by itself, other than and beside these many good things, which is in fact to all these the cause of their being good.

Now to sift all the opinions would be perhaps rather a fruitless task; so it shall suffice to sift those which are most generally current, or are thought to have some reason in them.

And here we must not forget the difference between reasoning from principles, and reasoning to principles: for with good cause did Plato too doubt about this, and inquire whether the right road is from principles or to principles, just as in the racecourse from the judges to the further end, or vice versa.

Of course, we must begin with what is known; but then this is of two kinds, what we *do* know, and what we *may* know: perhaps then as individuals we must begin with what we *do* know. Hence the necessity that he should have been well trained in habits, who is to study, with any tolerable chance of profit, the principles of nobleness and justice and moral philosophy generally. For a principle is a matter of fact, and if the fact is sufficiently clear to a man there will be no need in addition of the reason for the fact. And he that has been thus trained either has principles already, or can receive them easily: as for him who neither has nor can receive them, let him hear his sentence from Hesiod:

> He is best of all who of himself conceiveth all things;
> Good again is he too who can adopt a
> good suggestion;
> But whoso neither of himself conceiveth nor
> hearing from another
> Layeth it to heart; – he is a useless man.

5   But to return from this digression.

Now of the chief good (*i.e.* of happiness) men seem to form their notions from the different modes of life, as we might naturally expect : the many and most low conceive it to be pleasure, and hence they are content with the life of sensual enjoyment. For there are three lines of life which stand out prominently to view: that just mentioned, and the life in society, and, thirdly, the life of contemplation.

Now the many are plainly quite slavish, choosing a life like that of brute animals: yet they obtain some consideration, because many of the great share the tastes of Sardanapalus. The refined and active again conceive it to be honour: for this may be said to be the end of the life in society: yet it is plainly too superficial for the object of our search, because it is thought to rest with those who pay rather than with him who receives it, whereas the chief good we feel instinctively must be something which is our own, and not easily to be taken from us.

And besides, men seem to pursue honour, that they may believe themselves to be good: for instance, they seek to be honoured by the wise, and by those among whom they are known, and for virtue: clearly then, in the opinion at least of these men, virtue is higher than honour. In truth, one would be much more inclined to think this to be the end of the life in society; yet this itself is plainly not sufficiently final: for it is conceived possible, that a man possessed of virtue might sleep or be inactive all through his life, or, as a third case, suffer the greatest evils and misfortunes: and the man who should live thus no one would call happy, except for mere disputation's sake.

And for these let thus much suffice, for they have been treated of at sufficient length in my Encyclia.

A third line of life is that of contemplation, concerning which we shall make our examination in the sequel.

As for the life of money-making, it is one of constraint, and wealth manifestly is not the good we are seeking, because it is for use, that is, for the sake of something further: and hence one would rather conceive the forementioned ends to be the right ones, for men rest content with them for their own sakes. Yet, clearly, they are not the objects of our search either, though many words have been wasted on them. So much then for these.

6   Again, the notion of one universal good (the same, that is, in all things), it is better perhaps we should examine, and discuss the meaning of it, though such an inquiry is unpleasant, because they are friends of ours who have introduced these forms. Still perhaps it may appear better, nay to be our duty where the safety of the truth is concerned, to upset if need be even our own theories, specially as we are lovers of wisdom: for since both are dear to us, we are bound to prefer the truth. Now they who invented this doctrine of forms, did not apply it to those things in which they spoke of

priority and posteriority, and so they never made any idea of numbers; but good is predicated in the categories of substance, quality, and relation; now that which exists of itself, *i.e.* substance, is prior in the nature of things to that which is relative, because this latter is an off-shoot, as it were, and result of that which is; on their own principle then there cannot be a common idea in the case of these.

In the next place, since good is predicated in as many ways as there are modes of existence [for it is predicated in the category of substance, as god, intellect – and in that of quality, as the virtues – and in that of quantity, as the mean – and in that of relation, as the useful – and in that of time, as opportunity – and in that of place, as abode; and other such like things], it manifestly cannot be something common and universal and one in all: else it would not have been predicated in all the categories, but in one only.

Thirdly, since those things which range under one idea are also under the cognisance of one science, there would have been, on their theory, only one science taking cognisance of all goods collectively: but in fact there are many even for those which range under one category: for instance, of opportunity or seasonableness (which I have before mentioned as being in the category of time), the science is, in war, generalship; in disease, medical science; and of the mean (which I quoted before as being in the category of quantity), in food, the medical science; and in labour or exercise, the gymnastic science. A person might fairly doubt also what in the world they mean by very-this that or the other, since, as they would themselves allow, the account of the humanity is one and the same in the very-man, and in any individual man: for so far as the individual and the very-man are both man, they will not differ at all: and if so, then very-good and any particular good will not differ, in so far as both are good. Nor will it do to say, that the eternity of the very-good makes it to be more good; for what has lasted white ever so long, is no whiter than what lasts but for a day.

No. The Pythagoreans do seem to give a more credible account of the matter, who place 'one' among the goods in their double list of goods and bads: which philosophers, in fact, Speusippus seems to have followed.

But of these matters let us speak at some other time. Now there is plainly a loophole to object to what has been advanced, on the plea that the theory I have attacked is not by its advocates applied to all good: but those goods only are spoken of as being under one idea, which are pursued, and with which men rest content simply for their own sakes: whereas those things which have a tendency to produce or preserve them in any way, or to hinder their contraries, are called good because of these other goods, and after another fashion. It is manifest then that the goods may be so called in two senses, the one class for their own sakes, the other because of these.

Very well then, let us separate the independent goods from the instrumental, and see whether they are spoken of as under one idea. But the question next arises, what kind of goods are we to call independent? All such as are pursued even when separated from other goods, as, for instance, being wise, seeing, and certain pleasures and honours (for these, though we do pursue them with some further end in view, one would still place among the independent goods)? or does it come in fact to this, that we can call nothing independent good except the idea, and so the concrete of it will be nought?

If, on the other hand, these are independent goods, then we shall require that the account of the goodness be the same clearly in all, just as that of the whiteness is in snow and white lead. But how stands the fact? Why of honour and wisdom and pleasure the accounts are distinct and different in so far as they are good. The chief good then is not something common, and after one idea.

But then, how does the name come to be common (for it is not seemingly a case of fortuitous equivocation)? Are different individual things called good by virtue of being from one source, or all conducing to one end, or rather by way of analogy, for that intellect is to the soul as sight to the body, and so on? However, perhaps we ought to leave these questions now, for an accurate investigation of them is more properly the business of a different philosophy. And likewise respecting the idea: for even if there is some one good predicated in common of all things that are good, or separable and capable of existing independently, manifestly it cannot be the object of human action or attainable by man; but we are in search now of something that is so.

It may readily occur to anyone, that it would be better to attain a knowledge of it with a view to such concrete goods as are attainable and practical, because, with this as a kind of model in our hands, we shall the better know what things are good for us individually, and when we know them, we shall attain them.

Some plausibility, it is true, this argument possesses, but it is contradicted by the facts of the arts and sciences; for all these, though aiming at some good, and seeking that which is deficient, yet pretermit the knowledge of it; now it is not exactly probable that all artisans without exception should be ignorant of so great a help as this would be, and not even look after it; neither is it easy to see wherein a weaver or a carpenter will be profited in respect of his craft by knowing the very-good, or how a man will be the more apt to effect cures or to command an army for having seen the idea itself. For manifestly it is not health after this general and abstract fashion which is the subject of the physician's investigation, but the health of man, or rather perhaps of this or that man; for he has to heal individuals. – Thus much on these points.

7   And now let us revert to the good of which we are in search: what can it be? for manifestly it is different in different actions and arts: for it is different in the healing art and in the art military, and similarly in the rest. What then is the chief good in each? Is it not 'that for the sake of which the other things are done'? and this in the healing art is health, and in the art military victory, and in that of house-building a house, and in any other thing something else; in short, in every action and moral choice the end, because in all cases men do everything else with a view to this. So that if there is some one end of all things which are and may be done, this must be the good proposed by doing, or if more than one, then these.

Thus our discussion after some traversing about has come to the same point which we reached before. And this we must try yet more to clear up.

Now since the ends are plainly many, and of these we choose some with a view to others (wealth, for instance, musical instruments, and, in general, all instruments), it is clear that all are not final: but the chief good is manifestly something final; and so, if there is some one only which is final, this must be the object of our search: but if several, then the most final of them will be it.

Now that which is an object of pursuit in itself we call more final than that which is so with a view to something else; that again which is never an object of choice with a view to something else than those which are so both in themselves and with a view to this ulterior object: and so by the term 'absolutely final', we denote that which is an object of choice always in itself, and never with a view to any other.

And of this nature happiness is mostly thought to be, for this we choose always for its own sake, and never with a view to anything further: whereas honour, pleasure, intellect, in fact every excellence we choose for their own sakes, it is true (because we would choose each of these even if no result were to follow), but we choose them also with a view to happiness, conceiving that through their instrumentality we shall be happy: but no man chooses happiness with a view to them, nor in fact with a view to any other thing whatsoever.

The same result is seen to follow also from the notion of self-sufficiency, a quality thought to belong to the final good. Now by sufficient for self, we mean not for a single individual living a solitary life, but for his parents also and children and wife, and, in general, friends and countrymen; for man is by nature adapted to a social existence. But of these, of course, some limit must be fixed: for if one extends it to parents and descendants and friends' friends, there is no end to it.

This point, however, must be left for future investigation: for the present we define that to be self-sufficient 'which taken alone makes life choiceworthy, and to be in want of nothing'; now of such kind we think happiness to be: and further, to be most choiceworthy of all things; not being reckoned with any other thing, for if it were so reckoned, it is plain we must then allow it, with the addition of ever so small a good, to be more choiceworthy than it was before: because what is put to it becomes an addition of so much more good, and of goods the greater is ever the more choiceworthy.

So then happiness is manifestly something final and self-sufficient, being the end of all things which are and may be done.

But, it may be, to call happiness the chief good is a mere truism, and what is wanted is some clearer account of its real nature. Now this object may be easily attained, when we have discovered what is the work of man; for as in the case of flute-player, statuary, or artisan of any kind, or, more generally, all who have any work or course of action, their chief good and excellence is thought to reside in their work, so it would seem to be with man, if there is any work belonging to him.

Are we then to suppose, that while carpenter and cobbler have certain works and courses of action, man as man has none, but is left by nature without a work? Or would not one rather hold, that as eye, hand, and foot, and generally each of his members, has manifestly some special work; so too the whole man, as distinct from all these, has some work of his own?

What then can this be? Not mere life, because that plainly is shared with him even by vegetables, and we want what is peculiar to him. We must separate off then the life of mere nourishment and growth, and next will come the life of sensation: but this again manifestly is common to horses, oxen, and every animal. There remains then a kind of life of the rational nature apt to act: and of this nature there are two parts denominated rational, the one as being obedient to reason, the other as having and exerting it. Again, as this life is also spoken of in two ways, we must take that which is in the way of actual working, because this is thought to be most properly entitled to the name. If then the work of man is a working of the soul in accordance with reason, or at least not independently of reason, and we say that the work of any given subject, and of that subject good of its kind, are the same in kind (as, for instance, of a harp-player and a good harp-player, and so on in every case, adding to the work eminence in the way of excellence; I mean, the work of a harp-player is to play the harp, and of a good harp-player to play it well); if, I say, this is so, and we assume the work of man to be life of a certain kind, that is to say a working of the soul, and actions with reason, and of a good man to do these things well and nobly, and in fact everything is finished off well in the way of the excellence which peculiarly belongs to it: if all this is so, then the good of man comes to be 'a working of the soul in the way of excellence,' or, if excellence admits of degrees, in the way of the best and most perfect excellence.

And we must add, in a complete life; for as it is not one swallow or one fine day that makes a spring, so it is not one day or a short time that makes a man blessed and happy.

Let this then be taken for a rough sketch of the chief good: since it is probably the right way to give first the outline, and fill it in afterwards. And it would seem that any man may improve and connect what is good in the sketch, and that time is a good discoverer and co-operator in such matters: it is thus in fact that all improvements in the various arts have been brought about, for any man may fill up a deficiency.

You must remember also what has been already stated, and not seek for exactness in all matters alike, but in each according to the subject-matter, and so far as properly belongs to the system. The carpenter and geometrician, for instance, inquire into the right line in different fashion: the former so far as he wants it for his work, the latter inquires into its nature and properties, because he is concerned with the truth.

So then should one do in other matters, that the incidental matters may not exceed the direct ones.

And again, you must not demand the reason either in all things alike, because in some it is sufficient that the fact has been well demonstrated, which is the case with first principles; and the fact is the first step, *i.e.* starting-point or principle.

And of these first principles some are obtained by induction, some by perception, some by a course of habituation, others in other different ways. And we must try to trace up each in their own nature, and take pains to secure their being well defined, because they have great influence on what follows: it is thought, I mean, that the starting-point or principle is more than half the whole matter, and that many of the points of inquiry come simultaneously into view thereby.

8 We must now inquire concerning happiness, not only from our conclusion and the data on which

our reasoning proceeds, but likewise from what is commonly said about it: because with what is true all things which really are in harmony, but with that which is false the true very soon jars.

Now there is a common division of goods into three classes; one being called external, the other two those of the soul and body respectively, and those belonging to the soul we call most properly and specially good. Well, in our definition we assume that the actions and workings of the soul constitute happiness, and these of course belong to the soul. And so our account is a good one, at least according to this opinion, which is of ancient date, and accepted by those who profess philosophy. Rightly too are certain actions and workings said to be the end, for thus it is brought into the number of the goods of the soul instead of the external. Agreeing also with our definition is the common notion, that the happy man lives well and does well, for it has been stated by us to be pretty much a kind of living well and doing well.

But further, the points required in happiness are found in combination in our account of it.

For some think it is virtue, others practical wisdom, others a kind of scientific philosophy; others that it is these, or else some one of them, in combination with pleasure, or at least not independently of it; while others again take in external prosperity.

Of these opinions, some rest on the authority of numbers or antiquity, others on that of few, and those men of note: and it is not likely that either of these classes should be wrong in all points, but be right at least in some one, or even in most.

Now with those who assert it to be virtue (excellence), or some kind of virtue, our account agrees: for working in the way of excellence surely belongs to excellence.

And there is perhaps no unimportant difference between conceiving of the chief good as in possession or as in use, in other words, as a mere state or as a working. For the state or habit may possibly exist in a subject without effecting any good, as, for instance, in him who is asleep, or in any other way inactive; but the working cannot so, for it will of necessity act, and act well. And as at the Olympic games it is not the finest and strongest men who are crowned, but they who enter the lists, for out of these the prize-men are selected; so too in life, of the honourable and the good, it is they who act who rightly win the prizes.

Their life too is in itself pleasant: for the feeling of pleasure is a mental sensation, and that is to each pleasant of which he is said to be fond: a horse, for instance, to him who is fond of horses, and a sight to him who is fond of sights: and so in like manner just acts to him who is fond of justice, and more generally the things in accordance with virtue to him who is fond of virtue. Now in the case of the multitude of men the things which they individually esteem pleasant clash, because they are not such by nature, whereas to the lovers of nobleness those things are pleasant which are such by nature: but the actions in accordance with virtue are of this kind, so that they are pleasant both to the individuals and also in themselves.

So then their life has no need of pleasure as a kind of additional appendage, but involves pleasure in itself. For, besides what I have just mentioned, a man is not a good man at all who feels no pleasure in noble actions, just as no one would call that man just who does not feel pleasure in acting justly, or liberal who does not in liberal actions, and similarly in the case of the other virtues which might be enumerated: and if this be so, then the actions in accordance with virtue must be in themselves pleasurable. Then again they are certainly good and noble, and each of these in the highest degree; if we are to take as right the judgment of the good man, for he judges as we have said.

Thus then happiness is most excellent, most noble, and most pleasant, and these attributes are not separated as in the well-known Delian inscription –

'Most noble is that which is most just, but best
is health;
And naturally most pleasant is the obtaining
one's desires.'

For all these co-exist in the best acts of working: and we say that happiness is these, or one, that is, the best of them.

Still it is quite plain that it does require the addition of external goods, as we have said: because without appliances it is impossible, or at all events not easy, to do noble actions: for friends, money, and political influence are in a manner instruments whereby many things are done: some things there are again a deficiency in which mars blessedness; good birth, for instance, or fine offspring, or even personal beauty: for he is not at all capable of happiness who is very ugly, or is ill-born, or solitary and childless; and still less perhaps supposing him to have very bad children or friends, or to have lost good ones by death. As we have said already, the addition of prosperity of this kind does seem necessary to complete the idea of happiness; hence some rank good fortune, and others virtue, with happiness.

9   And hence too a question is raised, whether it is a thing that can be learned, or acquired by habituation or discipline of some other kind, or whether it comes in the way of divine dispensation, or even in the way of chance.

Now to be sure, if anything else is a gift of the gods to men, it is probable that happiness is a gift of theirs too, and specially because of all human goods it is the highest. But this, it may be, is a question belonging more properly to an investigation different from ours: and it is quite clear, that on the supposition of its not being sent from the gods direct, but coming to us by reason of virtue and learning of a certain kind, or discipline, it is yet one of the most godlike things; because the prize and end of virtue is manifestly somewhat most excellent, nay divine and blessed.

It will also on this supposition be widely participated, for it may through learning and diligence of a certain kind exist in all who have not been maimed for virtue.

And if it is better we should be happy thus than as a result of chance, this is in itself an argument that the case is so; because those things which are in the way of nature, and in like manner of art, and of every cause, and specially the best cause, are by nature in the best way possible: to leave them to chance what is greatest and most noble would be very much out of harmony with all these facts.

The question may be determined also by a reference to our definition of happiness, that it is a working of the soul in the way of excellence or virtue of a certain kind: and of the other goods, some we must have to begin with, and those which are co-operative and useful are given by nature as instruments.

These considerations will harmonise also with what

we said at the commencement: for we assumed the end of *politike* to be most excellent: now this bestows most care on making the members of the community of a certain character; good that is and apt to do what is honourable.

With good reason then neither ox nor horse nor any other brute animal do we call happy, for none of them can partake in such working: and for this same reason a child is not happy either, because by reason of his tender age he cannot yet perform such actions: if the term is applied, it is by way of anticipation.

For to constitute happiness, there must be, as we have said, complete virtue and a complete life: for many changes and chances of all kinds arise during a life, and he who is most prosperous may become involved in great misfortunes in his old age, as in the heroic poems the tale is told of Priam: but the man who has experienced such fortune and died in wretchedness, no man calls happy.

Section 10 to end

The accidents of fortune and whether they affect the balance of our happiness. The good man is not immune to the effects of misfortune but, bearing everything with honour, will never become entirely unhappy.

Additional argument that happiness is a fundamental good, valued for its own sake. Classification of parts of the soul.

BOOK TWO

Nature of moral virtue

1 Well: human excellence is of two kinds, intellectual and moral: now the intellectual springs originally, and is increased subsequently, from teaching (for the most part that is), and needs therefore experience and time; whereas the moral comes from custom, and so the Greek term denoting it is but a slight deflection from the term denoting custom in that language.

From this fact it is plain that not one of the moral virtues comes to be in us merely by nature: because of such things as exist by nature, none can be changed by custom: a stone, for instance, by nature gravitating downwards, could never by custom be brought to ascend, not even if one were to try and accustom it by throwing it up ten thousand times; nor could fire again be brought to descend, nor in fact could anything whose nature is in one way be brought by custom to be in another. The virtues then come to be in us neither by nature, nor in despite of nature, but we are furnished by nature with a capacity for receiving them, and are perfected in them through custom.

Again, in whatever cases we get things by nature, we get the faculties first and perform the acts of working afterwards; an illustration of which is afforded by the case of our bodily senses, for it was not from having often seen or heard that we got these senses, but just the reverse: we had them and so exercised them, but did not have them because we had exercised them. But the virtues we get by first performing single acts of working, which, again, is the case of other things, as the arts for instance; for what we have to make when we have learned how, these we learn how to make by making: men come to be builders, for instance, by building; harp-players, by playing on the harp: exactly so, by doing just actions we come to be just; by doing the actions of self-mastery we come to be perfected in self-mastery; and by doing brave actions brave.

And to the truth of this testimony is borne by what takes place in communities: because the law-givers make the individual members good men by habituation, and this is the intention certainly of every law-giver, and all who do not effect it well fail of their intent; and herein consists the difference between a good constitution and a bad.

Again, every virtue is either produced or destroyed from and by the very same circumstances: art too in like manner; I mean it is by playing the harp that both the good and the bad harp-players are formed: and similarly builders and all the rest; by building well men will become good builders; by doing it badly bad ones: in fact, if this had not been so, there would have been no need of instructors, but all men would have been at once good or bad in their several arts without them.

So too then is it with the virtues: for by acting in the various relations in which we are thrown with our fellow men, we come to be, some just, some unjust: and by acting in dangerous positions and being habituated to feel fear or confidence, we come to be, some brave, others cowards.

Similarly is it also with respect to the occasions of lust and anger: for some men come to be perfected in self-mastery and mild, others destitute of all self-control and passionate; the one class by behaving in one way under them, the other by behaving in another. Or, in one word, the habits are produced from the acts of working like to them: and so what we have to do is to give a certain character to these particular acts, because the habits formed correspond to the differences of these.

So then, whether we are accustomed this way or that straight from childhood, makes not a small but an important difference, or rather I would say it makes all the difference.

2   Since then the object of the present treatise is not mere speculation, as it is of some others (for we are inquiring not merely that we may know what virtue is but that we may become virtuous, else it would have been useless), we must consider as to the particular actions how we are to do them, because, as we have just said, the quality of the habits that shall be formed depends on these.

Now, that we are to act in accordance with right reason is a general maxim, and may for the present be taken for granted: we will speak of it hereafter, and say both what right reason is, and what are its relations to the other virtues.

But let this point be first thoroughly understood between us, that all which can be said on moral action must be said in outline, as it were, and not exactly: for as we remarked at the commencement, such reasoning only must be required as the nature of the subject-matter admits of, and matters of moral action and expediency have no fixedness any more than matters of health. And if the subject in its general maxims is such, still less in its application to particular cases is exactness attainable: because these fall not under any art or system of rules, but it must be left in each instance to the individual agents to look to the exigencies of the particular case, as it is in the art of healing, or that of navigating a ship. Still, though the present subject is confessedly such, we must try and do what we can for it.

First then this must be noted, that it is the nature of such things to be spoiled by defect and excess; as we see in the case of health and strength (since for the illustration of things which cannot be seen we must use those that can), for excessive training impairs the strength as well as deficient: meat and drink, in like manner, in too great or too small quantities, impair the health: while in due proportion they cause, increase, and preserve it.

Thus it is therefore with the habits of perfected self-mastery and courage and the rest of the virtues: for the man who flies from and fears all things, and never stands up against anything, comes to be a coward; and he who fears nothing, but goes at everything, comes to be rash. In like manner too, he that tastes of every pleasure and abstains from none comes to lose all self-control; while he who avoids all, as do the dull and clownish, comes as it were to lose his faculties of perception: that is to say, the habits of perfected self-mastery and courage are spoiled by the excess and defect, but by the mean state are preserved.

Furthermore, not only do the origination, growth, and marring of the habits come from and by the same circumstances, but also the acts of working after the habits are formed will be exercised on the same: for so it is also with those other things which are more directly matters of sight, strength for instance: for this comes by taking plenty of food and doing plenty of work, and the man who has attained strength is best able to do these: and so it is with the virtues, for not only do we by abstaining from pleasures come to be perfected in self-mastery, but when we have come to be so we can best abstain from them: similarly too with courage: for it is by accustoming ourselves to despise objects of fear and stand up against them that we come to be brave; and after we have come to be so we shall be best able to stand up against such objects.

3 And for a test of the formation of the habits we must take the pleasure or pain which succeeds the acts; for he is perfected in self-mastery who not only abstains from the bodily pleasures but is glad to do so; whereas he who abstains but is sorry to do it has not self-mastery: he again is brave who stands up against danger, either with positive pleasure or at least without any pain; whereas he who does it with pain is not brave.

For moral virtue has for its object-matter pleasures and pains, because by reason of pleasure we do what is bad, and by reason of pain decline doing what is right (for which cause, as Plato observes, men should have been trained straight from their childhood to receive pleasure and pain from proper objects, for this is the right education). Again: since virtues have to do with actions and feelings, and on every feeling and every action pleasure and pain follow, here again is another proof that virtue has for its object-matter pleasure and pain. The same is shown also by the fact that punishments are effected through the instrumentality of these; because they are of the nature of remedies, and it is the nature of remedies to be the contraries of the ills they cure. Again, to quote what we said before: every habit of the soul by its very nature has relation to, and exerts itself upon, things of the same kind as those by which it is naturally deteriorated or improved: now such habits do come to be vicious by reason of pleasures and pains, that is, by men pursuing or avoiding respectively, either such as they ought not, or at wrong times, or in wrong manner, and so forth (for which reason, by the way, some people define the virtues as certain states of impassibility and utter quietude, but they are wrong because they speak without modification, instead of adding 'as they ought', 'as they ought not', and 'when', and so on). Virtue then is assumed to be that habit which is such, in relation to pleasures and pains, as to effect the best results, and vice the contrary.

The following considerations may also serve to set this in a clear light. There are principally three things moving us to choice and three to avoidance, the honourable, the expedient, the pleasant; and their three contraries, the dishonourable, the hurtful, and the painful: now the good man is apt to go right, and the bad man wrong, with respect to all these of course, but most specially with respect to pleasure: because not only is this common to him with all animals but also it is a concomitant of all those things which move to choice, since both the honourable and the expedient give an impression of pleasure.

Again, it grows up with us all from infancy, and so it is a hard matter to remove from ourselves this feeling, engrained as it is into our very life.

Again, we adopt pleasure and pain (some of us more, and some less) as the measure even of actions: for this cause then our whole business must be with them, since to receive right or wrong impressions of pleasure and pain is a thing of no little importance in respect of the actions. Once more; it is harder, as Heraclitus says, to fight against pleasure than against anger: now it is about that which is more than commonly difficult that art comes into being, and virtue too, because in that which is difficult the good is of a higher order: and so for this reason too both virtue and moral philosophy generally must wholly busy themselves respecting pleasures and pains, because he that uses these well will be good, he that does so ill will be bad.

Let us then be understood to have stated, that virtue has for its object-matter pleasures and pains, and that it is either increased or marred by the same circumstances (differently used) by which it is originally generated, and that it exerts itself on the same circumstances out of which it was generated.

4   Now I can conceive a person perplexed as to the meaning of our statement, that men must do just actions to become just, and those of self-mastery to acquire the habit of self-mastery; 'for', he would say, 'if men are doing the actions they have the respective virtues already, just as men are grammarians or musicians when they do the actions of either art.' May we not reply by saying that it is not so even in the case of the arts referred to: because a man may produce something grammatical either by chance or the suggestion of another; but then only will he be a grammarian when he not only produces something grammatical but does so grammarian-wise, *i.e.* in virtue of the grammatical knowledge he himself possesses.

Again, the cases of the arts and the virtues are not

parallel: because those things which are produced by the arts have their excellence in themselves, and it is sufficient therefore that these when produced should be in a certain state: but those which are produced in the way of the virtues, are, strictly speaking, actions of a certain kind (say of justice or perfected self-mastery), not merely if in themselves they are in a certain state but if also he who does them does them being himself in a certain state, first if knowing what he is doing, next if with deliberate preference, and with such preference for the things' own sake; and thirdly if being himself stable and unapt to change. Now to constitute possession of the arts these requisites are not reckoned in, excepting the one point of knowledge: whereas for possession of the virtues knowledge avails little or nothing, but the other requisites avail not a little, but, in fact, are all in all, and these requisites as a matter of fact do come from oftentimes doing the actions of justice and perfected self-mastery.

The facts, it is true, are called by the names of these habits when they are such as the just or perfectly self-mastering man would do; but he is not in possession of the virtues who merely does these facts, but he who also so does them as the just and self-mastering do them.

We are right then in saying, that these virtues are formed in a man by his doing the actions; but no one, if he should leave them undone, would be even in the way to become a good man. Yet people in general do not perform these actions, but taking refuge in talk they flatter themselves they are philosophising, and that they will so be good men; acting in truth very like those sick people who listen to the doctor with great attention but do nothing that he tells them: just as these then cannot be well bodily under such a course of treatment, so neither can those be mentally by such philosophising.

5 Next, we must examine what virtue is. Well, since the things which come to be in the mind are, in all, of three kinds, feelings, capacities, states, virtue of course must belong to one of the three classes.

By feelings, I mean such as lust, anger, fear, confidence, envy, joy, friendship, hatred, longing, emulation, compassion, in short all such as are followed by pleasure or pain: by capacities, those in right of which we are said to be capable of these feelings; as by virtue of which we are able to have been made angry, or grieved, or to have compassionated; by states, those in right of which we are in a certain relation good or bad to the aforementioned feelings; to having been made angry, for instance, we are in a wrong relation if in our anger we were too violent or too slack, but if we were in the happy medium we are in a right relation to the feeling. And so on of the rest.

Now feelings neither the virtues nor vices are, because in right of the feelings we are not denominated either good or bad, but in right of the virtues and vices we are.

Again, in right of the feelings we are neither praised nor blamed (for a man is not commended for being afraid or being angry, nor blamed for being angry merely but for being so in a particular way), but in right of the virtues and vices we are.

Again, both anger and fear we feel without moral choice, whereas the virtues are acts of moral choice, or at least certainly not independent of it.

Moreover, in right of the feelings we are said to be

moved, but in right of the virtues and vices not to be moved, but disposed, in a certain way.

And for these same reasons they are not capacities, for we are not called good or bad merely because we are able to feel, nor are we praised or blamed.

And again, capacities we have by nature, but we do not come to be good or bad by nature, as we have said before.

Since then the virtues are neither feelings nor capacities, it remains that they must be states.

6 Now what the genus of virtue is has been said; but we must not merely speak of it thus, that it is a state, but say also what kind of a state it is.

We must observe then that all excellence makes that whereof it is the excellence both to be itself in a good state and to perform its work well. The excellence of the eye, for instance, makes both the eye good and its work also: for by the excellence of the eye we see well. So too the excellence of the horse makes a horse good, and good in speed, and in carrying his rider, and standing up against the enemy. If then this is universally the case, the excellence of man, *i.e.* virtue, must be a state whereby man comes to be good and whereby he will perform well his proper work. Now how this shall be it is true we have said already, but still perhaps it may throw light on the subject to see what is its characteristic nature.

In all quantity then, whether continuous or discrete, one may take the greater part, the less, or the exactly equal, and these either with reference to the thing itself, or relatively to us: and the exactly equal is a mean between excess and defect. Now by the mean of the thing, *i.e.* absolute mean, I denote that which is equidistant from either extreme (which of course is one and the same to all), and by the mean relatively to ourselves, that which is neither too much nor too little for the particular individual. This of course is not one nor the same to all: for instance, suppose ten is too much and two too little, people take six for the absolute mean; because it exceeds the smaller sum by exactly as much as it is itself exceeded by the larger, and this mean is according to arithmetical proportion.

But the mean relatively to ourselves must not be so found; for it does not follow, supposing ten minae is too large a quantity to eat and two too small, that the trainer will order his man six; because for the person who is to take it this also may be too much or too little: for Milo it would be too little, but for a man just commencing his athletic exercises too much: similarly too of the exercises themselves, as running or wrestling.

So then it seems everyone possessed of skill avoids excess and defect, but seeks for and chooses the mean, not the absolute but the relative.

Now if all skill thus accomplishes well its work by keeping an eye on the mean, and bringing the works to this point (whence it is common enough to say of such works as are in a good state, 'one cannot add to or take ought from them,' under the notion of excess or defect destroying goodness but the mean state preserving it), and good artisans, as we say, work with their eye on this, and excellence, like nature, is more exact and better than any art in the world, it must have an aptitude to aim at the mean.

It is moral excellence, *i.e.* virtue, of course which I mean, because this it is which is concerned with feelings and actions, and in these there can be excess and defect and the mean; it is possible, for instance, to feel the emotions of fear, confidence, lust, anger, compassion, and pleasure and pain generally, too much or too little, and in either case wrongly; but to feel them when we ought, on what occasions, towards whom, why, and as, we should do, is the mean, or in other words the best state, and this is the property of virtue.

In like manner too with respect to the actions, there may be excess and defect and the mean. Now virtue is concerned with feelings and actions, in which the excess is wrong and the defect is blamed but the mean is praised and goes right; and both these circumstances belong to virtue. Virtue then is in a sense a mean state, since it certainly has an aptitude for aiming at the mean.

Again, one may go wrong in many different ways (because, as the Pythagoreans expressed it, evil is of the class of the infinite, good of the finite), but right only in one; and so the former is easy, the latter difficult; easy to miss the mark, but hard to hit it: and for these reasons, therefore, both the excess and defect belong to vice, and the mean state to virtue; for, as the poet has it,

'Men may be bad in many ways,
    But good in one alone.'

Virtue then is 'a state apt to exercise deliberate choice, being in the relative mean, determined by reason, and as the man of practical wisdom would determine.'

It is a middle state between too faulty ones, in the way of excess on one side and of defect on the other: and it is so moreover, because the faulty states on one side fall short of, and those on the other exceed, what is right, both in the case of the feelings and the actions; but virtue finds, and when found adopts, the mean.

And so, viewing it in respect of its essence and definition, virtue is a mean state; but in reference to the chief good and to excellence it is the highest state possible.

But it must not be supposed that every action or every feeling is capable of subsisting in this mean state, because some there are which are so named as immediately to convey the notion of badness, as malevolence, shamelessness, envy; or, to instance in actions, adultery, theft, homicide; for all these and suchlike are blamed because they are in themselves bad, not the having too much or too little of them.

In these then you never can go right, but must always be wrong: nor in such does the right or wrong depend on the selection of a proper person, time, or manner (take adultery for instance), but simply doing any one soever of those things is being wrong.

You might as well require that there should be determined a mean state, an excess and a defect in respect of acting unjustly, being cowardly, or giving up all control of the passions: for at this rate there will be of excess and defect a mean state; of excess, excess; and of defect, defect.

But just as of perfected self-mastery and courage there is no excess and defect, because the mean is in one point of view the highest possible state, so neither of those faulty states can you have a mean state, excess, or defect, but howsoever done they are wrong: you cannot, in short, have of excess and defect a mean state, nor of a mean state excess and defect.

Section 7 to end

The definition of virtue above is applied to the particular virtues. Each virtue aims at the mean between an excess and a deficiency of a certain feeling or kind of conduct. But to strike the mean is a hard thing to achieve, particularly when pleasure is involved.

philanthropy

BOOK THREE

Voluntary and involuntary acts – choice, deliberation and wish – responsibility

1 Now since virtue is concerned with the regulation of feelings and actions, and praise and blame arise upon such as are voluntary, while for the involuntary allowance is made, and sometimes compassion is excited, it is perhaps a necessary task for those who are investigating the nature of virtue to draw out the distinction between what is voluntary and what involuntary; and it is certainly useful for legislators, with respect to the assigning of honours and punishments.

Involuntary actions then are thought to be of two kinds, being done either on compulsion, or by reason of ignorance.

An action is, properly speaking, compulsory, when the origination is external to the agent, being such that in it the agent (perhaps we may more properly say the patient) contributes nothing; as if a wind were to convey you anywhere, or men having power over your person.

But when actions are done, either from fear of greater evils, or from some honourable motive, as, for instance, if you were ordered to commit some base act by a despot who had your parents or children in his power, and they were to be saved upon your compliance or die upon your refusal, in such cases there is room for a question whether the actions are voluntary or involuntary.

A similar question arises with respect to cases of throwing goods overboard in a storm: abstractedly no man throws away his property willingly, but with a view to his own and his shipmates' safety anyone would who had any sense.

The truth is, such actions are of a mixed kind, but are most like voluntary actions; for they are choiceworthy at the time when they are being done, and the end or object of the action must be taken with reference to the actual occasion. Further, we must denominate an action voluntary or involuntary at the time of doing it: now in the given case the man acts voluntarily, because the originating of the motion of his limbs in such actions rests with himself; and where the origination is in himself it rests with himself to do or not to do.

Such actions then are voluntary, though in the abstract perhaps involuntary because no one would choose any of such things in and by itself.

But for such actions men sometimes are even praised, as when they endure any disgrace or pain to secure great and honourable equivalents; if vice versa, then they are blamed, because it shows a base mind to endure things very disgraceful for no honourable object, or for a trifling one.

For some again no praise is given, but allowance is made; as where a man does what he should not by reason of such things as overstrain the powers of human nature, or pass the limits of human endurance.

Some acts perhaps there are for which compulsion cannot be pleaded, but a man should rather suffer the worst and die; how absurd, for instance, are the pleas of compulsion with which Alcmaeon in Euripides' play excuses his matricide!

But it is difficult sometimes to decide what kind of thing should be chosen instead of what, or what endured in preference to what, and much more so to abide by one's decisions: for in general the alternatives are painful, and the actions required are base, and so praise or blame is awarded according as persons have been compelled or no.

What kind of actions then are to be called compulsory? May we say, simply and abstractedly whenever the cause is external and the agent contributes nothing; and that where the acts are in themselves such as one would not wish but choiceworthy at the present time and in preference to such and such things, and where the origination rests with the agent, the actions are in themselves involuntary but at the given time and in preference to such and such things voluntary; and they are more like voluntary than involuntary, because the actions consist of little details, and these are voluntary.

But what kind of things one ought to choose instead of what, it is not easy to settle, for there are many differences in particular instances.

But suppose a person should say, things pleasant and honourable exert a compulsive force (for that they are external and do compel); at that rate every action is on compulsion, because these are universal motives of action.

Again, they who act on compulsion and against their will do so with pain; but they who act by reason of what is pleasant or honourable act with pleasure.

It is truly absurd for a man to attribute his actions to external things instead of to his own capacity for being easily caught by them; or, again, to ascribe the honourable to himself, and the base ones to pleasure.

So then that seems to be compulsory 'whose origination is from without, the party compelled contributing nothing.'

Now every action of which ignorance is the cause is not-voluntary, but that only is involuntary which is attended with pain and remorse; for clearly the man who has done anything by reason of ignorance, but is not annoyed at his own action, cannot be said to have done it *with* his will because he did not know he was doing it, nor again *against* his will because he is not sorry for it.

So then of the class 'acting by reason of ignorance', he who feels regret afterwards is thought to be an involuntary agent, and him that has no such feeling, since he certainly is different from the other, we will call a not-voluntary agent; for as there is a real difference it is better to have a proper name.

Again, there seems to be a difference between acting *because of* ignorance and acting *with* ignorance: for instance, we do not usually assign ignorance as the cause of the actions of the drunken or angry man, but either the drunkenness or the anger, yet they act not knowingly but with ignorance.

Again, every bad man is ignorant what he ought to do and what to leave undone, and by reason of such error men become unjust and wholly evil.

Again, we do not usually apply the term involuntary when a man is ignorant of his own true interest; because ignorance which affects moral choice constitutes depravity but not involuntariness: nor does any ignorance of principle (because for this men are blamed) but ignorance in particular details, wherein consists the action and wherewith it is concerned, for in these there is both compassion and allowance, because he who acts in ignorance of any of them acts in a proper sense involuntarily.

It may be as well, therefore, to define these particular details; what they are, and how many; viz. who acts, what he is doing, with respect to what or in what, sometimes with what, as with what instrument, and with what result (as that of preservation, for instance), and how, as whether softly or violently.

All these particulars, in one and the same case, no man in his senses could be ignorant of; plainly not of the agent, being himself. But what he is doing a man may be ignorant, as men in speaking say a thing escaped them unawares; or as Aeschylus did with respect to the Mysteries, that he was not aware that it was unlawful to speak of them; or as in the case of that catapult accident the other day the man said he discharged it merely to display its operation. Or a person might suppose a son to be an enemy, as Merope did; or that the spear really pointed was rounded off; or that the stone was a pumice; or in striking with a view to save might kill; or might strike when merely wishing to show another, as people do in sham-fighting.

Now since ignorance is possible in respect to all these details in which the action consists, he that acted in ignorance of any of them is thought to have acted involuntarily, and he most so who was in ignorance as regards the most important, which are thought to be those in which the action consists, and the result.

Further, not only must the ignorance be of this kind, to constitute an action involuntary, but it must be also understood that the action is followed by pain and regret.

Now since all involuntary action is either upon compulsion or by reason of ignorance, voluntary action would seem to be 'that whose origination is in the agent, he being aware of the particular details in which the action consists.'

For, it may be, men are not justified by calling those actions involuntary, which are done by reason of anger or lust.

Because, in the first place, if this be so no other animal but man, and not even children, can be said to act voluntarily. Next, is it meant that we never act voluntarily when we act from lust or anger, or that we act voluntarily in doing what is right and involuntarily in doing what is discreditable? The latter supposition is absurd, since the cause is one and the same. Then as to the former, it is a strange thing to maintain actions to be involuntary which we are bound to grasp at: now there are occasions on which anger is a duty, and there are things which we are bound to lust after, health, for instant, and learning.

Again, whereas actions strictly involuntary are thought to be attended with pain, those which are done to gratify lust are thought to be pleasant.

Again: how does the involuntariness make any difference between wrong actions done from deliberate calculation, and those done by reason of anger? For both ought to be avoided, and the irrational feelings are thought to be just as natural to man as reason, and so of course must be such actions of the individual as are done from anger and lust. It is absurd then to class these actions among the involuntary.

2 Having thus drawn out the distinction between voluntary and involuntary action our next step is to examine into the nature of moral choice, because this seems most intimately connected with virtue and to be

a more decisive test of moral character than a man's acts are.

Now moral choice is plainly voluntary, but the two are not co-extensive, voluntary being the more comprehensive term; for first, children and all other animals share in voluntary action but not in moral choice; and next, sudden actions we call voluntary but do not ascribe them to moral choice.

Nor do they appear to be right who say it is lust or anger, or wish, or opinion of a certain kind; because, in the first place, moral choice is not shared by the irrational animals while lust and anger are. Next; the man who fails of self-control acts from lust but not from moral choice; the man of self-control, on the contrary, from moral choice, not from lust. Again: whereas lust is frequently opposed to moral choice, lust is not to lust.

Lastly: the object-matter of lust is the pleasant and the painful, but of moral choice neither the one nor the other. Still less can it be anger, because actions done from anger are thought generally to be least of all consequent on moral choice.

Nor is it wish either, though appearing closely connected with it; because, in the first place, moral choice has not for its objects impossibilities, and if a man were to say he chose them he would be thought to be a fool; but wish may have impossible things for its objects, immortality for instance.

Wish again may be exercised on things in the accomplishment of which one's self could have nothing to do, as the success of any particular actor or athlete; but no man chooses things of this nature, only such as he believes he may himself be instrumental in procuring.

Further: wish has for its object the end rather, but moral choice the means to the end; for instance, we wish to be healthy but we choose the means which will make us so; or happiness again we wish for, and commonly say so, but to say we choose is not an appropriate term, because, in short, the province of moral choice seems to be those things which are in our own power.

Neither can it be opinion; for opinion is thought to be unlimited in its range of objects, and to be exercised as well upon things eternal and impossible as on those which are in our own power: again, opinion is logically divided into true and false, not into good and bad as moral choice is.

However, nobody perhaps maintains its identity with opinion simply; but it is not the same with opinion of any kind, because by choosing good and bad things we are constituted of a certain character, but by having opinions on them we are not.

Again, we choose to take or avoid, and so on, but we opine what a thing is, or for what it is serviceable, or how; but we do not opine to take or avoid.

Further, moral choice is commended rather for having a right object than for being judicious, but opinion for being formed in accordance with truth.

Again, we choose such things as we pretty well know to be good, but we form opinions respecting such as we do not know at all.

And it is not thought that choosing and opining best always go together, but that some opine the better course and yet by reason of viciousness choose not the things which they should.

It may be urged, that opinion always precedes or accompanies moral choice; be it so, this makes no difference, for this is not the point in question, but whether moral choice is the same as opinion of a certain kind.

Since then it is none of the aforementioned things, what is it, or how is it characterised? Voluntary it plainly is, but not all voluntary action is an object of moral choice. May we not say then, it is 'that voluntary which has passed through a stage of previous deliberation'? because moral choice is attended with reasoning and intellectual process. The etymology of its Greek name seems to give a hint of it, being when analysed 'chosen in preference to somewhat else'.

3 Well then; do men deliberate about everything, and is anything soever the object of deliberation, or are there some matters with respect to which there is none? (It may be as well perhaps to say, that by 'object of deliberation' is meant such matter as a sensible man would deliberate upon, not what any fool or madman might.)

Well: about eternal things no one deliberates; as, for instance, the universe, or the incommensurability of the diameter and side of a square.

Nor again about things which are in motion but which always happen in the same way either necessarily, or naturally, or from some other cause, as the solstices or the sunrise.

Nor about those which are variable, as drought and rains; nor fortuitous matters, as finding of treasure.

Nor in fact even about all human affairs; no Lacedaemonian, for instance, deliberates as to the best course for the Scythian government to adopt; because in such cases we have no power over the result.

But we do deliberate respecting such practical matters as are in our own power (which are what are left after all our exclusions).

I have adopted this division because causes seem to be divisible into nature, necessity, chance, and moreover intellect, and all human powers.

And as man in general deliberates about what man in general can effect, so individuals do about such practical things as can be effected through their own instrumentality.

Again, we do not deliberate respecting such arts or sciences as are exact and independent: as, for instance, about written characters, because we have no doubt how they should be formed; but we do deliberate on all such things as are usually done through our own instrumentality, but not invariably in the same way; as, for instance, about matters connected with the healing art, or with money-making; and, again, more about piloting ships than gymnastic exercises, because the former has been less exactly determined, and so forth; and more about arts than sciences, because we more frequently doubt respecting the former.

So then deliberation takes place in such matters as are under general laws, but still uncertain how in any given case they will issue, *i.e.* in which there is some indefiniteness; and for great matters we associate co-adjutors in counsel, distrusting our ability to settle them alone.

Further, we deliberate not about ends, but means to ends. No physician, for instance, deliberates whether he will cure, nor orator whether he will persuade, nor statesman whether he will produce a good constitution, nor in fact any man in any other function about his particular end; but having set before them a certain end they look how and through what means it may be accomplished: if there is a choice of means, they examine further which are easiest and most creditable; or, if there is but one means of accomplishing the object, then how it may be through this, this again through what, till they come to the first cause; and this will be the last found; for a man engaged in a process of deliberation seems to seek and analyse, as a man, to solve a problem, analyses the figure given him. And plainly not every search is deliberation, those in mathematics to wit, but every deliberation is a search, and the last step in the analysis is the first in the constructive process. And if in the course of their search men come upon an impossibility, they give it up; if money, for instance, be necessary, but cannot be got: but if the thing appears possible they then attempt to do it.

And by possible I mean what may be done through our own instrumentality (of course what may be done through our friends is through our own instrumentality in a certain sense, because the origination in such cases rests with us). And the object of search is sometimes the necessary instruments, sometimes the method of using them; and similarly in the rest sometimes through what, and sometimes how or through what.

So it seems, as has been said, that man is the originator of his actions; and deliberation has for its object whatever may be done through one's own instrumentality, and the actions are with a view to other things; and so it is, not the end, but the means to ends on which deliberation is employed.

Nor, again, is it employed on matters of detail, as whether the substance before me is bread, or has been properly cooked; for these come under the province of sense, and if a man is to be always deliberating, he may go on *ad infinitum*.

Further, exactly the same matter is the object both of deliberation and moral choice; but that which is the object of moral choice is thenceforward separated off and definite, because by object of moral choice is denoted that which after deliberation has been preferred to something else: for each man leaves off searching how he shall do a thing when he has brought the origination up to himself, *i.e.* to the governing principle in himself, because it is this which makes the choice. A good illustration of this is furnished by the old regal constitutions which Homer drew from, in which the kings would announce to the commonalty what they had determined before.

Now since that which is the object of moral choice is something in our own power, which is the object of deliberation and the grasping of the will, moral choice must be 'a grasping after something in our own power consequent upon deliberation': because after having deliberated we decide, and then grasp by our will in accordance with the result of our deliberation.

Let this be accepted as a sketch of the nature and object of moral choice, that object being 'means to ends'.

4   That wish has for its object-matter the end, has been already stated; but there are two opinions respecting it; some thinking that its object is real good, others whatever impresses the mind with a notion of good.

Now those who maintain that the object of wish is real good are beset by this difficulty, that what is wished for by him who chooses wrongly is not really an object of wish (because, on their theory, if it is an object of wish, it must be good, but it is, in the case supposed, evil). Those who maintain, on the contrary, that that which impresses the mind with a notion of good is properly the object of wish, have to meet this difficulty, that there is nothing naturally an object of wish but to each individual whatever seems good to him; now different people have different notions, and it may chance contrary ones.

But, if these opinions do not satisfy us, may we not say that, abstractedly and as a matter of objective truth, the really good is the object of wish, but to each individual whatever impresses his mind with the notion of good. And so to the good man that is an object of wish which is really and truly so, but to the bad man anything may be; just as physically those things are wholesome to the healthy which are really so, but other things to the sick. And so too of bitter and sweet, and hot and heavy, and so on. For the good man judges in every instance correctly, and in every instance the notion conveyed to his mind is the true one.

For there are fair and pleasant things peculiar to, and so varying with, each state; and perhaps the most distinguishing characteristic of the good man is his seeing the truth in every instance, he being, in fact, the rule and measure of these matters.

The multitude of men seem to be deceived by reason of pleasure, because though it is not really a good it impresses their minds with the notion of goodness, so they choose what is pleasant as good and avoid pain as an evil.

5 Now since the end is the object of wish, and the means to the end of deliberation and moral choice, the

actions regarding these matters must be in the way of moral choice, *i.e.* voluntary: but the acts of working out the virtues are such actions, and therefore virtue is in our power.

And so too is vice: because wherever it is in our power to do it is also in our power to forbear doing, and vice versa: therefore if the doing (being in a given case creditable) is in our power, so too is the forbearing (which is in the same case discreditable), and vice versa.

But if it is in our power to do and to forbear doing what is creditable or the contrary, and these respectively constitute the being good or bad, then the being good or vicious characters is in our power.

As for the well-known saying, 'No man voluntarily is wicked or involuntarily happy,' it is partly true, partly false; for no man is happy against his will, of course, but wickedness is voluntary. Or must we dispute the statements lately made, and not say that man is the originator or generator of his actions as much as of his children?

But if this is matter of plain manifest fact, and we cannot refer our actions to any other originations beside those in our own power, those things must be in our own power, and so voluntary, the originations of which are in ourselves.

Moreover, testimony seems to be borne to these positions both privately by individuals, and by law-givers too, in that they chastise and punish those who do wrong (unless they do so on compulsion, or by reason of ignorance which is not self-caused), while they honour those who act rightly, under the notion of being likely to encourage the latter and restrain the former. But such things as are not in our own power, *i.e.* not voluntary, no one thinks of encouraging us to do, knowing it to be of no avail for one to have been persuaded not to be hot (for instance), or feel pain, or be hungry, and so forth, because we shall have those sensations all the same.

And what makes the case stronger is this: that they chastise for the very fact of ignorance, when it is thought to be self-caused; to the drunken, for instance, penalties are double, because the origination in such case lies in a man's own self: for he might have helped getting drunk, and this is the cause of his ignorance.

Again, those also who are ignorant of legal regulations which they are bound to know, and which are not hard to know, they chastise; and similarly in all other cases where neglect is thought to be the cause of the ignorance, under the notion that it was in their power to prevent their ignorance, because they might have paid attention.

But perhaps a man is of such a character that he cannot attend to such things: still men are themselves the causes of having become such characters by living carelessly, and also of being unjust or destitute of self-control, the former by doing evil actions, the latter by spending their time in drinking and such-like; because the particular acts of working form corresponding characters, as is shown by those who are practising for any contest or particular course of action, for such men persevere in the acts of working.

As for the plea, that a man did not know that habits are produced from separate acts of working, we reply, such ignorance is a mark of excessive stupidity.

Furthermore, it is wholly irrelevant to say that the man who acts unjustly or dissolutely does not *wish* to attain the habits of these vices: for if a man wittingly does those things whereby he must become unjust he is to all intents and purposes unjust voluntarily; but he cannot with a wish cease to be unjust and become just. For, to take the analogous case, the sick man cannot with a wish be well again, yet in a supposable case he is voluntarily ill because he has produced his sickness by living intemperately and disregarding his physicians. There was a time then when he might have helped being ill, but now he has let himself go he cannot any longer; just as he who has let a stone out of his hand cannot recall it, and yet it rested with him to aim and throw it, because the origination was in his power. Just so the unjust man, and he who has lost all self-control, might originally have helped being what they are, and so they are voluntarily what they are; but now that they are become so they no longer have the power of being otherwise.

And not only are mental diseases voluntary, but the bodily are so in some men, whom we accordingly blame: for such as are naturally deformed no one blames, only such as are so by reason of want of exercise, and neglect: and so too of weakness and maiming: no one would think of upbraiding, but would rather compassionate, a man who is blind by nature, or from disease, or from an accident; but every one would blame him who was so from excess of wine, or any other kind of intemperance. It seems, then, that in respect of bodily diseases, those which depend on ourselves are censured, those which do not are not censured; and if so, then in the case of the mental disorders, those which are censured must depend upon ourselves.

But suppose a man to say, 'that (by our own admission) all men aim at that which conveys to their minds an impression of good, and that men have no control over this impression, but that the end impresses each with a notion correspondent to his own individual character; that to be sure if each man is in a way the cause of his own moral state, so he will be also of the kind of impression he receives: whereas, if this is not so, no one is the cause to himself of doing evil actions, but he does them by reason of ignorance of the true end, supposing that through their means he will secure the chief good. Further, that this aiming at the end is no matter of one's own choice, but one must be born with a power of mental vision, so to speak, whereby to judge fairly and choose that which is really good; and he is blessed by nature who has this naturally well: because it is the most important thing and the fairest, and what a man cannot get or learn from another but will have such as nature has given it; and for this to be so given well and fairly would be excellence of nature in the highest and truest sense.'

If all this be true, how will virtue be a whit more voluntary than vice? Alike to the good man and the bad, the end gives its impression and is fixed by nature or howsoever you like to say, and they act so and so, referring everything else to this end.

Whether then we suppose that the end impresses each man's mind with certain notions not merely by nature, but that there is somewhat also dependent on himself; or that the end is given by nature, and yet virtue is voluntary because the good man does all the rest voluntarily, vice must be equally so; because his own agency equally attaches to the bad man in the actions, even if not in the selection of the end.

If then, as is commonly said, the virtues are voluntary (because we at least co-operate in producing our moral states, and we assume the end to be a certain kind according as we are ourselves of certain characters), the vices must be voluntary also, because the cases are exactly similar.

Well now, we have stated generally respecting the moral virtues, the genus (in outline), that they are mean states, and that they are habits, and how they are formed, and that they are of themselves calculated to act upon the circumstances out of which they were formed, and that they are in our own power and voluntary, and are to be done so as right reason may direct.

But the particular actions and the habits are not voluntary in the same sense; for of the actions we are masters from beginning to end (supposing of course a knowledge of the particular details), but only of the origination of the habits, the addition by small particular accessions not being cognisable (as is the case with sicknesses): still they are voluntary because it rested with us to use our circumstances this way or that.

Here we will resume the particular discussion of the moral virtues, and say what they are, what is their object-matter, and how they stand respectively related to it: of course their number will be thereby shown.

Section 6 to end

Examination of the particular virtues, beginning with (1) courage, and (2) self-restraint in relation to sensual pleasures.

70

The other moral virtues are treated in turn: liberality, munificence, greatness of spirit, proper ambition, good temper, agreeableness, correct appreciation of one's merits, wittiness, modesty.

BOOK FIVE

Justice and injustice

1   Now the points for our inquiry in respect of justice and injustice are, what kind of actions are their object-matter, and what kind of a mean state justice is, and between what points the abstract principle of it, *i.e.* the just, is a mean. And our inquiry shall be, if you please, conducted in the same method as we have observed in the foregoing parts of this treatise.

We see then that all men mean by the term justice a moral state such that in consequence of it men have the capacity of doing what is just, and actually do it, and wish it: similarly also with respect to injustice, a moral state such that in consequence of it men do unjustly and wish what is unjust: let us also be content then with these as a ground-work sketched out.

I mention the two, because the same does not hold with regard to states whether of mind or body as with regard to sciences or faculties; I mean that whereas it is thought that the same faculty or science embraces contraries, a state will not: from health, for instance, not the contrary acts are done but the healthy ones only; we say a man walks healthily when he walks as the healthy man would.

However, of the two contrary states the one may be frequently known from the other, and oftentimes the states from their subject-matter: if it be seen clearly what a good state of body is, then is it also seen what a bad state is, and from the things which belong to a good state of body the good state itself is seen, and vice versa. If, for instance, the good state is firmness of flesh it follows that the bad state is flabbiness of flesh; and whatever causes firmness of flesh is connected with the good state.

It follows moreover in general, that if of two contrary terms the one is used in many senses so also will the other be; as, for instance, if 'the just', then also 'the unjust'. Now justice and injustice do seem to be used respectively in many senses, but, because the line of demarcation between these is very fine and minute, it commonly escapes notice that they are thus used, and it is not plain and manifest as where the various significations of terms are widely different: for in these last the visible difference is great; for instance, the word *kleis* is used equivocally to denote the bone which is under the neck of animals and the instrument with which people close doors.

Let it be ascertained then in how many senses the term 'unjust man' is used. Well, he who violates the law, and he who is a grasping man, and the unequal man, are all thought to be unjust: and so manifestly the just man will be the man who acts according to law, and the equal man. 'The just' then will be the lawful and the equal, and 'the unjust' the unlawful and the unequal.

Well, since the unjust man is also a grasping man, he will be so, of course, with respect to good things, but not of every kind, only those which are the subject-matter of good and bad fortune and which are in themselves always good but not always to the individual. Yet men pray for and pursue these things: this they should not do but pray that things which are in the abstract good may be so also to them, and choose what is good for themselves.

But the unjust man does not always choose actually the greater part, but even sometimes the less; as in the case of things which are simply evil: still, since the less evil is thought to be in a manner a good and the grasping is after good, therefore even in this case he is thought to be a grasping man, *i.e.* one who strives for more good than fairly falls to his share: of course he is also an unequal man, this being an inclusive and common term.

We said that the violator of law is unjust, and the keeper of the law just: further, it is plain that all lawful things are in a manner just, because by lawful we understand what have been defined by the legislative power and each of these we say is just. The laws too give directions on all points, aiming either at the common good of all, or that of the best, or that of those in power (taking for the standard real goodness or adopting some other estimate); in one way we mean by just, those things which are apt to produce and preserve happiness and its ingredients for the social community.

Further, the law commands the doing the deeds not only of the brave man (as not leaving the ranks, nor flying, nor throwing away one's arms), but those also of the perfectly self-mastering man, as abstinence from adultery and wantonness; and those of the meek man, as refraining from striking others or using abusive language: and in like manner in respect of the other virtues and vices commanding some things and forbidding others, rightly if it is a good law, in a way somewhat inferior if it is one extemporised.

Now this justice is in fact perfect virtue, yet not

simply so but as exercised towards one's neighbour: and for this reason justice is thought oftentimes to be the best of the virtues, and

> 'neither Hesper nor the Morning-star
> So worthy of our admiration:'

and in a proverbial saying we express the same;

> 'All virtue is in justice comprehended.'

And it is in a special sense perfect virtue because it is the practice of perfect virtue. And perfect it is because he that has it is able to practise his virtue towards his neighbour and not merely on himself; I mean, there are many who can practise virtue in the regulation of their own personal conduct who are wholly unable to do it in transactions with their neighbour. And for this reason that saying of Bias is thought to be a good one,

> 'Rule will show what a man is;'

for he who bears rule is necessarily in contact with others, *i.e.* in a community. And for this same reason justice alone of all the virtues is thought to be a good to others, because it has immediate relation to some other person, inasmuch as the just man does what is advantageous to another, either to his ruler or fellow-subject. Now he is the basest of men who practises vice not only in his own person but towards his friends also; but he the best who practises virtue not merely in his own person but towards his neighbour, for this is a matter of some difficulty.

However, justice in this sense is not a part of virtue but is co-extensive with virtue; nor is the injustice which answers to it a part of vice but co-extensive with vice. Now wherein justice in this sense differs from virtue appears from what has been said: it is the same really, but the point of view is not the same: in so far as it has respect to one's neighbour it is justice, in so far as it is such and such a moral state it is simply virtue.

2 But the object of our inquiry is justice, in the sense in which it is a part of virtue (for there is such a thing, as we commonly say), and likewise with respect to particular injustice. And of the existence of this last the following consideration is a proof: there are many vices by practising which a man acts unjustly, of course, but does not grasp at more than his share of good; if, for instance, by reason of cowardice he throws away his shield, or by reason of ill-temper he uses abusive language, or by reason of stinginess does not give a friend pecuniary assistance; but whenever he does a grasping action, it is often in the way of none of these vices, certainly not in all of them, still in the way of some vice or other (for we blame him), and in the way of injustice. There is then some kind of injustice distinct from that co-extensive with vice and related to it as a part to a whole, and some 'unjust' related to that which is co-extensive with violation of the law as a part to a whole.

Again, suppose one man seduces a man's wife with a view to gain and actually gets some advantage by it, and another does the same from impulse of lust, at an expense of money and damage; this latter will be thought to be rather destitute of self-mastery than a grasping man, and the former unjust but not destitute of self-mastery: now why? Plainly because of his gaining.

Again, all other acts of injustice we refer to some particular depravity, as, if a man commits adultery, to abandonment to his passions; if he deserts his comrade, to cowardice; if he strikes another, to anger: but if he gains by the act to no other vice than to injustice.

Thus it is clear that there is a kind of injustice different from and besides that which includes all vice, having the same name because the definition is in the same genus; for both have their force in dealings with others, but the one acts upon honour, or wealth, or safety, or by whatever one name we can include all these things, and is actuated by pleasure attendant on gain, while the other acts upon all things which constitute the sphere of the good man's action.

Now that there is more than one kind of justice, and that there is one which is distinct from and besides that which is co-extensive with virtue, is plain: we must next ascertain what it is, and what are its characteristics.

Well, the unjust has been divided into the unlawful and the unequal, and the just accordingly into the lawful and the equal: the aforementioned injustice is in the way of the unlawful. And as the unequal and the more are not the same, but differing as part to whole (because all more is unequal, but not all unequal more), so the unjust and the injustice we are now in search of are not the same with, but other than, those before mentioned, the one being the parts, the other the wholes; for this particular injustice is a part of the injustice co-extensive with vice, and likewise this justice of the justice co-extensive with virtue. So that what we have now to speak of is the particular justice and injustice, and likewise the particular just and unjust.

Here then let us dismiss any further consideration of the justice ranking as co-extensive with virtue (being the practice of virtue in all its bearings towards others), and of the co-relative injustice (being similarly the practice of vice). It is clear too, that we must separate off the just and the unjust involved in these: because one may pretty well say that most lawful things are those which naturally result in action from virtue in its fullest sense, because the law enjoins the living in accordance with each virtue and forbids living in accordance with each vice. And the producing causes of virtue in all its bearings are those enactments which have been made respecting education for society.

By the way, as to individual education, in respect of which a man is simply good without reference to others, whether it is the province of *politike* or some other science we must determine at a future time: for it may be it is not the same thing to be a good man and a good citizen in every case.

Now of the particular justice, and the just involved in it, one species is that which is concerned in the distributions of honour, or wealth, or such other things as are to be shared among the members of the social community (because in these one man as compared with another may have either an equal or an unequal share), and the other is that which is corrective in the various transactions between man and man. And of this latter there are two parts: because of transactions some are voluntary and some involuntary; voluntary, such as follow; selling, buying, use, bail, borrowing, deposit, hiring: and this class is called voluntary because the origination of these transactions is voluntary.

The involuntary again are either such as effect secrecy; as theft, adultery, poisoning, pimping, kidnapping of slaves, assassination, false witness; or accompanied with open violence; as insult, bonds, death, plundering, maiming, foul language, slanderous abuse.

3 Well, the unjust man we have said is unequal, and the abstract 'unjust' unequal: further, it is plain that there is some mean of the unequal, that is to say, the equal or exact half (because in whatever action there is the greater and the less there is also the equal, *i.e.* the exact half). If then the unjust is unequal the just is equal, which all must allow without further proof: and as the equal is a mean the just must be also a mean. Now the equal implies two terms at least: it follows then that the just is both a mean and equal, and these to certain persons; and, in so far as it is a mean, between certain things (that is, the greater and the less), and, so far as it is equal, between two, and in so far as it is just it is so to certain persons. The just then must imply four terms at least, for those to which it is just are two, and the terms representing the things are two.

And there will be the same equality between the terms representing the persons, as between those representing the things: because as the latter are to one another so are the former: for if the persons are not equal they must not have equal shares; in fact this is the very source of all the quarrelling and wrangling in the world, when either they who are equal have and get awarded to them things not equal, or being not equal those things which are equal. Again, the necessity of this equality of ratios is shown by the common phrase 'according to rate,' for all agree that the just in distributions ought to be according to some rate: but what that rate is to be, all do not agree; the democrats are for freedom, oligarchs for wealth, others for nobleness of birth, and the aristocratic party for virtue.

The just, then, is a certain proportionable thing. For proportion does not apply merely to number in the abstract, but to number generally, since it is equality of ratios, and implies four terms at least (that this is the case in what may be called discrete proportion is plain and obvious, but it is true also in continual proportion, for this uses the one term as two, and mentions it twice; thus $A : B : C$ may be expressed $A : B :: B : C$. In the first, B is named twice; and so, if, as in the second, B is actually written twice, the proportionals will be four): and the just likewise implies four terms at the least, and the ratio between the two pairs of terms is the same, because the persons and the things are divided similarly. It will stand then thus, $A : B :: C : D$, and then permutando $A : C :: B : D$, and then (supposing C and D to represent the things) $A + C : B + D :: A : B$. The distribution in fact consisting in putting together these terms thus: and if they are put together so as to preserve this same ratio, the distribution puts them together justly. So then the joining together of the first and third and second and fourth proportionals is the just in the distribution, and this just is the mean relatively to that which violates the proportionate, for the proportionate is a mean and the just is proportionate. Now mathematicians call this kind of proportion geometrical: for in geometrical proportion the whole is to the whole as each part to each part. Furthermore this proportion is not continual, because the person and thing do not make up one term.

The just then is this proportionate, and the unjust that which violates the proportionate; and so there comes to be the greater and the less: which in fact is the case in actual transactions, because he who acts unjustly has the greater share and he who is treated unjustly has the less of what is good: but in the case of what is bad this is reversed: for the less evil compared with the greater comes to be reckoned for good, because the less evil is more choiceworthy than the greater, and what is choiceworthy is good, and the more so the greater good.

This then is the one species of the just.

4 And the remaining one is the corrective, which arises to voluntary as well as involuntary transactions. Now this just has a different form from the afore-mentioned; for that which is concerned in distribution of common property is always according to the afore-mentioned proportion: I mean that, if the division is made out of common property, the shares will bear the same proportion to one another as the original contributions did: and the unjust which is opposite to this just is that which violates the proportionate.

But the just which arises in transactions between men is an equal in a certain sense, and the unjust an unequal, only not in the way of that proportion but of arithmetical. Because it makes no difference whether a robbery, for instance, is committed by a good man on a bad or by a bad man on a good, nor whether a good or a bad man has committed adultery: the law looks only to the difference created by the injury and treats the men as previously equal, where the one does and the other suffers injury, or the one has done and the other suffered harm. And so this unjust, being unequal, the judge endeavours to reduce to equality again, because really when the one party has been wounded and the other has struck him, or the one kills and the other dies, the suffering and the doing are divided into unequal shares; well, the judge tries to restore equality by penalty, thereby taking from the gain.

For these terms gain and loss are applied to these cases, though perhaps the term in some particular instance may not be strictly proper, as gain, for instance, to the man who has given a blow, and loss to him who has received it: still, when the suffering has been estimated, the one is called loss and the other gain.

And so the equal is a mean between the more and the less, which represent gain and loss in contrary ways (I mean, that the more of good and the less of evil is gain, the less of good and the more of evil is loss): between which the equal was stated to be a mean, which equal we say is just: and so the corrective just must be the mean between loss and gain. And this is the reason why, upon a dispute arising, men have recourse to the judge: going to the judge is in fact going to the just, for the judge is meant to be the personification of the just. And men seek a judge as one in the mean, which is expressed in a name given by some to judges (*mesidioi*, or middle-men) under the notion that if they can hit on the mean they shall hit on the just. The just is then surely a mean since the judge is also.

So it is the office of a judge to make things equal, and the line, as it were, having been unequally divided, he takes from the greater part that by which it exceeds the half, and adds this on to the less. And when the whole is divided into two exactly equal portions then men say they have their own, when they have gotten the equal; and the equal is a mean between the greater and the less according to arithmetical equality.

This, by the way, accounts for the etymology of the term by which we in Greek express the ideas of just and judge; (*dikaion* quasi *dichaion*, that is in two parts, and *dikastes* quasi *dichastes*, he who divides into two parts). For when from one of two equal magnitudes somewhat has been taken and added to the other, this latter exceeds the former by twice that portion: if it had been merely taken from the former and not added to the latter, then the latter would have exceeded the former only by that one portion; but in the other case, the greater exceeds the mean by one, and the mean exceeds also by one that magnitude from which the portion was taken. By this illustration, then, we obtain a rule to determine what one ought to take from him who has the greater, and what to add to him who has the less. The excess of the mean over the less must be added to the less, and the excess of the greater over the mean be taken: from the greater.

Thus let there be three straight lines equal to one another. From one of them cut off a portion, and add as much to another of them. The whole line thus made will exceed the remainder of the first-named line, by twice the portion added, and will exceed the untouched line by that portion. And these terms loss and gain are derived from voluntary exchange: that is to say, the having more than what was one's own is called gaining, and the having less than one's original stock is called losing; for instance, in buying or selling, or any other transactions which are guaranteed by law: but when the result is neither more nor less, but exactly the same as there was originally, people say they have their own, and neither lose nor gain.

So then the just we have been speaking of is a mean between loss and gain arising in involuntary trans-actions; that is, it is the having the same after the transaction as one had before it took place.

5 There are people who have a notion that reciprocation is simply just, as the Pythagoreans said: for they defined the just simply and without qualification as 'that which reciprocates with another'. But this simple reciprocation will not fit on either to the distributive just, or the corrective (and yet this is the interpretation they put on the Rhadamanthian rule of just,

'If a man should suffer what he hath done, then there would be straightforward justice');

for in many cases differences arise: as, for instance, suppose one in authority has struck a man, he is not to be struck in turn; or if a man has struck one in authority, he must not only be struck but punished also. And again, the voluntariness or involuntariness of actions makes a great difference.

But in dealings of exchange such a principle of justice as this reciprocation forms the bond of union; but then it must be reciprocation according to proportion and not exact equality, because by proportionate reciprocity of action the social community is held together. For either reciprocation of evil is meant, and if this be not allowed it is thought to be a servile condition of things: or else reciprocation of good, and if this be not effected then there is no admission to participation which is the very bond of their union.

And this is the moral of placing the Temple of the Graces (*kharites*) in the public streets; to impress the notion that there may be requital, this being peculiar to *kharis*, because a man ought to requite with a good turn the man who has done him a favour and then to become himself the originator of another *kharis*, by doing him a favour.

Now the acts of mutual giving in due proportion may be represented by the diameters of a parallelogram, at the four angles of which the parties and their wares are so placed that the side connecting the parties be opposite to that connecting the wares, and each party be connected by one side with his own ware, as in the accompanying diagram.

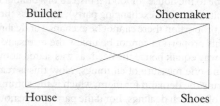

Builder   Shoemaker

House   Shoes

The builder is to receive from the shoemaker of his ware, and to give him of his own: if then there be first proportionate equality, and *then* the reciprocation takes place, there will be the just result which we are speaking of: if not, there is not the equal, nor will the connection stand: for there is no reason why the ware of the one may not be better than that of the other, and therefore before the exchange is made they must have been equalised. And this is so also in the other arts: for they would have been destroyed entirely if there were not a correspondence in point of quantity and quality between the producer and the consumer. For, we must remember, no dealing arises between two of the same kind, two physicians, for instance; but say between a physician and agriculturist, or, to state it generally, between those who are different and not equal, but these of course must have been equalised before the exchange can take place.

It is therefore indispensable that all things which can be exchanged should be capable of comparison, and for this purpose money has come in, and comes to be a kind of medium, for it measures all things and so likewise the excess and defect; for instance, how many shoes are equal to a house or a given quantity of food. As then the builder to the shoemaker, so many shoes must be to the house (or food, if instead of a builder an agriculturist be the exchanging party); for unless there is this proportion there cannot be exchange or dealing, and this proportion cannot be unless the terms are in some way equal; hence the need, as was stated above, of some one measure of all things. Now this is really and truly the demand for them, which is the common bond of all such dealings. For if the parties were not in want at all or not similarly of one another's wares, there would either not be any exchange, or at least not the same.

And money has come to be, by general agreement, a representative of demand: and the account of its Greek name *nomisma* is this, that it is what it is not naturally but by custom or law (*nomos*), and it rests with us to change its value, or make it wholly useless.

Very well then, there will be reciprocation when the terms have been equalised so as to stand in this proportion; Agriculturist : Shoemaker : : wares of Shoemaker : wares of Agriculturist; but you must bring them to this form of proportion when they exchange, otherwise the one extreme will combine both exceedings of the mean: but when they have exactly their own then they are equal and have dealings, because the same equality can come to be in their case. Let A represent an agriculturist, C food, B a shoemaker, D his wares equalised with A's. Then the proportion will be correct, $A : B :: C : D$; *now* reciprocation will be practicable, if it were not, there would have been no dealing.

Now that what connects men in such transactions is demand, as being some one thing, is shown by the fact that, when either one does not want the other or neither want one another, they do not exchange at all: whereas they do when one wants what the other man has, wine for instance, giving in return corn for exportation.

And further, money is a kind of security to us in respect of exchange at some future time (supposing that one wants nothing now that we shall have it when we do): the theory of money being that whenever one brings it one can receive commodities in exchange: of course this too is liable to depreciation, for its purchasing power is not always the same, but still it is of a more permanent nature than the commodities it represents. And this is the reason why all things should have a price set upon them, because thus there may be exchange at any time, and if exchange then dealing. So money, like a measure, making all things commensurable equalises them: for if there was not exchange there would not have been dealing, nor exchange if there were not equality, nor equality if there were not the capacity of being commensurate: it is impossible that things so greatly different should be really commensurate, but we can approximate sufficiently for all practical purposes in reference to demand. The common measure must be some one thing, and also from agreement (for which reason it is called *nomisma*), for this makes all things commensurable: in fact, all things are measured by money. Let B represent ten minae, A a house worth five minae, or in other words half B, C a bed worth A a tenth of B: it is clear then how many beds are equal to one house, namely, five.

It is obvious also that exchange was thus conducted before the existence of money: for it makes no difference whether you give for a house five beds or the price of five beds.

We have now said then what the abstract just and unjust are, and these having been defined it is plain that just acting is a mean between acting unjustly and being acted unjustly towards: the former being equivalent to having more, and the latter to having less.

But justice, it must be observed, is a mean state not after the same manner as the forementioned virtues, but because it aims at producing the mean, while injustice occupies *both* the extremes.

And justice is the moral state in virtue of which the just man is said to have the aptitude for practising the just in the way of moral choice, and for making division between himself and another, or between two other men, not so as to give to himself the greater and to his neighbour the less share of what is choiceworthy and contrariwise of what is hurtful, but what is proportionably equal, and in like manner when adjudging the rights of two other men.

Injustice is all this with respect to the unjust: and since the unjust is excess or defect of what is good or hurtful respectively, in violation of the proportionate, therefore injustice is both excess and defect because it aims at producing excess and defect; excess, that is, in a man's own case of what is simply advantageous, and defect of what is hurtful: and in the case of other men in like manner generally speaking, only that the proportionate is violated not always in one direction as before but whichever way it happens in the given case. And of the unjust act the less is being acted unjustly towards, and the greater the acting unjustly towards others.

Let this way of describing the nature of justice and injustice, and likewise the just and the unjust generally, be accepted as sufficient.

6 Again, since a man may do unjust acts and not yet have formed a character of injustice, the question arises whether a man is unjust in each particular form of injustice, say a thief, or adulterer, or robber, by doing acts of a given character.

We may say, I think, that this will not of itself make any difference; a man may, for instance, have had connection with another's wife, knowing well with whom he was sinning, but he may have done it not of deliberate choice but from the impulse of passion: of course he acts unjustly, but he has not necessarily formed an unjust character: that is, he may have stolen yet not be a thief; or committed an act of adultery but still not be an adulterer, and so on in other cases which might be enumerated.

Of the relation which reciprocation bears to the just we have already spoken: and here it should be noticed that the just which we are investigating is both the just in the abstract and also as exhibited in social relations, which latter arises in the case of those who live in communion with a view to independence and who are free and equal either proportionately or numerically.

It follows then that those who are not in this position have not among themselves the social just, but still just of some kind and resembling that other. For just implies mutually acknowledged law, and law the possibility of injustice, for adjudication is the act of distinguishing between the just and the unjust.

And among whomsoever there is the possibility of injustice among these there is that of acting unjustly; but it does not hold conversely that injustice attaches to all among whom there is the possibility of acting unjustly, since by the former we mean giving one's self the larger share of what is abstractedly good and the less of what is abstractedly evil.

This, by the way, is the reason why we do not allow a man to govern, but principle, because a man governs for himself and comes to be a despot: but the office of a ruler is to be guardian of the just and therefore of the equal. Well then, since he seems to have no peculiar personal advantage, supposing him a just man, for in this case he does not allot to himself the larger share of what is abstractedly good unless it falls to his share proportionately (for which reason he really governs for others, and so justice, men say, is a good not to one's self so much as to others, as was mentioned before), therefore some compensation must be given him, as there actually is in the shape of honour and privilege; and wherever these are not adequate there rulers turn into despots.

But the just which arises in the relations of master and father, is not identical with, but similar to, these; because there is no possibility of injustice towards those things which are absolutely one's own; and a slave or child (so long as this last is of a certain age and not separated into an independent being), is, as it were, part of a man's self, and no man chooses to hurt himself, for which reason there cannot be injustice towards one's own self: therefore neither is there the social unjust or just, which was stated to be in accordance with law and to exist between those among whom law naturally exists, and these were said to be they to whom belongs equality of ruling and being ruled.

Hence also there is just rather between a man and his wife than between a man and his children or slaves; this is in fact the just arising in domestic relations: and this too is different from the social just.

7 Further, this last-mentioned just is of two kinds, natural and conventional; the former being that which has everywhere the same force and does not depend upon being received or not; the latter being that which originally may be this way or that indifferently but not after enactment: for instance, the price of ransom being fixed at a mina, or the sacrificing a goat instead of two sheep; and again, all cases of special enactment, as the sacrificing to Brasidas as a hero; in short, all matters of special decree.

But there are some men who think that all the justs are of this latter kind, and on this ground: whatever exists by nature, they say, is unchangeable and has everywhere the same force; fire, for instance, burns not here only but in Persia as well, but the justs they see changed in various places.

Now this is not really so, and yet it is in a way (though among the gods perhaps by no means): still even amongst ourselves there is somewhat existing by nature: allowing that everything is subject to change, still there is that which does exist by nature, and that which does not.

Nay, we may go further, and say that it is practically plain what among things which can be otherwise does exist by nature, and what does not but is dependent upon enactment and conventional, even granting that both are alike subject to be changed: and the same distinctive illustration will apply to this and other cases; the right hand is naturally the stronger, still some men may become equally strong in both.

A parallel may be drawn between the justs which depend upon convention and expedience, and measures; for wine and corn measures are not equal in all places, but where men buy they are large, and where these same sell again they are smaller: well, in like manner the justs which are not natural, but of human invention, are not everywhere the same, for not even the forms of government are, and yet there is one only which by nature would be best in all places.

Now of justs and lawfuls each bears to the acts which embody and exemplify it the relation of an universal to a particular; the acts being many, but each of the principles only singular because each is an universal. And so there is a difference between an unjust act and the abstract unjust, and the just act and the abstract just: I mean, a thing is unjust in itself, by nature or by ordinance; well, when this has been embodied in act, there is an unjust act, but not till then, only some unjust thing. And similarly of a just act. (Perhaps *dikaiopragma* is more correctly the common or generic term for just act, the word *dikaioma*, which I have here used, meaning generally and properly the act corrective of the unjust act.) Now as to each of them, what kinds there are, and how many, and what is their object-matter, we must examine afterwards.

8   For the present we proceed to say that, the justs and the unjusts being what have been mentioned, a man is said to act unjustly or justly when he embodies these abstracts in voluntary actions, but when in involuntary, then he neither acts unjustly or justly except accidentally; I mean that the being just or unjust is really only accidental to the agents in such cases.

So both unjust and just actions are limited by the being voluntary or the contrary: for when an embodying of the unjust is voluntary, then it is blamed and is at the same time also an unjust action: but, if voluntariness does not attach, there will be a thing which is in itself unjust but not yet an unjust action.

By voluntary, I mean, as we stated before, whatso-ever of things in his own power a man does with knowledge, and the absence of ignorance as to the person to whom, or the instrument with which, or the result with which he does; as, for instance, whom he strikes, what he strikes him with, and with what probable result; and each of these points again, not accidentally nor by compulsion; as supposing another man were to seize his hand and strike a third person with it, here, of course, the owner of the hand acts not voluntarily, because it did not rest with him to do or leave undone: or again, it is conceivable that the person struck may be his father, and he may know that it is a man, or even one of the present company, whom he is striking, but not know that it is his father. And let these same distinctions be supposed to be carried into the case of the result and in fact the whole of any given action. In fine then, that is involuntary which is done through ignorance, or which, not resulting from ignorance, is not in the agent's control or is done on compulsion.

I mention these cases, because there are many natural things which we do and suffer knowingly but still no one of which is either voluntary or involuntary, growing old, or dying, for instance.

Again, accidentality may attach to the unjust in like manner as to the just acts. For instance, a man may have restored what was deposited with him, but against his will and from fear of the consequences of a refusal: we must not say that he either does what is just, or does justly, except accidentally: and in like manner the man who through compulsion and against his will fails to restore a deposit, must be said to do unjustly, or to do what is unjust, accidentally only.

Again, voluntary actions we do either from deliberate choice or without it; from it, when we act from previous deliberation; without it, when without any previous deliberation. Since then hurts which may be done in transactions between man and man are threefold, those mistakes which are attended with ignorance are, when a man either does a thing not to the man to whom he meant to do it, or not the thing he meant to do, or not with the instrument, or not with the result which he intended: either he did not think he should hit him at all, or not with this, or this is not the man he thought he should hit, or he did not think this would be the result of the blow but a result has followed which he did not anticipate; as, for instance, he did it not to wound but merely to prick him; or it is not the man whom, or the way in which, he meant.

Now when the hurt has come about contrary to all reasonable expectation, it is a misadventure; when though not contrary to expectation yet without any viciousness, it is a mistake; for a man makes a mistake when the origination of the cause rests with himself, he has a misadventure when it is external to himself. When again he acts with knowledge, but not from previous deliberation, it is an unjust action; for instance, whatever happens to men from anger or other passions which are necessary or natural: for when doing these hurts or making these mistakes they act unjustly of course and their actions are unjust, still they are not yet confirmed unjust or wicked persons by reason of these, because the hurt did not arise from depravity in the doer of it: but when it does arise from deliberate choice, then the doer is a confirmed unjust and depraved man.

And on this principle acts done from anger are fairly judged not to be from malice prepense, because it is not the man who acts in wrath who is the originator really but he who caused his wrath. And again, the question at issue in such cases is not respecting the fact but respecting the justice of the case, the occasion of anger being a notion of injury. I mean, that the parties do not dispute about the fact, as in questions of contract (where one of the two must be a rogue, unless real forgetfulness can be pleaded), but, admitting the fact, they dispute on which side the justice of the case lies (the one who plotted against the other, *i.e.* the real aggressor, of course, cannot be ignorant), so that the one thinks there is injustice committed while the other does not.

Well then, a man acts unjustly if he has hurt another of deliberate purpose, and he who commits such acts of injustice is *ipso facto* an unjust character when they are in violation of the proportionate or the equal; and in like manner also a man is a just character when he acts justly of deliberate purpose, and he does act justly if he acts voluntarily.

Then as for involuntary acts of harm, they are either such as are excusable or such as are not: under the former head come all errors done not merely in ignorance but from ignorance; under the latter all that are done not from ignorance but in ignorance caused by some passion which is neither natural nor fairly attributable to human infirmity.

Section 9 to end

Can a person suffer wrong voluntarily? It would seem not. Neither is it possible for any person to act unjustly towards himself.

The relation of equity, or fairness, to justice, and how this sheds further light on the questions raised above.

BOOK SIX

Virtues of the intellect

1 Having stated in a former part of this treatise that men should choose the mean instead of either the excess or defect, and that the mean is according to the dictates of right reason; we will now proceed to explain this term.

For in all the habits which we have expressly mentioned, as likewise in all the others, there is, so to speak, a mark with his eye fixed on which the man who has reason tightens or slacks his rope; and there is a certain limit of those mean states which we say are in accordance with right reason, and lie between excess on the one hand and defect on the other.

Now to speak thus is true enough but conveys no very definite meaning: as, in fact, in all other pursuits requiring attention and diligence on which skill and science are brought to bear; it is quite true of course to say that men are neither to labour nor relax too much or too little, but in moderation, and as right reason directs; yet if this were all a man had he would not be greatly the wiser; as, for instance, if in answer to the question, what are proper applications to the body, he were to be told, 'Oh! of course, whatever the science of medicine, and in such manner as the physician, directs.'

And so in respect of the mental states it is requisite not merely that this should be true which has been already stated, but further that it should be expressly laid down what right reason is, and what is the definition of it.

Now in our division of the excellences of the soul, we said there were two classes, the moral and the intellectual: the former we have already gone through; and we will now proceed to speak of the others, premising a few words respecting the soul itself. It was stated before, you will remember, that the soul consists of two parts, the rational, and irrational: we must now make a similar division of the rational.

Let it be understood then that there are two parts of the soul possessed of reason; one whereby we realise those existences whose causes cannot be otherwise than they are, and one whereby we realise those which can be otherwise than they are (for there must be, answering to things generically different, generically different parts of the soul naturally adapted to each, since these parts of the soul possess their knowledge in virtue of a certain resemblance and appropriateness in themselves to the objects of which they are percipients); and let us name the former, 'that which is apt to know', the latter, 'that which is apt to calculate' (because deliberating and calculating are the same, and no one ever deliberates about things which cannot be otherwise than they are: and so the calculative will be one part of the rational faculty of the soul).

We must discover, then, which is the best state of each of these, because that will be the excellence of each; and this again is relative to the work each has to do.

2 There are in the soul three functions on which depend moral action and truth; sense, intellect, appetition, whether vague desire or definite will. Now of these sense is the originating cause of no moral action, as is seen from the fact that brutes have sense but are in no way partakers of moral action.

[Intellect and will are thus connected,] what in the intellectual operation is affirmation and negation, that in the will is pursuit and avoidance. And so, since moral virtue is a state apt to exercise moral choice and moral choice is will consequent on deliberation, the reason must be true and the will right, to constitute good moral choice, and what the reason affirms the will must pursue.

Now this intellectual operation and this truth is what bears upon moral action; of course truth and falsehood must be the good and the bad of that intellectual operation which is purely speculative and concerned neither with action nor production, because this is manifestly the work of every intellectual faculty, while of the faculty which is of a mixed practical and intellectual nature the work is that truth which, as I have described above, corresponds to the right movement of the will.

Now the starting-point of moral action is moral choice (I mean, what actually sets it in motion, not the final cause), and of moral choice, appetition, and reason directed to a certain result: and thus moral choice is neither independent of intellect, *i.e.* intellectual operation, nor of a certain moral state: for right or wrong action cannot exist independently of operation of the intellect and moral character.

But operation of the intellect by itself moves nothing, only when directed to a certain result, *i.e.*

exercised in moral action (I say nothing of its being exercised in production, because this function is originated by the former: everyone who makes, makes with a view to somewhat further; and that which is or may be made is not an end in itself, but only relatively to somewhat else, and belonging to someone: whereas that which is or may be done is an end in itself, because acting well is an end in itself, and this is the object of the will): and so moral choice is either intellect put in a position of willing, or appetition subjected to an intellectual process. And such a cause is man.

But nothing which is done and past can be the object of moral choice; for instance, no man chooses to have sacked Troy; because, in fact, no one ever deliberates about what is past but only about that which is future and which may therefore be influenced, whereas what has been cannot not have been: and so Agathon is right in saying,

'Of this alone is Deity bereft,
To make undone whatever hath been done.'

Thus then the truth is the work of both the intellectual parts of the soul; those states therefore are the excellences of each in which each will best attain truth.

3 Commencing then from the point stated above we will now speak of these excellences again. Let those faculties whereby the soul attains truth in affirmation or negation, be assumed to be in number five: viz. art, knowledge, practical wisdom, science, intuition (supposition and opinion I do not include, because by these one may go wrong).

What knowledge is is plain from the following considerations, if one is to speak accurately instead of being led away by resemblances. We all conceive that what we strictly speaking *know* cannot be otherwise than it is, because as to those things which can be otherwise than they are we are uncertain whether they are or are not the moment they cease to be within the sphere of our actual observation.

So then, whatever comes within the range of knowledge is by necessity, and therefore eternal (because all things are so which exist necessarily), and all eternal things are without beginning and indestructible.

Again, all knowledge is thought to be capable of being taught, and what comes within its range capable of being learned. And all teaching is based upon previous knowledge (a statement you will find in the *Analytics* also); for there are two ways of teaching, by syllogism and by induction. In fact, induction is the source of universal propositions, and syllogism reasons from these universals. syllogism then may reason from principles which cannot be themselves proved syllogistically; and therefore must be proved by induction.

So knowledge is 'a state or mental faculty apt to demonstrate syllogistically', etc., as in the *Analytics*: because a man, strictly and properly speaking, *knows*, when he establishes his conclusion in a certain way and the principles are known to him: for if they are not better known to him than the conclusion such knowledge as he has will be merely accidental.

4 Let thus much be accepted as a definition of knowledge.

Matter which may exist otherwise than it actually

does in any given case (commonly called contingent) is of two kinds, that which is the object of making, and that which is the object of doing; now making and doing are two different things (as we show in the exoteric treatise), and so that state of mind, conjoined with reason, which is apt to do, is distinct from that also conjoined with reason, which is apt to make: and for this reason they are not included one by the other, that is, doing is not making, nor making doing. Now as architecture is an art, and is the same as 'a certain state of mind, conjoined with reason, which is apt to make,' and as there is no art which is not such a state, nor any such state which is not an art, art, in its strict and proper sense, must be 'a state of mind, conjoined with true reason, apt to make'.

Now all art has to do with production, and contrivance, and seeing how any of those things may be produced which may either be or not be, and the origination of which rests with the maker and not with the thing made.

And, so neither things which exist or come into being necessarily, nor things in the way of nature, come under the province of art, because these are self-originating. And since making and doing are distinct, art must be concerned with the former and not the latter. And in a certain sense art and fortune are concerned with the same things, as Agathon says by the way,'

'Art fortune loves, and is of her beloved.'

So art, as has been stated, is 'a certain state of mind, apt to make, conjoined with true reason'; its absence, on the contrary, is the same state conjoined with false reason, and both are employed upon contingent matter.

5   As for practical wisdom, we shall ascertain its nature by examining to what kind of persons we in common language ascribe it.

It is thought then to be the property of the practically wise man to be able to deliberate well respecting what is good and expedient for himself, not in any definite line, as what is conducive to health or strength, but what to living well. A proof of this is that we call men wise in this or that, when they calculate well with a view to some good end in a case where there is no definite rule. And so, in a general way of speaking, the man who is good at deliberation will be practically wise. Now no man deliberates respecting things which cannot be otherwise than they are, nor such as lie not within the range of his own action: and so, since knowledge requires strict demonstrative reasoning, of which contingent matter does not admit (I say contingent matter, because all matters of deliberation must be contingent and deliberation cannot take place with respect to things which are necessarily), practical wisdom cannot be knowledge nor art; not the former, because what falls under the province of doing must be contingent; not the latter, because doing and making are different in kind.

It remains then that it must be 'a state of mind true, conjoined with reason, and apt to do, having for its object those things which are good or bad for man': because of making something beyond itself is always the object, but cannot be of doing because the very well-doing is in itself an end.

For this reason we think pericles and men of that stamp to be practically wise, because they can see what is good for themselves and for men in general, and we also think those to be such who are skilled in domestic management or civil government. In fact, this is the reason why we call the habit of perfected self-mastery by the name which in Greek it bears, etymologically signifying 'that which preserves the practical wisdom': for what it does preserve is the notion I have mentioned, *i.e,* of one's own true interest.

For it is not every kind of notion which the pleasant and the painful corrupt and pervert, as, for instance, that 'the three angles of every rectilineal triangle are equal to two right angles', but only those bearing on moral action.

For the principles of the matters of moral action are the final cause of them: now to the man who has been corrupted by reason of pleasure or pain the principle immediately becomes obscured, nor does he see that it is his duty to choose and act in each instance with a view to this final cause and by reason of it: for viciousness has a tendency to destroy the moral principle: and so practical wisdom must be 'a state conjoined with reason, true, having human good for its object, and apt to do'.

Then again art admits of degrees of excellence, but practical wisdom does not: and in art he who goes wrong purposely is preferable to him who does so unwittingly, but not so in respect of practical wisdom or the other virtues. It plainly is then an excellence of a certain kind, and not an art.

Now as there are two parts of the soul which have reason, it must be the excellence of the opinionative [which we called before calculative or deliberative], because both opinion and practical wisdom are exercised upon contingent matter. And further, it is not simply a state conjoined with reason, as is proved by the fact that such a state may be forgotten and so lost while practical wisdom cannot.

6   Now knowledge is a conception concerning universals and necessary matter, and there, are of course certain first principles in all trains of demonstrative reasoning (that is of all knowledge because this is connected with reasoning): that faculty, then, which takes in the first principles of that which comes under the range of knowledge, cannot be either knowledge, or art, or practical wisdom: not knowledge, because what is the object of knowledge must be derived from demonstrative reasoning; not either of the other two, because they are exercised upon contingent matter only. Nor can it be science which takes in these, because the scientific man must in some cases depend on demonstrative reasoning.

It comes then to this: since the faculties whereby we always attain truth and are never deceived when dealing with matter necessary or even contingent are knowledge, practical wisdom, science, and intuition, and the faculty which takes in first principles cannot be any of the three first; the last, namely intuition, must be it which performs this function.

7   Science is a term we use principally in two meanings: in the first place, in the arts we ascribe it to those who carry their arts to the highest accuracy; Phidias, for instance, we call a scientific or cunning sculptor; Polycleitus a scientific or cunning statuary; meaning, in this instance, nothing else by science than an excellence of art: in the other sense, we think some to be scientific in a general way, not in any particular line or in any particular thing, just as Homer says of a man

in his *Margites*: 'Him the gods made neither a digger of the ground, nor ploughman, nor in any other way scientific.'

So it is plain that science must mean the most accurate of all knowledge; but if so, then the scientific man must not merely know the deductions from the first principles but be in possession of truth respecting the first principles. So that science must be equivalent to intuition and knowledge; it is, so to speak, knowledge of the most precious objects, *with a head on.*

I say of the most precious things, because it is absurd to suppose *politike*, or practical wisdom, to be the highest, unless it can be shown that man is the most excellent of all that exists in the universe. Now if 'healthy' and 'good' are relative terms, differing when applied to men or to fish, but 'white' and 'straight' are the same always, men must allow that the scientific is the same always, but the practically wise varies: for whatever provides all things well for itself, to this they would apply the term practically wise, and commit these matters to it; which is the reason, by the way, that they call some brutes practically wise, such that is as plainly have a faculty of forethought respecting their own subsistence.

And it is quite plain that science and *politike* cannot be identical: because if men give the name of science to that faculty which is employed upon what is expedient for themselves, there will be many instead of one, because there is not one and the same faculty employed on the good of all animals collectively, unless in the same sense as you may say there is one art of healing with respect to all living beings.

If it is urged that man is superior to all other animals, that makes no difference: for there are many other things more godlike in their nature than man, as, most obviously, the elements of which the universe is composed.

It is plain then that science is the union of knowledge and intuition, and has for its objects those things which are most precious in their nature. Accordingly, Anaxagoras, Thales, and men of that stamp, people call scientific, but not practically wise because they see them ignorant of what concerns themselves; and they say that what they know is quite out of the common run certainly, and wonderful, and hard, and very fine no doubt, but still useless because they do not seek after what is good for them as men.

But practical wisdom is employed upon human matters, and such as are objects of deliberation (for we say, that to deliberate well is most peculiarly the work of the man who possesses this wisdom), and no man deliberates about things which cannot be otherwise than they are, nor about any save those that have some definite end and this end good resulting from moral action; and the man to whom we should give the name of good in counsel, simply and without modification, is he who in the way of calculation has a capacity for attaining that of practical goods which is the best for man.

Nor again does practical wisdom consist in a knowledge of general principles only, but it is necessary that one should know also the particular details, because it is apt to act, and action is concerned with details: for which reason sometimes men who have not much knowledge are more practical than others who have; among others, they who derive all they know from actual experience: suppose a man to know, for instance, that light meats are easy of digestion and wholesome, but not what kinds of meat are light, he will not produce a healthy state; that man will have a much better chance of doing so, who knows that the flesh of birds is light and wholesome. Since then practical wisdom is apt to act, one ought to have both kinds of knowledge, or, if only one, the knowledge of details rather than of principles. So there will be in respect of practical wisdom the distinction of supreme and subordinate.

Section 8 to end

Practical wisdom and its relation to intelligence. Aspects of practical wisdom: excellence in deliberation, understanding, judgement. How the virtues of the intellect contribute to happiness.

BOOK SEVEN

Self-control and weakness of will

1 Next we must take a different point to start from, and observe that of what is to be avoided in respect of moral character there are three forms; vice, imperfect self-control, and brutishness. Of the two former it is plain what the contraries are, for we call the one virtue, the other self-control; and as answering to brutishness it will be most suitable to assign superhuman, *i.e.* heroical and godlike virtue, as, in Homer, Priam says of Hector 'that he was very excellent, nor was he like the offspring of mortal man, but of a god': and so, if, as is commonly said, men are raised to the position of gods by reason of very high excellence in virtue, the state opposed to the brutish will plainly be of this nature: because as brutes are not virtuous or vicious so neither are gods; but the state of these is something more precious than virtue, of the former something different in kind from vice.

And as, on the one-hand, it is a rare thing for a man to be godlike (a term the Lacedaemonians are accustomed to use when they admire a man exceedingly; *seios* they call him), so the brutish man is rare; the character is found most among barbarians, and some cases of it are caused by disease or maiming; also such men as exceed in vice all ordinary measures we therefore designate by this opprobrious term. Well, we must in a subsequent place make some mention of this disposition, and vice has been spoken of before: for the present we must speak of imperfect self-control and its kindred faults of softness and luxury, on the one hand, and of self-control and endurance on the other; since we are to conceive of them, not as being the same states exactly as virtue and vice respectively, nor again as differing in kind.

And we should adopt the same course as before, *i.e.* state the phenomena, and, after raising and discussing difficulties which suggest themselves, then exhibit, if possible, all the opinions afloat respecting these affections of the moral character; or, if not all, the greater part and the most important: for we may consider we have illustrated the matter sufficiently when the difficulties have been solved, and such theories as are most approved are left as a residuum.

The chief points may be thus enumerated. It is thought,

1 That self-control and endurance belong to the class of things good and praiseworthy, while imperfect self-control and softness belong to that of things low and blameworthy.

2 That the man of self-control is identical with the man who is apt to abide by his resolution, and the man of imperfect self-control with him who is apt to depart from his resolution.

3 That the man of imperfect self-control does things at the instigation of his passions, knowing them to be wrong, while the man of self-control, knowing his lusts to be wrong, refuses, by the influence of reason, to follow their suggestions.

4 That the man of perfected self-mastery unites the qualities of self-control and endurance, and some

say that everyone who unites these is a man of perfect self-mastery, others do not.

5 Some confound the two characters of the man who has *no* self-control, and the man of *imperfect* self-control, while others distinguish between them.

6 It is sometimes said that the man of practical wisdom cannot be a man of imperfect self-control, sometimes that men who are practically wise and clever are of imperfect self-control.

7 Again, men are said to be of imperfect self-control, not simply but with the addition of the thing wherein, as in respect of anger, of honour, and gain.

These then are pretty well the common statements.

2 Now a man may raise a question as to the nature of the right conception in violation of which a man fails of self-control.

That he can so fail when *knowing* in the strict sense what is right some say is impossible: for it is a strange thing, as Socrates thought, that while knowledge is present in his mind something else should master him and drag him about like a slave. Socrates in fact contended generally against the theory, maintaining there is no such state as that of imperfect self-control, for that no one acts contrary to what is best conceiving it to be best but by reason of ignorance what is best.

With all due respect to Socrates, his account of the matter is at variance with plain facts, and we must inquire with respect to the affection, if it be caused by ignorance what is the nature of the ignorance; for that the man so failing does not suppose his acts to be right before he is under the influence of passion is quite plain.

There are people who partly agree with Socrates

and partly not: that nothing can be stronger than knowledge they agree, but that no man acts in contravention of his conviction of what is better they do not agree; and so they say that it is not knowledge, but only opinion, which the man in question has and yet yields to the instigation of his pleasures.

But then, if it is opinion and not knowledge, that is if the opposing conception be not strong but only mild (as in the case of real doubt), the not abiding by it in the face of strong lusts would be excusable: but wickedness is not excusable, nor is anything which deserves blame.

Well then, is it practical wisdom which in this case offers opposition: for that is the strongest principle? The supposition is absurd, for we shall have the same man uniting practical wisdom and imperfect self-control, and surely no single person would maintain that it is consistent with the character of practical wisdom to do voluntarily what is very wrong; and besides we have shown before that the very mark of a man of this character is aptitude to act, as distinguished from mere knowledge of what is right; because he is a man conversant with particular details, and possessed of all the other virtues.

Again, if the having strong and bad lusts is necessary to the idea of the man of self-control, this character cannot be identical with the man of perfected self-mastery, because the having strong desires or bad ones does not enter into the idea of this latter character: and yet the man of self-control must have such: for suppose them good; then the moral state which should hinder a man from following their suggestions must be bad, and so self-control would not be in all cases good: suppose them on the other hand to be weak and not wrong, it would be nothing grand; nor anything great, supposing them to be wrong and weak.

Again, if self-control makes a man apt to abide by all opinions without exception, it may be bad, as suppose the case of a false opinion: and if imperfect self-control makes a man apt to depart from all without exception, we shall have cases where it will be good; take that of Neoptolemus in the *Philoctetes* of Sophocles, for instance: he is to be praised for not abiding by what he was persuaded to by Ulysses, because he was pained at being guilty of falsehood.

Or again, false sophistical reasoning presents a difficulty: for because men wish to prove paradoxes that they may be counted clever when they succeed, the reasoning that has been used becomes a difficulty: for the intellect is fettered; a man being unwilling to abide by the conclusion because it does not please his judgment, but unable to advance because he cannot disentangle the web of sophistical reasoning.

Or again, it is conceivable on this supposition that folly joined with imperfect self-control may turn out, in a given case, goodness: for by reason of his imperfection of self-control a man acts in a way which contradicts his notions; now his notion is that what is really good is bad and ought not to be done; and so he will eventually do what is good and not what is bad.

Again, on the same supposition, the man who acting on conviction pursues and chooses things because they are pleasant must be thought a better man than he who does so not by reason of a quasi-rational conviction but of imperfect self-control: because he is more open to cure by reason of the possibility of his receiving a contrary conviction. But to the man of imperfect self-control would apply the proverb, 'when water chokes, what should a man drink then?' For had he never been convinced at all in respect of what he does, then by a conviction in a contrary direction he might have stopped in his course; but now though he has had convictions he notwithstanding acts against them.

Again, if any and every thing is the object-matter of imperfect and perfect self-control, who is the man of imperfect self-control simply? Because no one unites all cases of it, and we commonly say that some men are so simply, not adding any particular thing in which they are so.

Well, the difficulties raised are pretty near such as I have described them, and of these theories we must remove some and leave others as established; because the solving of a difficulty is a positive act of establishing something as true.

3 Now we must examine first whether men of imperfect self-control act with a knowledge of what is right or not: next, if with such knowledge, in what sense; and next what are we to assume is the object-matter of the man of imperfect self-control, and of the man of self-control; I mean, whether pleasure and pain of all kinds or certain definite ones; and as to self-control and endurance, whether these are designations of the same character or different. And in like manner we must go into all questions which are connected with the present.

But the real starting point of the inquiry is, whether the two characters of self-control and imperfect self-control are distinguished by their object-matter, or their respective relations to it. I mean, whether the man of imperfect self-control is such simply by virtue of having such and such object-matter; or not, but by virtue of his being related to it in such and such a way, or by virtue of both: next, whether self-control and imperfect self-control are unlimited in their object-matter: because he who is designated without any addition a man of imperfect self-control is not unlimited in his object-matter, but has exactly the same as the man who has lost all self-control: nor is he so designated because of his relation to this object-matter merely (for then his character would be identical with that just mentioned, loss of all self-control), but because of his relation to it being such and such. For the man who has lost all self-control is led on with deliberate moral choice, holding that it is his line to pursue pleasure as it rises: while the man of imperfect self-control does not think that he ought to pursue it, but does pursue it all the same.

Now as to the notion that it is true opinion and not knowledge in contravention of which men fail in self-control, it makes no difference to the point in question, because some of those who hold opinions have no doubt about them but suppose themselves to have accurate knowledge; if then it is urged that men holding opinions will be more likely than men who have knowledge to act in contravention of their conceptions, as having but a moderate belief in them; we reply, knowledge will not differ in this respect from opinion: because some men believe their own opinions no less firmly than others do their positive knowledge: Heraclitus is a case in point.

Rather the following is the account of it: the term *knowing* has two senses; both the man who does not use his knowledge, and he who does, are said to *know*: there will be a difference between a man's acting wrongly, who though possessed of knowledge does not call it into operation, and his doing so who has it and actually exercises it: the latter is a strange case, but the mere having, if not exercising, presents no anomaly.

Again, as there are two kinds of propositions affecting action, universal and particular, there is no reason why a man may not act against his knowledge, having both propositions in his mind, using the universal but not the particular, for the particulars are the objects of moral action.

There is a difference also in universal propositions; a universal proposition may relate partly to a man's self and partly to the thing in question: take the following for instance; 'dry food is good for every man', this may have the two minor premises, 'this is a man', and 'so and so is dry food'; but whether a given substance is so and so a man either has not the knowledge or does not exert it. According to these different senses there will be an immense difference, so that for a man to *know* in the one sense, and yet act wrongly, would be nothing strange, but in any of the other senses it would be a matter for wonder.

Again, men may have knowledge in a way different from any of those which have been now stated: for we constantly see a man's state so differing by having and not using knowledge, that he has it in a sense and also has not; when a man is asleep, for instance, or mad, or drunk: well, men under the actual operation of passion are in exactly similar conditions; for anger, lust, and some other such-like things, manifestly make changes even in the body, and in some they even cause madness; it is plain then that we must say the men of imperfect self-control are in a state similar to these.

And their saying what embodies knowledge is no proof of their actually then exercising it, because they who are under the operation of these passions repeat demonstrations; or verses of Empedocles, just as children, when first learning, string words together, but as yet know nothing of their meaning, because they must grow into it, and this is a process requiring time: so that we must suppose these men who fail in self-control to say these moral sayings just as actors do.

Furthermore, a man may look at the account of the phenomenon in the following way, from an examination of the actual working of the mind: all action may be analysed into a syllogism, in which the one premiss is an universal maxim and the other concerns particulars of which sense [moral or physical, as the case may be] is cognisant: now when one results from these two, it follows necessarily that, as far as theory goes the mind must assert the conclusion, and in practical propositions the man must act accordingly.

For instance, let the universal be, 'All that is sweet should be tasted', the particular, 'This is sweet'; it follows necessarily that he who is able and is not hindered should not only draw, but put in practice, the conclusion 'This is to be tasted'. When then there is in the mind one universal proposition forbidding to taste, and the other 'All that is sweet is pleasant' with its minor 'This is sweet' (which is the one that really works), and desire happens to be in the man, the first universal bids him avoid this but the desire leads him on to taste; for it has the power of moving the various organs: and so it results that he fails in self-control, in a certain sense under the influence of reason and opinion not contrary in itself to reason but only accidentally so;

117

because it is the desire that is contrary to right reason, but not the opinion: and so for this reason brutes are not accounted of imperfect self-control, because they have no power of conceiving universals but only of receiving and retaining particular impressions.

As to the manner in which the ignorance is removed and the man of imperfect self-control recovers his knowledge, the account is the same as with respect to him who is drunk or asleep, and is not peculiar to this affection, so physiologists are the right people to apply to. But whereas the minor premiss of every practical syllogism is an opinion on matter cognisable by sense and determines the actions; he who is under the influence of passion either has not this, or so has it that his having does not amount to *knowing* but merely saying, as a man when drunk might repeat Empedocles' verses; and because the minor term is neither universal, nor is thought to have the power of producing knowledge in like manner as the universal term: and so the result which Socrates was seeking comes out, that is to say, the affection does not take place in the presence of that which is thought to be specially and properly knowledge, nor is this dragged about by reason of the affection, but in the presence of that knowledge which is conveyed by sense.

Let this account then be accepted of the question respecting the failure in self-control, whether it is with knowledge or not; and, if with knowledge, with what kind of knowledge such failure is possible.

4   The next question to be discussed is whether there is a character to be designated by the term 'of imperfect self-control' simply, or whether all who are so are to be accounted such, in respect of some particular thing;

and, if there is such a character, what is his object-matter.

Now that pleasures and pains are the object-matter of men of self-control and of endurance, and also of men of imperfect self-control and softness, is plain.

Further, things which produce pleasure are either necessary, or objects of choice in themselves but yet admitting of excess. All bodily things which produce pleasure are necessary; and I call such those which relate to food and other grosser appetites, in short such bodily things as we assumed were the object-matter of absence of self-control and of perfected self-mastery.

The other class of objects are not necessary, but objects of choice in themselves: I mean, for instance, victory, honour, wealth, and such-like good or pleasant things. And those who are excessive in their liking for such things contrary to the principle of right reason which is in their own breasts we do not designate men of imperfect self-control simply, but with the addition of the thing wherein, as in respect of money, or gain, or honour, or anger, and not simply; because we consider them as different characters and only having that title in right of a kind of resemblance (as when we add to a man's name 'conqueror in the Olympic games' the account of him as man differs but little from the account of him as the man who conquered in the Olympic games, but still it is different). And a proof of the real difference between these so designated with an addition and those simply so called is this, that imperfect self-control is blamed, not as an error merely but also as being a vice, either wholly or partially; but none of these other cases is so blamed.

But of those who have for their object-matter the

bodily enjoyments, which we say are also the object-matter of the man of perfected self-mastery and the man who has lost all self-control, he that pursues excessive pleasures and too much avoids things which are painful (as hunger and thirst, heat and cold, and everything connected with touch and taste), not from moral choice but in spite of his moral choice and intellectual conviction, is termed 'a man of imperfect self-control,' not with the addition of any particular object-matter as we do in respect of want of control of anger but simply.

And a proof that the term is thus applied is that the kindred term 'soft' is used in respect of these enjoyments but not in respect of any of those others. And for this reason we put into the same rank the man of imperfect self-control, the man who has lost it entirely, the man who has it, and the man of perfected self-mastery; but not any of those other characters, because the former have for their object-matter the same pleasures and pains: but though they have the same object-matter, they are not related to it in the same way, but two of them act upon moral choice, two without it. And so we should say that man is more entirely given up to his passions who pursues excessive pleasures, and avoids moderate pains, being either not at all, or at least but little, urged by desire, than the man who does so because his desire is very strong: because we think what would the former be likely to do if he had the additional stimulus of youthful lust and violent pain consequent on the want of those pleasures which we have denominated necessary?

Well then, since of desires and pleasures there are some which are in kind honourable and good (because things pleasant are divisible, as we said before, into such as are naturally objects of choice, such as are naturally objects of avoidance, and such as are in themselves indifferent, money, gain, honour, victory, for instance); in respect of all such and those that are indifferent, men are blamed not merely for being affected by or desiring or liking them, but for exceeding in any way in these feelings.

And so they are blamed, whosoever in spite of reason are mastered by, that is pursue, any object, though in its nature noble and good; they, for instance, who are more earnest than they should be respecting honour, or their children or parents; not but what these are good objects and men are praised for being earnest about them: but still they admit of excess; for instance, if anyone, as Niobe did, should fight even against the gods, or feel towards his father as Satyrus, who got therefrom the nickname of *philopator*, because he was thought to be very foolish.

Now depravity there is none in regard of these things, for the reason assigned above, that each of them in itself is a thing naturally choiceworthy, yet the excesses in respect of them are wrong and matter for blame: and similarly there is no imperfect self-control in respect of these things; that being not merely a thing that should be avoided but blameworthy.

But because of the resemblance of the affection to the imperfection of self-control the term is used with the addition in each case of the particular object-matter, just as men call a man a bad physician, or bad actor, whom they would not think of calling simply bad. As then in these cases we do not apply the term simply because each of the states is not a vice, but only like a vice in the way of analogy, so it is plain that in respect of imperfect self-control and self-control we must limit the names to those states which have the same object-matter as perfected self-mastery and utter loss of self-control, and that we do apply it to the case of anger only in the way of resemblance: for which reason, with an addition, we designate a man of imperfect self-control in respect of anger, as of honour or of gain.

5 As there are some things naturally pleasant, and of these two kinds; those, namely, which are pleasant generally, and those which are so relatively to particular kinds of animals and men; so there are others which are not naturally pleasant but which come to be so in consequence either of maimings, or custom, or depraved natural tastes: and one may observe moral states similar to those we have been speaking of, having respectively these classes of things for their object-matter.

I mean the brutish, as in the case of the female who, they say, would rip up women with child and eat the foetus; or the tastes which are found among the savage tribes bordering on the Pontus, some liking raw flesh, and some being cannibals, and some lending one another their children to make feasts of; or what is said of Phalaris. These are instances of brutish states, caused in some by disease or madness; take, for instance, the man who sacrificed and ate his mother, or him who devoured the liver of his fellow-servant. Instances again of those caused by disease or by custom, would be, plucking out of hair, or eating one's nails, or eating coals and earth . . . Now wherever nature is really the cause no one would think of calling men of imperfect self-control . . . nor, in like manner, such as are in a diseased state through custom.

Obviously the having any of these inclinations is something foreign to what is denominated vice, just as brutishness is: and when a man has them his mastering them is not properly self-control, nor his being mastered by them imperfection of self-control in the proper sense, but only in the way of resemblance; just as we may say a man of ungovernable wrath fails of self-control in respect of anger but not simply fails of self-control. For all excessive folly, cowardice, absence of self-control, or irritability, are either brutish or morbid. The man, for instance, who is naturally afraid of all things, even if a mouse should stir, is cowardly after a brutish sort; there was a man again who, by reason of disease, was afraid of a cat: and of the fools, they who are naturally destitute of reason and live only by sense are brutish, as are some tribes of the far-off barbarians, while others who are so by reason of diseases, epileptic or frantic, are in morbid states.

So then, of these inclinations, a man may sometimes merely have one without yielding to it: I mean, suppose that Phalaris had restrained his unnatural desire to eat a child: or he may both have and yield to it. As then vice when such as belongs to human nature is called vice simply, while the other is so called with the addition of 'brutish' or 'morbid', but not simply vice, so manifestly there is brutish and morbid imperfection of self-control, but that alone is entitled to the name without any qualification which is of the nature of utter absence of self-control, as it is found in man.

6   It is plain then that the object-matter of imperfect self-control and self-control is restricted to the same as that of utter absence of self-control and that of perfected self-mastery, and that the rest is the object-matter of a different species so named metaphorically and not simply: we will now examine the position, 'that imperfect self-control in respect of anger is less disgraceful than that in respect of lusts'.

In the first place, it seems that anger does in a way listen to reason but mishears it; as quick servants who run out before they have heard the whole of what is said and then mistake the order; dogs, again, bark at the slightest stir, before they have seen whether it be friend or foe; just so anger, by reason of its natural heat and quickness, listening to reason, but without having heard the command of reason, rushes to its revenge. That is to say, reason or some impression on the mind shows there is insolence or contempt in the offender, and then anger, reasoning as it were that one ought to fight against what is such, fires up immediately: whereas lust, if reason or sense, as the case may be, merely says a thing is sweet, rushes to the enjoyment of it: and so anger follows reason in a manner, but lust does not and is therefore more disgraceful: because he that cannot control his anger yields in a manner to reason, but the other to his lust and not to reason at all.

Again, a man is more excusable for following such desires as are natural, just as he is for following such lusts as are common to all and to that degree in which they are common. Now anger and irritability are more natural than lusts when in excess and for objects not necessary. (This was the ground of the defence the man made who beat his father. 'My father,' he said, 'used to beat his, and his father his again, and this little fellow here,' pointing to his child, 'will beat me when he is grown a man: it runs in the family.' And the father, as he was being dragged along, bid his son leave off beating him at the door, because he had himself been used to drag his father so far and no farther.)

Again, characters are less unjust in proportion as they involve less insidiousness. Now the angry man is not insidious, nor is anger, but quite open: but lust is: as they say of Venus,

'Cyprus-born goddess, *weaver of deceits.*'

Or Homer of the girdle called the Cestus,

'Persuasiveness *cheating* e'en the subtlest mind.'

And so since this kind of imperfect self-control is more unjust, it is also more disgraceful than that in respect of anger, and is simply imperfect self-control, and vice in a certain sense.

Again, no man feels pain in being insolent, but everyone who acts through anger does act with pain; and he who acts insolently does it with pleasure. If then those things are most unjust with which we have most right to be angry, then imperfect self-control, arising from lust, is more so than that arising from anger: because in anger there is no insolence.

Well then, it is clear that imperfect self-control in respect of lusts is more disgraceful than that in respect of anger, and that the object-matter of self-control, and the imperfection of it, are bodily lusts and pleasures; but of these last we must take into account the differences; for, as was said at the commencement, some are proper to the human race and natural both in kind and degree, others brutish, and others caused by maimings and diseases.

Now the first of these only are the object-matter of perfected self-mastery and utter absence of self-control; and therefore we never attribute either of these states to brutes (except metaphorically, and whenever any one kind of animal differs entirely from another in insolence, mischievousness, or voracity), because they have not moral choice or process of deliberation, but are quite different from that kind of creature just as are madmen from other men.

Brutishness is not so low in the scale as vice, yet it is to be regarded with more fear: because it is not that the highest principle has been corrupted, as in the human creature, but the subject has it not at all.

It is much the same, therefore, as if one should compare an inanimate with an animate being, which were the worse: for the badness of that which has no principle of origination is always less harmful; now intellect is a principle of origination. A similar case would be the comparing injustice and an unjust man together: for in different ways each is the worst: a bad man would produce ten thousand times as much harm as a bad brute.

7 Now with respect to the pleasures and pains which come to a man through touch and taste, and the desiring or avoiding such (which we determined before to constitute the object-matter of the states of utter absence of self-control and perfected self-mastery), one may be so disposed as to yield to temptations to which most men would be superior, or to be superior to those to which most men would yield: in respect of pleasures, these characters will be respectively the man

of imperfect self-control, and the man of self-control; and, in respect of pains, the man of softness and the man of endurance: but the moral state of most men is something between the two, even though they lean somewhat to the worse characters.

Again, since of the pleasures indicated some are necessary and some are not, others are so to a certain degree but not the excess or defect of them, and similarly also of lusts and pains, the man who pursues the excess of pleasant things, or such as are in themselves excess, or from moral choice, for their own sake, and not for anything else which is to result from them, is a man utterly void of self-control: for he must be incapable of remorse, and so incurable, because he that has not remorse is incurable. (He that has too little love of pleasure is the opposite character, and the man of perfected self-mastery the mean character.) He is of a similar character who avoids the bodily pains, not because he *cannot*, but because he *chooses not to*, withstand them.

But of the characters who go wrong without *choosing so* to do, the one is led on by reason of pleasure, the other because he avoids the pain it would cost him to deny his lust; and so they are different the one from the other. Now everyone would pronounce a man worse for doing something base without any impulse of desire, or with a very slight one, than for doing the same from the impulse of a very strong desire; for striking a man when not angry than if he did so in wrath: because one naturally says, 'What would he have done had he been under the influence of passion?' (and on this ground, by the bye, the man utterly void of self-control is worse than he who has it imperfectly). However, of the two characters which have been mentioned [as included in that of utter absence of self-control], the one is rather softness, the other properly the man of no self-control.

Furthermore, to the character of imperfect self-control is opposed that of self-control, and to that of softness that of endurance: because endurance consists in continued resistance but self-control in actual mastery, and continued resistance and actual mastery are as different as not being conquered is from conquering; and so self-control is more choiceworthy than endurance.

Again, he who fails when exposed to those temptations against which the common run of men hold out, and are well able to do so, is soft and luxurious (luxury being a kind of softness): the kind of man, I mean, to let his robe drag in the dirt to avoid the trouble of lifting it, and who, aping the sick man, does not however suppose himself wretched though he is like a wretched man. So it is too with respect to self-control and the imperfection of it: if a man yields to pleasures or pains which are violent and excessive it is no matter for wonder, but rather for allowance if he made what resistance he could (instances are, Philoctetes in Theodectes' drama when wounded by the viper; or Cercyon in the *Alope* of Carcinus, or men who in trying to suppress laughter burst into a loud continuous fit of it, as happened, you remember, to Xenophantus), but it is a matter for wonder when a man yields to and cannot contend against those pleasures or pains which the common herd are able to resist; always supposing his failure not to be owing to natural constitution or disease, I mean, as the Scythian kings are constitutionally soft, or the natural difference between the sexes.

Again, the man who is a slave to amusement is commonly thought to be destitute of self-control, but he really is soft; because amusement is an act of relaxing, being an act of resting, and the character in question is one of those who exceed due bounds in respect of this.

Moreover of imperfect self-control there are two forms, precipitancy and weakness: those who have it in the latter form though they have made resolutions do not abide by them by reason of passion; the others are led by passion because they have never formed any resolutions at all: while there are some who, like those who by tickling themselves beforehand get rid of ticklishness, having felt and seen beforehand the approach of temptation, and roused up themselves and their resolution, yield not to passion; whether the temptation be somewhat pleasant or somewhat painful. The precipitate form of imperfect self-control they are most liable to who are constitutionally of a sharp or melancholy temperament: because the one by reason of the swiftness, the other by reason of the violence, of their passions, do not wait for reason, because they are disposed to follow whatever notion is impressed upon their minds.

Section 8 to end

Different forms of imperfect self-control. Change of mind does not always arise from failure of self-control.

Discussion of pleasure (for another treatment of the same topic, see Book Ten, sections 1–5). Current opinions on whether pleasure is a good, and if so whether it is the supreme good.

BOOK EIGHT

Friendship

1 Next would seem properly to follow a dissertation on friendship: because, in the first place, it is either itself a virtue or connected with virtue; and next it is a thing most necessary for life, since no one would choose to live without friends though he should have all the other good things in the world: and, in fact, men who are rich or possessed of authority and influence are thought to have special need of friends: for where is the use of such prosperity if there be taken away the doing of kindnesses of which friends are the most usual and most commendable objects? Or how can it be kept or preserved without friends? because the greater it is so much the more slippery and hazardous: in poverty moreover and all other adversities men think friends to be their only refuge.

Furthermore, friendship helps the young to keep from error: the old, in respect of attention and such deficiencies in action as their weakness makes them liable to; and those who are in their prime, in respect of noble deeds ('They *two* together going,' Homer says, you may remember), because they are thus more able to devise plans and carry them out.

Again, it seems to be implanted in us by nature: as, for instance, in the parent towards the offspring and the offspring towards the parent (not merely in the human species, but likewise in birds and most animals), and in those of the same tribe towards one another, and specially in men of the same nation; for which reason we commend those men who love their fellows: and one may see in the course of travel how close of kin and how friendly man is to man.

Furthermore, friendship seems to be the bond of social communities, and legislators seem to be more anxious to secure it than justice even. I mean, unanimity is somewhat like to friendship, and this they certainly aim at and specially drive out faction as being inimical.

Again, where people are in friendship justice is not required; but, on the other hand, though they are just they need friendship in addition, and that principle which is most truly just is thought to partake of the nature of friendship.

Lastly, not only is it a thing necessary but honourable likewise: since we praise those who are fond of friends, and the having numerous friends is thought a matter of credit to a man; some go so far as to hold, that 'good man' and 'friend' are terms synonymous.

Yet the disputed points respecting it are not few: some men lay down that it is a kind of resemblance, and that men who are like one another are friends: whence come the common sayings, 'Like will to like', 'Birds of a feather', and so on. Others, on the contrary, say, that all such come under the maxim, 'Two of a trade never agree.'

Again, some men push their inquiries on these points higher and reason physically: as Euripides, who says,

'The earth by drought consumed doth love the rain,
And the great heaven, overcharged with rain,
Doth love to fall in showers upon the earth.'

Heraclitus, again, maintains that 'contrariety is expedient, and that the best agreement arises from things differing, and that all things come into being in the way of the principle of antagonism.'

Empedocles, among others, in direct opposition to these, affirms, that 'like aims at like.'

These physical questions we will take leave to omit, inasmuch as they are foreign to the present inquiry; and we will examine such as are proper to man and concern moral characters and feelings: as, for instance, 'Does friendship arise among all without distinction, or is it impossible for bad men to be friends?' and, 'Is there but one species of friendship, or several?' For they who ground the opinion that there is but one on the fact that friendship admits of degrees hold that upon insufficient proof; because things which are different in species admit likewise of degrees (on this point we have spoken before).

2 Our view will soon be cleared on these points when we have ascertained what is properly the object-matter of friendship: for it is thought that not everything indiscriminately, but some peculiar matter alone, is the object of this affection; that is to say, what is good, or pleasurable, or useful. Now it would seem that that is useful through which accrues any good or pleasure, and so the objects of friendship, as absolute ends, are the good and the pleasurable.

A question here arises; whether it is good absolutely or that which is good to the individuals, for which men feel friendship (these two being sometimes distinct): and similarly in respect of the pleasurable. It seems then that each individual feels it towards that which is good to himself, and that abstractedly it is the real good which is the object of friendship, and to each individual that which is good to each. It comes then to this; that each individual feels friendship not for what *is* but for that which *conveys to his mind the impression of being* good to himself. But this will make no real difference, because that which is truly the object of friendship will also convey this impression to the mind.

There are then three causes from which men feel friendship : but the term is not applied to the case of fondness for things inanimate because there is no requital of the affection nor desire for the good of those objects: it certainly savours of the ridiculous to say that a man fond of wine wishes well to it: the only sense in which it is true being that he wishes it to be kept safe and sound for his own use and benefit. But to the friend they say one should wish all good for his sake. And when men do thus wish good to another (he not reciprocating the feeling), people call them kindly; because friendship they describe as being 'kindliness between persons who reciprocate it'. But must they not add that the feeling must be mutually known? For many men are kindly disposed towards those whom they have never seen but whom they conceive to be amiable or useful: and this notion amounts to the same thing as a real feeling between them.

Well, these are plainly kindly-disposed towards one another: but how can one call them friends while their mutual feelings are unknown to one another? To complete the idea of friendship, then, it is requisite that they have kindly feelings towards one another, and wish one another good from one of the afore-mentioned causes, and that these kindly feelings should be mutually known.

3   As the motives to friendship differ in kind so do the respective feelings and friendships. The species then of friendship are three, in number equal to the objects of it, since in the line of each there may be 'mutual affection mutually known'.

Now they who have friendship for one another desire one another's good according to the motive of their friendship; accordingly they whose motive is utility have no friendship for one another really, but only in so far as some good arises to them from one another.

And they whose motive is pleasure are in like case: I mean, they have friendship for men of easy pleasantry, not because they are of a given character but because they are pleasant to themselves. So then they whose motive to friendship is utility love their friends for what is good to themselves; they whose motive is pleasure do so for what is pleasurable to themselves; that is to say, not in so far as the friend beloved *is* but in so far as he is useful or pleasurable. These friendships then are a matter of result: since the object is not beloved in that he is the man he is but in that he furnishes advantage or pleasure as the case may be.

Such friendships are of course very liable to dissolution if the parties do not continue alike: I mean, that the others cease to have any friendship for them when they are no longer pleasurable or useful. Now it is the nature of utility not to be permanent but constantly varying: so, of course, when the motive which made them friends is vanished, the friendship likewise dissolves; since it existed only relatively to those circumstances.

Friendship of this kind is thought to exist principally among the old (because men at that time of life pursue not what is pleasurable but what is profitable); and in such, of men in their prime and of the young, as are given to the pursuit of profit. They that are such have no intimate intercourse with one another; for sometimes they are not even pleasurable to one another: nor, in fact, do they desire such intercourse unless their friends are profitable to them, because they are pleasurable only in so far as they have hopes of advantage. With these friendships is commonly ranked that of hospitality.

But the friendship of the young is thought to be based on the motive of pleasure: because they live at the beck and call of passion and generally pursue what is pleasurable to themselves and the object of the present moment: and as their age changes so likewise do their pleasures.

This is the reason why they form and dissolve friendships rapidly: since the friendship changes with the pleasurable object and such pleasure changes quickly.

The young are also much given up to love; this passion being, in great measure, a matter of impulse and based on pleasure: for which cause they conceive friendships and quickly drop them, changing often in the same day: but these wish for society and intimate intercourse with their friends, since they thus attain the object of their friendship.

That then is perfect friendship which subsists between those who are good and whose similarity consists in their goodness: for these men wish one another's good in similar ways; in so far as they are good (and good they are in themselves); and those are specially friends who wish good to their friends for their sakes, because they feel thus towards them on their own account and not as a mere matter of result;

so the friendship between these men continues to subsist so long as they are good; and goodness, we know, has in it a principle of permanence.

Moreover, each party is good abstractedly and also relatively to his friend, for all good men are not only abstractedly good but also useful to one another. Such friends are also mutually pleasurable because all good men are so abstractedly, and also relatively to one another, inasmuch as to each individual those actions are pleasurable which correspond to his nature, and all such as are like them. Now when men are good these will be always the same, or at least similar.

Friendship then under these circumstances is permanent, as we should reasonably expect, since it combines in itself all the requisite qualifications of friends. I mean, that friendship of whatever kind is based upon good or pleasure (either abstractedly or relatively to the person entertaining the sentiment of friendship), and results from a similarity of some sort; and to this kind belong all the aforementioned requisites in the parties themselves, because in this the parties are similar, and so on: moreover, in it there is the abstractedly good and the abstractedly pleasant, and as these are specially the object-matter of friendship so the feeling and the state of friendship is found most intense and most excellent in men thus qualified.

Rare it is probable friendships of this kind will be, because men of this kind are rare. Besides, all requisite qualifications being presupposed, there is further required time and intimacy: for, as the proverb says, men cannot know one another 'till they have eaten the requisite quantity of salt together'; nor can they in fact admit one another to intimacy, much less be friends, till each has appeared to the other and been proved to be a fit object of friendship. They who speedily commence an interchange of friendly actions may be said to wish to be friends, but they are not so unless they are also proper objects of friendship and mutually known to be such: that is to say, a desire for friendship may arise quickly but not friendship itself.

4   Well, this friendship is perfect both in respect of the time and in all other points; and exactly the same and similar results accrue to each party from the other; which ought to be the case between friends.

The friendship based upon the pleasurable is, so to say, a copy of this, since the good are sources of pleasure to one another: and that based on utility likewise, the good being also useful to one another. Between men thus connected friendships are most permanent when the same result accrues to both from one another, pleasure, for instance; and not merely so but from the same source, as in the case of two men of easy pleasantry; and not as it is in that of a lover and the object of his affection, these not deriving their pleasure from the same causes, but the former from seeing the latter and the latter from receiving the attentions of the former: and when the bloom of youth fades the friendship sometimes ceases also, because then the lover derives no pleasure from seeing and the object of his affection ceases to receive the attentions which were paid before: in many cases, however, people so connected continue friends, if being of similar tempers they have come from custom to like one another's disposition.

Where people do not interchange pleasure but profit in matters of love, the friendship is both less intense in degree and also less permanent: in fact, they

who are friends because of advantage commonly part
when the advantage ceases; for, in reality, they never
were friends of one another but of the advantage.

So then it appears that from motives of pleasure or
profit bad men may be friends to one another, or good
men to bad men, or men of neutral character to one of
any character whatever: but disinterestedly, for the
sake of one another, plainly the good alone can be
friends; because bad men have no pleasure even in
themselves unless in so far as some advantage arises.

And further, the friendship of the good is alone
superior to calumny; it not being easy for men to
believe a third person respecting one whom they have
long tried and proved: there is between good men
mutual confidence, and the feeling that one's friend
would never have done one wrong, and all other such
things as are expected in friendship really worthy the
name; but in the other kinds there is nothing to
prevent all such suspicions.

I call them friendships, because since men commonly give the name of friends to those who are
connected from motives of profit (which is justified by
political language, for alliances between states are
thought to be contracted with a view to advantage),
and to those who are attached to one another by the
motive of pleasure (as children are), we may perhaps
also be allowed to call such persons friends, and say
there are several species of friendship; primarily and
specially that of the good, in that they are good, and
the rest only in the way of resemblance: I mean,
people connected otherwise are friends in that way in
which there arises to them somewhat good and some
mutual resemblance (because, we must remember the
pleasurable is good to those who are fond of it).

These secondary friendships, however, do not combine very well; that is to say, the same persons do not become friends by reason of advantage and by reason of the pleasurable, for these matters of result are not often combined. And friendship having been divided into these kinds, bad men will be friends by reason of pleasure or profit, this being their point of resemblance; while the good are friends for one another's sake, that is, in so far as they are good.

These last may be termed abstractedly and simply friends, the former as a matter of result and termed friends from their resemblance to these last.

5 Further; just as in respect of the different virtues some men are termed good in respect of a certain inward state, others in respect of acts of working, so is it in respect of friendship: I mean, they who live together take pleasure in, and impart good to, one another: but they who are asleep or are locally separated do not perform acts, but only are in such a state as to act in a friendly way if they acted at all: distance has in itself no direct effect upon friendship, but only prevents the acting it out: yet, if the absence be protracted, it is thought to cause a forgetfulness even of the friendship: and hence it has been said, 'many and many a friendship doth want of intercourse destroy.'

Accordingly, neither the old nor the morose appear to be calculated for friendship, because the pleasurableness in them is small, and no one can spend his days in company with that which is positively painful or even not pleasurable; since to avoid the painful and aim at the pleasurable is one of the most obvious tendencies of human nature. They who get on with one another very fairly, but are not in habits of intimacy, are rather like people having kindly feelings towards one another than friends; nothing being so characteristic of friends as the living with one another, because the necessitous desire assistance, and the happy companionship, they being the last persons in the world for solitary existence: but people cannot spend their time together unless they are mutually pleasurable and take pleasure in the same objects, a quality which is thought to appertain to the friendship of companionship.

The connection then subsisting between the good is friendship *par excellence*, as has already been frequently said: since that which is abstractedly good or pleasant is thought to be an object of friendship and choiceworthy, and to each individual whatever is such to him; and the good man to the good man for both these reasons.

(Now the entertaining the sentiment is like a feeling, but friendship itself like a state: because the former may have for its object even things inanimate, but requital of friendship is attended with moral choice which proceeds from a moral state: and again, men wish good to the objects of their friendship for their sakes, not in the way of a mere feeling but of moral state.)

And the good, in loving their friend, love their own good (inasmuch as the good man, when brought into that relation, becomes a good to him with whom he is so connected), so that either party loves his own good, and repays his friend equally both in wishing well and in the pleasurable: for equality is said to be a tie of friendship. Well, these points belong most to the friendship between good men.

6 But between morose or elderly men friendship is less apt to arise, because they are somewhat awkward-

tempered, and take less pleasure in intercourse and society; these being thought to be specially friendly and productive of friendship; and so young men become friends quickly, old men not so (because people do not become friends with any, unless they take pleasure in them); and in like manner neither do the morose. Yet men of these classes entertain kindly feelings towards one another: they wish good to one another and render mutual assistance in respect of their needs, but they are not quite friends, because they neither spend their time together nor take pleasure in one another, which circumstances are thought specially to belong to friendship.

To be a friend to many people, in the way of the perfect friendship, is not possible; just as you cannot be in love with many at once: it is, so to speak, a state of excess which naturally has but one object; and besides, it is not an easy thing for one man to be very much pleased with many people at the same time, nor perhaps to find many really good. Again, a man needs experience, and to be in habits of close intimacy, which is very difficult.

But it *is* possible to please many on the score of advantage and pleasure: because there are many men of the kind, and the services may be rendered in a very short time.

Of the two imperfect kinds that which most resembles the perfect is the friendship based upon pleasure, in which the same results accrue from both and they take pleasure in one another or in the same objects; such as are the friendships of the young, because a generous spirit is most found in these. The friendship because of advantage is the connecting link of shopkeepers.

Then again, the very happy have no need of persons who are profitable, but of pleasant ones they have because they wish to have people to live intimately with; and what is painful they bear for a short time indeed, but continuously no one could support it, nay, not even the chief good itself, if it were painful to him individually: and so they look out for pleasant friends: perhaps they ought to require such to be good also; and good moreover to themselves individually, because then they will have all the proper requisites of friendship.

Men in power are often seen to make use of several distinct friends: for some are useful to them and others pleasurable, but the two are not often united: because they do not, in fact, seek such as shall combine pleasantness and goodness, nor such as shall be useful for honourable purposes: but with a view to attain what is pleasant they look out for men of easy-pleasantry; and again, for men who are clever at executing any business put into their hands: and these qualifications are not commonly found united in the same man.

It has been already stated that the good man unites the qualities of pleasantness and usefulness: but then such an one will not be a friend to a superior unless he be also his superior in goodness: for if this be not the case, he cannot, being surpassed in one point, make things equal by a proportionate degree of friendship. And characters who unite superiority of station and goodness are not common.

Now all the kinds of friendship which have been already mentioned exist in a state of equality, inasmuch as either the same results accrue to both and they wish the same things to one another, or else they barter one thing against another; pleasure, for instance, against profit: it has been said already that friendships of this latter kind are less intense in degree and less permanent.

And it is their resemblance or dissimilarity to the same thing which makes them to be thought to be and not to be friendships: they show like friendships in right of their likeness to that which is based on virtue (the one kind having the pleasurable, the other the profitable, both of which belong also to the other); and again, they do not show like friendships by reason of their unlikeness to that true kind; which unlikeness consists herein, that while that is above calumny and so permanent these quickly change and differ in many other points.

7 But there is another form of friendship, that, namely, in which the one party is superior to the other; as between father and son, elder and younger, husband and wife, ruler and ruled. These also differ one from another: I mean, the friendship between parents and children is not the same as between ruler and the ruled, nor has the father the same towards the son as the son towards the father, nor the husband towards the wife as she towards him; because the work, and therefore the excellence, of each of these is different, and different therefore are the causes of their feeling friendship; distinct and different therefore are their feelings and states of friendship.

And the same results do not accrue to each from the other, nor in fact ought they to be looked for: but, when children render to their parents what they ought to the authors of their being, and parents to their sons what they ought to their offspring, the friendship between such parties will be permanent and equitable.

Further; the feeling of friendship should be in a due proportion in all friendships which are between superior and inferior; I mean, the better man, or the more profitable, and so forth, should be the object of a stronger feeling than he himself entertains, because when the feeling of friendship comes to be after a certain rate then equality in a certain sense is produced, which is thought to be a requisite in friendship.

(It must be remembered, however, that the equal is not in the same case as regards justice and friendship: for in strict justice the exactly proportioned equal ranks first, and the actual numerically equal ranks second, while in friendship this is exactly reversed.)

And that equality is thus requisite is plainly shown by the occurrence of a great difference of goodness or badness, or prosperity, or something else: for in this case, people are not any longer friends, nay they do not even feel that they ought to be. The clearest illustration is perhaps the case of the gods, because they are most superior in all good things. It is obvious too, in the case of kings, for they who are greatly their inferiors do not feel entitled to be friends to them; nor do people very insignificant to be friends to those of very high excellence or wisdom. Of course, in such cases it is out of the question to attempt to define up to what point they may continue friends: for you may remove many points of agreement and the friendship last nevertheless; but when one of the parties is very far separated (as a god from men), it cannot continue any longer.

This has given room for a doubt, whether friends do really wish to their friends the very highest goods, as that they may be gods: because, in case the wish were accomplished, they would no longer have them for friends, nor in fact would they have the good things they had, because friends are good things. If then it has been rightly said that a friend wishes to his friend good things for that friend's sake, it must be understood that he is to remain such as he now is: that is to say, he will wish the greatest good to him of which as man he is capable: yet perhaps not all, because each man desires good for himself most of all.

Section 8 to end

Inequality between friends may be reduced when the inferior partner offers the greater affection.

Friendship provides us with an analogy for political relationships and the types of constitution. The same types also occur in families: there are different kinds of affection between kinsmen, comrades, parents and children, brothers, husbands and wives. Friendship imposes a variety of claims both on equals and unequals.

BOOK NINE

Friendship (continued)

Sections 1 to 6

Further treatment of the claims of friendship. How is the due return for a service to be measured? Judging between conflicting claims of different friends. When is it justified to terminate a friendship?

Friendship is characterised by the kinds of feelings the good person has towards himself: self-esteem and a desire to bring about his own benefit. It has similarities to goodwill and concord but is distinct from them.

7 Benefactors are commonly held to have more friendship for the objects of their kindness than these for them: and the fact is made a subject of discussion and inquiry, as being contrary to reasonable expectation.

The account of the matter which satisfies most persons is that the one are debtors and the others creditors: and therefore that, as in the case of actual loans the debtors wish their creditors out of the way while the creditors are anxious for the preservation of their debtors, so those who have done kindnesses desire the continued existence of the people they have done them to, under the notion of getting a return of their good offices, while these are not particularly anxious about requital.

Epicharmus, I suspect, would very probably say that they who give this solution judge from their own baseness; yet it certainly is like human nature, for the generality of men have short memories on these points, and aim rather at receiving than conferring benefits.

But the real cause, it would seem, rests upon nature, and the case is not parallel to that of creditors; because in this there is no affection to the persons, but merely a wish for their preservation with a view to the return: whereas, in point of fact, they who have done kindnesses feel friendship and love for those to whom they have done them, even though they neither are, nor can by possibility hereafter be, in a position to serve their benefactors.

And this is the case also with artisans; everyone, I mean, feels more affection for his own work than that work possibly could for him if it were animate. It is perhaps specially the case with poets: for these entertain very great affection for their poems, loving them as their own children. It is to this kind of thing I should be inclined to compare the case of benefactors: for the object of their kindness is their own work, and so they love this more than this loves its creator.

And the account of this is that existence is to all a thing choiceworthy and an object of affection; now we exist by acts of working, that is, by living and acting; he then that has created a given work exists, it may be said, by his act of working: therefore he loves his work because he loves existence. And this is natural, for the work produced displays in act what existed before potentially.

Then again, the benefactor has a sense of honour in right of his action, so that he may well take pleasure in him in whom this resides; but to him who has received the benefit there is nothing honourable in respect of his benefactor, only something advantageous which is both less pleasant and less the object of friendship.

Again, pleasure is derived from the actual working out of a present action, from the anticipation of a future one, and from the recollection of a past one: but the highest pleasure and special object of affection is that which attends on the actual working. Now the benefactor's work abides (for the honourable is enduring), but the advantage of him who has received the kindness passes away.

Again, there is pleasure in recollecting honourable actions, but in recollecting advantageous ones there is none at all or much less (by the way though, the contrary is true of the expectation of advantage).

Further, the entertaining the feeling of friendship is like acting on another; but being the object of the feeling is like being acted upon.

So then, entertaining the sentiment of friendship, and all feelings connected with it, attend on those who, in the given case of a benefaction, are the superior party.

Once more: all people value most what has cost them much labour in the production; for instance, people who have themselves made their money are fonder of it than those who have inherited it: and receiving kindness is, it seems, unlaborious, but doing it is laborious. And this is the reason why the female parents are most fond of their offspring; for their part in producing them is attended with most labour, and they know more certainly that they are theirs. This feeling would seem also to belong to benefactors.

8   A question is also raised as to whether it is right to love one's self best, or someone else: because men find fault with those who love themselves best, and call them in a disparaging way lovers of self; and the bad man is thought to do everything he does for his own sake merely, and the more so the more depraved he is; accordingly men reproach him with never doing anything unselfish: whereas the good man acts from a sense of honour (and the more so the better man he is), and for his friend's sake, and is careless of his own interest.

But with these theories facts are at variance, and not unnaturally: for it is commonly said also that a man is to love most him who is most his friend, and he is most a friend who wishes good to him to whom he wishes it for that man's sake even though no one knows. Now these conditions, and in fact all the rest by which a friend is characterised, belong specially to each individual in respect of his self: for we have said before that all the friendly feelings are derived to others from those which have self primarily for their object. And all the current proverbs support this view; for instance, 'one soul', 'the goods of friends are common', 'equality is a tie of friendship', 'the knee is nearer than the shin'. For all these things exist specially with reference to a man's own self: he is specially a friend to himself and so he is bound to love himself the most.

It is with good reason questioned which of the two parties one should follow, both having plausibility on their side. Perhaps then, m respect of theories of this kind, the proper course is to distinguish and define how far each is true, and in what way. If we could ascertain the sense in which each uses the term 'self-loving', this point might be cleared up.

Well now, they who use it disparagingly give the name to those who, in respect of wealth, and honours, and pleasures of the body, give to themselves the larger share: because the mass of mankind grasp after these and are earnest about them as being the best things; which is the reason why they are matters of contention. They who are covetous in regard to these gratify their lusts and passions in general, that is to say the irrational part of their soul: now the mass of mankind are so disposed, for which reason the appellation has taken its rise from that mass which is low and bad. Of course they are justly reproached who are self-loving in this sense.

And that the generality of men are accustomed to apply the term to denominate those who do give such things to themselves is quite plain: suppose, for instance, that a man were anxious to do, more than other men, acts of justice, or self-mastery, or any other virtuous acts, and, in general, were to secure to himself that which is abstractedly noble and honourable, no one would call him self-loving, nor blame him.

Yet might such an one be judged to be more truly self-loving: certainly he gives to himself the things which are most noble and most good, and gratifies that principle of his nature which is most rightfully authoritative, and obeys it in everything: and just as that which possesses the highest authority is thought to constitute a community or any other system, so also in the case of man: and so he is most truly self-loving who loves and gratifies this principle.

Again, men are said to have, or to fail of having, self-control, according as the intellect controls or not, it being plainly implied thereby that this principle constitutes each individual; and people are thought to have done of themselves, and voluntarily, those things specially which are done with reason.

It is plain, therefore, that this principle does, either entirely or specially, constitute the individual man, and that the good man specially loves this. For this reason then he must be specially self-loving, in a kind other than that which is reproached, and as far superior to it as living in accordance with reason is to living at the beck and call of passion, and aiming at the truly noble to aiming at apparent advantage.

Now all approve and commend those who are eminently earnest about honourable actions, and if all would vie with one another in respect of the *kalon* and be intent upon doing what is most truly noble and honourable, society at large would have all that is proper while each individual in particular would have the greatest of goods, virtue being assumed to be such.

And so the good man ought to be self-loving: because by doing what is noble he will have advantage himself and will do good to others: but the bad man ought not to be, because he will harm himself and his neighbours by following low and evil passions. In the case of the bad man, what he ought to do and what he does are at variance, but the good man does what he ought to do, because all intellect chooses what is best for itself and the good man puts himself under the direction of intellect.

Of the good man it is true likewise that he does many things for the sake of his friends and his country, even to the extent of dying for them, if need be: for money and honours, and, in short, all the good things which others fight for, he will throw away while eager to secure to himself the *kalon*; he will prefer a brief and great joy to a tame and enduring one, and to live nobly for one year rather than ordinarily for many, and one great and noble action to many trifling ones. And this is perhaps that which befalls men who die for their country and friends; they choose great glory for themselves: and they will lavish their own money that their friends may receive more, for hereby the friend gets the money but the man himself the *kalon*; so, in fact, he gives to himself the greater good. It is the same with honours and offices; all these things he will give up to his friend, because this reflects honour and praise on himself: and so with good reason is he esteemed a fine character since he chooses the honourable before all things else. It is possible also to give up the opportunities of action to a friend; and to have caused a friend's doing a thing may be more noble than having done it one's self.

In short, in all praiseworthy things the good man does plainly give to himself a larger share of the honourable. In this sense it is right to be self-loving, in the vulgar acceptation of the term it is not.

9   A question is raised also respecting the happy man, whether he will want friends, or no?

Some say that they who are blessed and independent have no need of friends, for they already have all that is good, and so, as being independent, want nothing further: whereas the notion of a friend's office is to be as it were a second self and procure for a man what he cannot get by himself: hence the saying,

'When Fortune gives us good, what need we
                                    friends?'

On the other hand, it looks absurd, while we are assigning to the happy man all other good things, not to give him friends, which are, after all, thought to be the greatest of external goods.

Again, if it is more characteristic of a friend to confer than to receive kindnesses, and if to be beneficent belongs to the good man and to the character of virtue, and if it is more noble to confer kindnesses on friends than strangers, the good man will need objects for his benefactions. And out of this last consideration springs a question whether the need of friends be greater in prosperity or adversity, since the unfortunate man wants people to do him kindnesses and they who are fortunate want objects for their kind acts.

Again, it is perhaps absurd to make our happy man a solitary, because no man would choose the possession of all goods in the world on the condition of solitariness, man being a social animal and formed by nature for living with others: of course the happy man has this qualification since he has all those things which are good by nature: and it is obvious that the society of friends and good men must be preferable to that of strangers and ordinary people, and we conclude, therefore, that the happy man does need friends.

But then, what do they mean whom we quoted first, and how are they right? Is it not that the mass of mankind mean by friends those who are useful? and of course the happy man will not need such because he has all good things already; neither will he need such as are friends with a view to the pleasurable, or at least only to a slight extent; because his life, being already pleasurable, does not want pleasure imported from without; and so, since the happy man does not need friends of these kinds, he is thought not to need any at all.

But it may be, this is not true: for it was stated

originally, that happiness is a kind of working; now working plainly is something that must come into being, not be already there like a mere piece of property.

If then the being happy consists in living and working, and the good man's working is in itself excellent and pleasurable (as we said at the commencement of the treatise), and if what is our own reckons among things pleasurable, and if we can view our neighbours better than ourselves and their actions better than we can our own, then the actions of their friends who are good men are pleasurable to the good; inasmuch as they have both the requisites which are naturally pleasant. So the man in the highest state of happiness will need friends of this kind, since he desires to contemplate good actions, and actions of his own, which those of his friend, being a good man, are.

Again, common opinion requires that the happy man live with pleasure to himself: now life is burthensome to a man in solitude, for it is not easy to work continuously by one's self, but in company with, and in regard to others, it is easier, and therefore the working, being pleasurable in itself, will be more continuous (a thing which should be in respect of the happy man); for the good man, in that he is good, takes pleasure in the actions which accord with virtue and is annoyed at those which spring from vice, just as a musical man is pleased with beautiful music and annoyed by bad. And besides, as Theognis says, virtue itself may be improved by practice, from living with the good.

And, upon the following considerations more purely metaphysical, it will probably appear that the good friend is naturally choiceworthy to the good man. We have said before, that whatever is naturally good is also in itself good and pleasant to the good man; now the fact of living, so far as animals are concerned, is characterised generally by the power of sentience, in man it is characterised by that of sentience, or of rationality (the faculty of course being referred to the actual operation of the faculty, certainly the main point is the actual operation of it); so that living seems mainly to consist in the act of sentience or exerting rationality: now the fact of living is in itself one of the things that are good and pleasant (for it is a definite totality, and whatever is such belongs to the nature of good), but what is naturally good is good to the good man: for which reason it seems to be pleasant to all. (Of course one must not suppose a life which is depraved and corrupted, nor one spent in pain, for that which is such is indefinite as are its inherent qualities: however, what is to be said of pain will be clearer in what is to follow.)

If then the fact of living is in itself good and pleasant (and this appears from the fact that all desire it, and specially those who are good and in high happiness; their course of life being most choiceworthy and their existence most choiceworthy likewise), then also he that sees perceives that he sees: and he that hears perceives that he hears; and he that walks perceives that he walks; and in all the other instances in like manner there is a faculty which reflects upon and perceives the fact that we are working, so that we can perceive that we perceive and intellectually know that we intellectually know: but to perceive that we perceive or that we intellectually know is to perceive that we exist, since existence was defined to be perceiving or intellectually knowing. Now to perceive that one lives is a thing pleasant in itself, life being a thing naturally good, and the perceiving of the presence in ourselves of things naturally good being pleasant.

Therefore the fact of living is choiceworthy, and to the good specially so since existence is good and pleasant to them: for they receive pleasure from the internal consciousness of that which in itself is good.

But the good man is to his friend as to himself, friend being but a name for a second self; therefore as his own existence is choiceworthy to each so too, or similarly at least, is his friend's existence. But the ground of one's own existence being choiceworthy is the perceiving of one's self being good, any such perception being in itself pleasant. Therefore one ought to be thoroughly conscious of one's friend's existence, which will result from living with him, that is sharing in his words and thoughts: for this is the meaning of the term as applied to the human species, not mere feeding together as in the case of brutes.

If then to the man in a high state of happiness existence is in itself choiceworthy, being naturally good and pleasant, and so too a friend's existence, then the friend also must be among things choiceworthy. But whatever is choiceworthy to a man he should have or else he will be in this point deficient. The man therefore who is to come up to our notion 'happy' will need good friends.

Are we then to make our friends as numerous as possible? Or, as in respect of acquaintance it is thought to have been well said 'have not thou many acquaintances yet be not without;' so too in respect of friendship may we adopt the precept, and say that a man should not be without friends, nor again have exceeding many friends?

Now as for friends who are intended for use, the

maxim I have quoted will, it seems, fit in exceedingly well, because to requite the services of many is a matter of labour, and a whole life would not be long enough to do this for them. So that, if more numerous than what will suffice for one's own life, they become officious, and are hindrances in respect of living well: and so we do not want them. And again, of those who are to be for pleasure a few are quite enough, just like sweetening in our food.

10　But of the good are we to make as many as ever we can, or is there any measure of the number of friends, as there is of the number to constitute a political community? I mean, you cannot make one out of ten men, and if you increase the number to one hundred thousand it is not any longer a community. However, the number is not perhaps some one definite number but any between certain extreme limits.

Well, of friends likewise there is a limited number, which perhaps may be laid down to be the greatest number with whom it would be possible to keep up intimacy; this being thought to be one of the greatest marks of friendship, and it being quite obvious that it is not possible to be intimate with many, in other words, to part one's self among many. And besides it must be remembered that they also are to be friends to one another if they are all to live together: but it is a matter of difficulty to find this in many men at once.

It comes likewise to be difficult to bring home to one's self the joys and sorrows of many: because in all probability one would have to sympathise at the same time with the joys of this one and the sorrows of that other.

Perhaps then it is well not to endeavour to have very

many friends but so many as are enough for intimacy: because, in fact, it would seem not to be possible to be very much a friend to many at the same time: and, for the same reason, not to be in love with many objects at the same time: love being a kind of excessive friendship which implies but one object: and all strong emotions must be limited in the number towards whom they are felt.

And if we look to facts this seems to be so: for not many at a time become friends in the way of companionship, all the famous friendships of the kind are between *two* persons: whereas they who have many friends, and meet everybody on the footing of intimacy, seem to be friends really to no one except in the way of general society; I mean the characters denominated as over-complaisant.

To be sure, in the way merely of society, a man may be a friend to many without being necessarily over-complaisant, but being truly good: but one cannot be a friend to many because of their virtue, and for the persons' own sake; in fact, it is a matter for contentment to find even a few such.

11 Again: are friends most needed in prosperity or in adversity? They are required, we know, in both states, because the unfortunate need help and the prosperous want people to live with and to do kindnesses to: for they have a desire to act kindly to some one.

To have friends is more necessary in adversity, and therefore in this case useful ones are wanted; and to have them in prosperity is more honourable, and this is why the prosperous want good men for friends, it being preferable to confer benefits on, and to live with, these. For the very presence of friends is pleasant even in adversity: since men when grieved are comforted by the sympathy of their friends.

And from this, by the way, the question might be raised, whether it is that they do in a manner take part of the weight of calamities, or only that their presence, being pleasurable, and the consciousness of their sympathy, make the pain of the sufferer less.

However, we will not further discuss whether these which have been suggested or some other causes produce the relief, at least the effect we speak of is a matter of plain fact.

But their presence has probably a mixed effect: I mean, not only is the very seeing friends pleasant, especially to one in misfortune, and actual help towards lessening the grief is afforded (the natural tendency of a friend, if he is gifted with tact, being to comfort by look and word, because he is well acquainted with the sufferer's temper and disposition and therefore knows what things give him pleasure and pain), but also the perceiving a friend to be grieved at his misfortunes causes the sufferer pain, because everyone avoids being cause of pain to his friends. And for this reason they who are of a manly nature are cautious not to implicate their friends in their pain; and unless a man is exceedingly callous to the pain of others he cannot bear the pain which is thus caused to his friends: in short, he does not admit men to wail with him, not being given to wail at all: women, it is true, and men who resemble women, like to have others to groan with them, and love such as friends and sympathisers. But it is plain that it is our duty in all things to imitate the highest character.

On the other hand, the advantages of friends in our prosperity are the pleasurable intercourse and the consciousness that they are pleased at our good fortune.

It would seem, therefore, that we ought to call in friends readily on occasion of good fortune, because it is noble to be ready to do good to others: but on occasion of bad fortune, we should do so with reluctance; for we should as little as possible make others share in our ills; on which principle goes the saying, 'I am unfortunate, let that suffice.' The most proper occasion for calling them in is when with small trouble or annoyance to themselves they can be of very great use to the person who needs them.

But, on the contrary, it is fitting perhaps to go to one's friends in their misfortunes unasked and with alacrity (because kindness is the friend's office and specially towards those who are in need and who do not demand it as a right, this being more creditable and more pleasant to both); and on occasion of their good fortune to go readily, if we can forward it in any way (because men need their friends for this likewise), but to be backward in sharing it, any great eagerness to receive advantage not being creditable.

One should perhaps be cautious not to present the appearance of sullenness in declining the sympathy or help of friends, for this happens occasionally.

It appears then that the presence of friends is, under all circumstances, choiceworthy.

12 May we not say then that, as seeing the beloved object is most prized by lovers and they choose this sense rather than any of the others because Love

> 'Is engendered in the eyes,
>   With gazing fed,'

in like manner intimacy is to friends most choice-worthy, friendship being communion? Again, as a man is to himself so is he to his friend; now with respect to himself the perception of his own existence is choiceworthy, therefore is it also in respect of his friend.

And besides, their friendship is acted out in intimacy, and so with good reason they desire this. And whatever in each man's opinion constitutes existence, or whatsoever it is for the sake of which they choose life, herein they wish their friends to join with them; and so some men drink together, others gamble, others join in gymnastic exercises or hunting, others study philosophy together: in each case spending their days together in that which they like best of all things in life, for since they wish to be intimate with their friends they do and partake in those things whereby they think to attain this object.

Therefore the friendship of the wicked comes to be depraved; for, being unstable, they share in what is bad and become depraved in being made like to one another: but the friendship of the good is good, growing with their intercourse; they improve also, as it seems, by repeated acts, and by mutual correction, for they receive impress from one another in the points which give them pleasure ; whence says the poet,

'Thou from the good, good things shalt
                        surely learn.'

Here then we will terminate our discourse of friendship. The next thing is to go into the subject of pleasure.

BOOK TEN

Pleasure – happiness reviewed

1 Next, it would seem, follows a discussion respecting pleasure, for it is thought to be most closely bound up with our kind: and so men train the young, guiding them on their course by the rudders of pleasure and pain. And to like and dislike what one ought is judged to be most important for the formation of good moral character: because these feelings extend all one's life through, giving a bias towards and exerting an influence on the side of virtue and happiness, since men choose what is pleasant and avoid what is painful.

Subjects such as these then, it would seem, we ought by no means to pass by, and specially since they involve much difference of opinion. There are those who call pleasure the chief good; there are others who on the contrary maintain that it is exceedingly bad; some perhaps from a real conviction that such is the case, others from a notion that it is better, in reference to our life and conduct, to show up pleasure as bad, even if it is not so really; arguing that, as the mass of men have a bias towards it and are the slaves of their pleasures, it is right to draw them to the contrary, for that so they may possibly arrive at the mean.

I confess I suspect the soundness of this policy; in matters respecting men's feelings and actions theories are less convincing than facts: whenever, therefore, they are found conflicting with actual experience, they not only are despised but involve the truth in their fall: he, for instance, who deprecates pleasure, if once seen to aim at it, gets the credit of backsliding to it as being universally such as he said it was, the mass of men being incapable of nice distinctions.

Real accounts, therefore, of such matters seem to be most expedient, not with a view to knowledge merely but to life and conduct: for they are believed as being in harmony with facts, and so they prevail with the wise to live in accordance with them.

But of such considerations enough: let us now proceed to the current maxims respecting pleasure.

2 Now Eudoxus thought pleasure to be the chief good because he saw all, rational and irrational alike, aiming at it: and he argued that, since in all what was the object of choice must be good and what most so the best, the fact of all being drawn to the same thing proved this thing to be the best for all: 'For each,' he said, 'finds what is good for itself just as it does its proper nourishment, and so that which is good for all, and the object of the aim of all, is their chief good.'

(And his theories were received, not so much for their own sake, as because of his excellent moral character; for he was thought to be eminently possessed of perfect self-mastery, and therefore it was not thought that he said these things because he was a lover of pleasure but that he really was so convinced.)

And he thought his position was not less proved by the argument from the contrary: that is, since pain was in itself an object of avoidance to all the contrary must be in like manner an object of choice,

Again he urged that that is most choiceworthy which we choose, not by reason of, or with a view to, anything further; and that pleasure is confessedly of this kind because no one ever goes on to ask to what purpose he is pleased, feeling that pleasure is in itself choiceworthy.

Again, that when added to any other good it makes it more choiceworthy; as, for instance, to actions of justice, or perfected self-mastery; and good can only be increased by itself.

However, this; argument at least seems to prove only that it belongs to the class of goods, and not that it does so more than anything else: for every good is more choiceworthy in combination with some other than when taken quite alone. In fact, it is by just such an argument that Plato prove that pleasure is not the chief good: 'For,' says he, 'the life of pleasure is more choiceworthy in combination with practical wisdom than apart from it; but, if the compound be better, then simple pleasure cannot be the chief good because the very chief good cannot by any addition become more choiceworthy than it is already:' and it is obvious that nothing else can be the chief good, which by combination with any of the things in themselves good comes to be more choiceworthy.

What is there then of such a nature? (meaning, of course, whereof we can partake; because that which we are in search of must be such).

As for those who object that 'what all aim at is not necessarily good,' I confess I cannot see much in what they say, because what all *think* we say *is*. And he who would cut away this ground from under us will not bring forward things more dependable: because if the argument had rested on the desires of irrational creatures there might have been something in what he says, but, since the rational also desire pleasure, how can his objection be allowed any weight? And it may be that, even in the lower animals, there is some natural good principle above themselves which aims at the good peculiar to them.

Nor does that seem to be sound which is urged respecting the argument from the contrary: I mean, some people say 'it does not follow that pleasure must be good because pain is evil, since evil may be opposed to evil, and both evil and good to what is indifferent:' now what they say is right enough in itself but does not hold in the present instance. If both pleasure and pain were bad both would have been objects of avoidance; or if neither then neither would have been, at all events they must have fared alike: but now men do plainly avoid the one as bad and choose the other as good, and so there is a complete opposition.

3 Nor again is pleasure therefore excluded from being a good because it does not belong to the class of qualities: the acts of virtue are not qualities, neither is happiness [yet surely both are goods],

Again, they say the chief good is limited but pleasure unlimited, in that it admits of degrees.

Now if they judge this from the act of feeling pleasure then the same thing will apply to justice and all the other virtues, in respect of which clearly it is said that men are more or less of such and such characters (according to the different virtues), they are more just or more brave, or one may practise justice and self-mastery more or less.

If, on the other hand, they judge in respect of the pleasures themselves then it may be they miss the true cause, namely, that some are unmixed and others mixed: for just as health, being in itself limited, admits of degrees, why should not pleasure do so and yet be limited? In the former case we account for it by the fact that there is not the same adjustment of parts in all men, nor one and the same always in the same individual: but health, though relaxed, remains up to a certain point, and differs in degrees; and of course the same may be the case with pleasure.

Again, assuming the chief good to be perfect and all movements and generations imperfect, they try to show that pleasure is a movement and a generation.

Yet they do not seem warranted in saying even that it is a movement: for to every movement are thought to belong swiftness and slowness, and if not in itself, as to that of the universe, yet relatively: but to pleasure neither of these belongs: for though one may have got quickly into the state of pleasure, as into that of anger, one cannot be in the state quickly, nor relatively to the state of any other person; but we can walk or grow, and so on, quickly or slowly.

Of course it is possible to change into the state of pleasure quickly or slowly, but to act in the state (by which, I mean, have the perception of pleasure) quickly, is not possible.

And how can it be a generation? Because, according to notions generally held, not *anything* is generated from *anything*, but a thing resolves itself into that out of which it was generated: whereas of that of which pleasure is a generation pain is a destruction.

Again, they say that pain is a lack of something suitable to nature and pleasure a supply of it.

But these are affections of the body: now if pleasure really is a supplying of somewhat suitable to nature, that must feel the pleasure in which the supply takes place, therefore the body of course: yet this is not thought to be so: neither then is pleasure a supplying, only a person of course will be pleased when a supply takes place just as he will be pained when he is cut.

This notion would seem to have arisen out of the pains and pleasures connected with natural nourishment; because, when people have felt a lack and so have had pain first, they, of course, are pleased with the supply of their lack.

But this is not the case with all pleasures: those attendant on mathematical studies, for instance, are unconnected with any pain; and of such as attend on the senses those which arise through the sense of smell; and again, many sounds, and sights, and memories, and hopes: now of what can these be generations? Because there has been here no lack of anything to be afterwards supplied.

And to those who bring forward disgraceful pleasures we may reply that these are not really pleasant things; for it does not follow because they are pleasant to the ill-disposed that we are to admit that they are pleasant except to them; just as we should not say that those things are really wholesome, or sweet, or bitter, which are so to the sick, or those objects really white which give that impression to people labouring under ophthalmia.

Or we might say thus, that the pleasures are choiceworthy but not as derived from these sources: just as wealth is, but not as the price of treason; or health, but not on the terms of eating anything however loathsome.

Or again, may we not say that pleasures differ in kind? Those derived from honourable objects, for instance, are different from those arising from disgraceful ones; and it is not possible to experience the pleasure of the just man without being just, or of the musical man without being musical; and so on of others.

The distinction commonly drawn between the friend and the flatterer would seem to show clearly either that pleasure is not a good, or that there are different kinds of pleasure: for the former is thought to have good as the object of his intercourse, the latter pleasure only; and this last is reproached, but the former men praise as having different objects in his intercourse.

Again, no one would choose to live with a child's intellect all his life through, though receiving the highest possible pleasure from such objects as children receive it from; or to take pleasure in doing any of the most disgraceful things, though sure never to be pained.

There are many things also about which we should be diligent even though they brought no pleasure; as seeing, remembering, knowing, possessing the various excellences; and the fact that pleasures do follow on these naturally makes no difference, because we should certainly choose them even though no pleasure resulted from them.

It seems then to be plain that pleasure is not the chief good, nor is every kind of it choiceworthy: and that there are some choiceworthy in themselves, differing in kind, *i.e.* in the sources from which they are derived. Let this then suffice by way of an account of the current maxims respecting pleasure and pain.

4 Now what it is, and how characterised, will be more plain if we take up the subject afresh.

An act of sight is thought to be complete at any moment; that is to say, it lacks nothing the accession of which subsequently will complete its whole nature.

Well, pleasure resembles this: because it is a whole, as one may say; and one could not at any moment of time take a pleasure whose whole nature would be completed by its lasting for a longer time. And for this reason it is not a movement: for all movement takes place in time of certain duration and has a certain end to accomplish; for instance, the movement of house-building is then only complete when the builder has produced what he intended, that is, either in the whole time [necessary to complete the whole design], or in a given portion. But all the subordinate movements are incomplete in the parts of the time, and are different in kind from the whole movement and from one another (I mean, for instance, that the fitting the stones together is a movement different from that of fluting the column, and both again from the construction of the temple as a whole: but this last is complete as lacking nothing to the result proposed; whereas that of the basement, or of the triglyph, is incomplete, because each is a movement of a part merely).

As I said then, they differ in kind, and you cannot at any time you choose find a movement complete in its whole nature, but, if at all, in the whole time requisite.

And so it is with the movement of walking and all others: for, if motion be a movement from one place to another place, then of it too there are different kinds, flying, walking, leaping, and such-like. And not only so, but there are different kinds even in walking: the where-from and where-to are not the same in the whole course as in a portion of it; nor in one portion as in another; nor is crossing this line the same as crossing that: because a man is not merely crossing a line but a line in a given place, and this is in a different place from that.

Of movement I have discoursed exactly in another treatise. I will now therefore only say that it seems not to be complete at any given moment; and that most movements are incomplete and specifically different, since the whence and whither constitute different species.

But of pleasure the whole nature is complete at any given moment: it is plain then that pleasure and movement must be different from one another, and that pleasure belongs to the class of things whole and complete. And this might appear also from the impossibility of moving except in a definite time, whereas there is none with respect to the sensation of pleasure, for what exists at the very present moment is a kind of 'whole'.

From these considerations then it is plain that people are not warranted in saying that pleasure is a movement or a generation: because these terms are not applicable to all things, only to such as are divisible and not 'wholes': I mean that of an act of sight there is no generation, nor is there of a point, nor of a monad, nor is any one of these a movement or a generation: neither then of pleasure is there movement or generation, because it is, as one may say, 'a whole'.

Now since every percipient faculty works upon the object answering to it, and perfectly the faculty in a good state upon the most excellent of the objects within its range (for perfect working is thought to be much what I have described; and we will not raise any question about saying 'the faculty' works, instead of, 'that subject wherein the faculty resides'), in each case the best working is that of the faculty in its best state upon the best of the objects answering to it. And this will be, further, most perfect and most pleasant: for pleasure is attendant upon every percipient faculty, and in like manner on every intellectual operation and speculation; and that is most pleasant which is most perfect, and that most perfect which is the working of the best faculty upon the most excellent of the objects within its range.

And pleasure perfects the working. But pleasure does not perfect it in the same way as the faculty and object of perception do, being good; just as health and the physician are not in similar senses causes of a healthy state.

And that pleasure does arise upon the exercise of every percipient faculty is evident, for we commonly say that sights and sounds are pleasant; it is plain also that this is especially the case when the faculty is most excellent and works upon a similar object: and when both the object and faculty of perception are such, pleasure will always exist, supposing of course an agent and a patient.

Furthermore, pleasure perfects the act of working not in the way of an inherent state but as a supervening finish, such as is bloom in people at their prime. Therefore so long as the object of intellectual or sensitive perception is such as it should be and also the faculty which discerns or realises the object, there will be pleasure in the working: because when that which has the capacity of being acted on and that which is apt to act are alike and similarly related, the same result follows naturally.

How is it then that no one feels pleasure continuously? Is it not that he wearies, because all human faculties are incapable of unintermitting exertion; and so, of course, pleasure does not arise either, because that follows upon the act of working. But there are some things which please when new, but afterwards not in the like way, for exactly the same reason: that at first the mind is roused and works on these objects with its powers at full tension; just as they who are gazing steadfastly at anything; but afterwards the act of working is not of the kind it was at first, but careless, and so the pleasure too is dulled.

Again, a person may conclude that all men grasp at pleasure, because all aim likewise at life and life is an act of working, and every man works at and with those things which also he best likes; the musical man, for instance, works with his hearing at music; the studious man with his intellect at speculative questions, and so forth. And pleasure perfects the acts of working, and so life after which men grasp. No wonder then that they aim also at pleasure, because to each it perfects life, which is itself choiceworthy. (We will take leave to omit the question whether we choose life for pleasure's sake or pleasure for life's sake; because these two plainly are closely connected and admit not of separation; since pleasure comes not into being without working, and again, every working pleasure perfects.)

5   And this is one reason why pleasures are thought to differ in kind, because we suppose that things which differ in kind must be perfected by things so differing: it plainly being the case with the productions of nature and art; as animals, and trees, and pictures, and statues, and houses, and furniture; and so we suppose that in like manner acts of working which are different in kind are perfected by things differing in kind. Now

intellectual workings differ specifically from those of the senses, and these last from one another; therefore so do the pleasures which perfect them.

This may be shown also from the intimate connection subsisting between each pleasure and the working which it perfects: I mean, that the pleasure proper to any working increases that working; for they who work with pleasure sift all things more closely and carry them out to a greater degree of nicety; for instance, those men become geometricians who take pleasure in geometry, and they apprehend particular points more completely: in like manner men who are fond of music, or architecture, or anything else, improve each on his own pursuit, because they feel pleasure in them. Thus the pleasures aid in increasing the workings, and things which do so aid are proper and peculiar; but the things which are proper and peculiar to others specifically different are themselves also specifically different.

Yet even more clearly may this be shown from the fact that the pleasures arising from one kind of workings hinder other workings; for instance, people who are fond of flute-music cannot keep their attention to conversation or discourse when they catch the sound of a flute; because they take more pleasure in flute-playing than in the working they are at the time engaged on; in other words, the pleasure attendant on flute-playing destroys the working of conversation or discourse.

Much the same kind of thing takes place in other cases, when a person is engaged in two different workings at the same time: that is, the pleasanter of the two keeps pushing out the other, and, if the disparity in pleasantness be great, then more and more till a man even ceases altogether to work at the other.

This is the reason why, when we are very much pleased with anything whatever, we do nothing else, and it is only when we are but moderately pleased with one occupation that we vary it with another: people, for instance, who eat sweetmeats in the theatre do so most when the performance is indifferent.

Since then the proper and peculiar pleasure gives accuracy to the workings and makes them more enduring and better of their kind, while those pleasures which are foreign to them mar them, it is plain there is a wide difference between them: in fact, pleasures foreign to any working have pretty much the same effect as the pains proper to it, which, in fact, destroy the workings; I mean, if one man dislikes writing, or another calculation, the one does not write, the other does not calculate; because, in each case, the working is attended with some pain: so then contrary effects are produced upon the workings by the pleasures and pains proper to them, by which I mean those which arise upon the working, in itself, independently of any other circumstances. As for the pleasures foreign to a working, we have said already that they produce a similar effect to the pain proper to it; that is they destroy the working, only not in like way.

Well then, as workings differ from one another in goodness and badness, some being fit objects of choice, others of avoidance, and others in their nature indifferent, pleasures are similarly related; since its own proper pleasure attends on each working: of course that proper to a good working is good, that proper to a bad, bad: for even the desires for what is noble are praiseworthy, and for what is base blameworthy.

Furthermore, the pleasures attendant on workings

are more closely connected with them even than the desires after them: for these last are separate both in time and nature, but the former are close to the workings, and so indivisible from them as to raise a question whether the working and the pleasure are identical; but pleasure does not seem to be an intellectual operation nor a faculty of perception, because that is absurd; but yet it gives some the impression of being the same from not being separated from these.

As then the workings are different so are their pleasures; now sight differs from touch in purity, and hearing and smelling from taste; therefore, in like manner, do their pleasures; and again, intellectual pleasures from these sensual, and the different kinds both of intellectual and sensual from one another.

It is thought, moreover, that each animal has a pleasure proper to itself, as it has a proper work; that pleasure of course which is attendant on the working. And the soundness of this will appear upon particular inspection: for horse, dog, and man have different pleasures; as Heraclitus says, an ass would sooner have hay than gold; in other words, provender is pleasanter to asses than gold. So then the pleasures of animals specifically different are also specifically different, but those of the same, we may reasonably suppose, are without difference.

Yet in the case of human creatures they differ not a little: for the very same things please some and pain others: and what are painful and hateful to some are pleasant to and liked by others. The same is the case with sweet things: the same will not seem so to the man in a fever as to him who is in health: nor will the invalid and the person in robust health have the same notion of warmth. The same is the case with other things also.

Now in all such cases that is held to *be* which impresses the good man with the notion of being such and such; and if this is a second maxim (as it is usually held to be), and virtue, that is, the good man, in that he is such, is the measure of everything, then those must be real pleasures which give him the impression of being so and those things pleasant in which he takes pleasure. Nor is it at all astonishing that what are to him unpleasant should give another person the impression of being pleasant, for men are liable to many corruptions and marrings; and the things in question are not pleasant really, only to these particular persons, and to them only as being thus disposed.

Well, of course, you may say, it is obvious that we must not assert those which are confessedly disgraceful to be real pleasures, except to depraved tastes: but of those which are thought to be good what kind, or which, must we say is *the pleasure of man*? Is not the answer plain from considering the workings, because the pleasures follow upon these?

Whether then there be one or several workings which belong to the perfect and blessed man, the pleasures which perfect these workings must be said to be specially and properly *the pleasures of man*; and all the rest in a secondary sense, and in various degrees according as the workings are related to those highest and best ones.

6   Now that we have spoken about the excellences of both kinds, and friendship in its varieties, and pleasures, it remains to sketch out happiness, since we assume that to be the one end of all human things: and we shall save time and trouble by recapitulating what was stated before.

Well then, we said that it is not a state merely; because, if it were, it might belong to one who slept all his life through and merely vegetated, or to one who fell into very great calamities: and so, if these possibilities displease us and we would rather put it into the rank of some kind of working (as was also said before), and workings are of different kinds (some being necessary and choiceworthy with a view to other things, while others are so in themselves), it is plain we must rank happiness among those choiceworthy for their own sakes and not among those which are so with a view to something further: because happiness has no lack of anything but is self-sufficient.

By choiceworthy in themselves are meant those from which nothing is sought beyond the act of working: and of this kind are thought to be the actions according to virtue, because doing what is noble and excellent is one of those things which are choiceworthy for their own sake alone.

And again, such amusements as are pleasant; because people do not choose them with any further purpose: in fact they receive more harm than profit from them, neglecting their persons and their property. Still the common run of those who are judged happy take refuge in such pastimes, which is the reason why they who have varied talent in such are highly esteemed among despots; because they make themselves pleasant in those things which these aim at, and these accordingly want such men.

Now these things are thought to be appurtenances of happiness because men in power spend their leisure herein: yet, it may be, we cannot argue from the example of such men: because there is neither virtue nor intellect necessarily involved in having power, and yet these are the only sources of good workings: nor does it follow that because these men, never having tasted pure and generous pleasure, take refuge in bodily ones, we are therefore to believe them to be more choiceworthy: for children too believe that those things are most excellent which are precious in their eyes.

We may well believe that as children and men have different ideas as to what is precious so too have the bad and the good: therefore; as we have many times said, those things are really precious and pleasant which seem so to the good man: and as to each individual that working is most choiceworthy which is in accordance with his own state to the good man that is so which is in accordance with virtue.

Happiness then stands not in amusement; in fact the very notion is absurd of the end being amusement, and of one's toiling and enduring hardness all one's life long with a view to amusement: for everything in the world, so to speak, we choose with some further end in view, except happiness, for that is the end comprehending all others. Now to take pains and to labour with a view to amusement is plainly foolish and very childish: but to amuse one's self with a view to steady employment afterwards, as Anacharsis says, is thought to be right: for amusement is like rest, and men want rest because unable to labour continuously.

Rest, therefore, is not an end, because it is adopted with a view to working afterwards.

Again, it is held that the happy life must be one in the way of excellence, and this is accompanied by earnestness and stands not in amusement. Moreover those things which are done in earnest, we say, are better than things merely ludicrous and joined with amusement: and we say that the working of the better part, or the better man, is more earnest; and the working of the better is at once better and more capable of happiness.

Then, again, as for bodily pleasures, any ordinary person, or even a slave, might enjoy them, just as well as the best man living: but happiness no one supposes a slave to share except so far as it is implied in life: because happiness stands not in such pastimes but in the workings in the way of excellence, as has also been stated before.

7   Now if happiness is a working in the way of excellence of course that excellence must be the highest, that is to say, the excellence of the best principle. Whether then this best principle is intellect or some other which is thought naturally to rule and to lead and to conceive of noble and divine things, whether being in its own nature divine or the most divine of all our internal principles, the working of this in accordance with its own proper excellence must be the perfect happiness.

That it is contemplative has been already stated: and this would seem to be consistent with what we said before and with truth: for, in the first place, this working is of the highest kind, since the intellect is the highest of our internal principles and the subjects with which it is conversant the highest of all which fall within the range of our knowledge.

Next, it is also most continuous: for we are better able to contemplate than to do anything else whatever, continuously.

Again, we think pleasure must be in some way an ingredient in happiness, and of all workings in accordance with excellence that in the way of science is confessedly most pleasant: at least the pursuit of science is thought to contain pleasures admirable for purity and permanence; and it is reasonable to suppose that the employment is more pleasant to those who have mastered than to those who are yet seeking for it.

And the self-sufficiency which people speak of will attach chiefly to the contemplative working: of course the actual necessaries of life are needed alike by the man of science, and the just man, and all the other characters; but, supposing all sufficiently supplied with these, the just man needs people towards whom, and in concert with whom, to practise his justice; and in like manner the man of perfected self-mastery, and the brave man, and so on of the rest; whereas the man of science can contemplate and speculate even when quite alone, and the more entirely he deserves the appellation the more able is he to do so: it may be he can do better for having fellow-workers but still he is certainly most self-sufficient.

Again, this alone would seem to be rested in for its own sake, since nothing results from it beyond the fact of having contemplated; whereas from all things which are objects of moral action we do mean to get something beside the doing them, be the same more or less.

Also, happiness is thought to stand in perfect rest; for we toil that we may rest, and war that we may be at peace. Now all the practical virtues require either society or war for their working, and the actions regarding these are thought to exclude rest; those of war entirely, because no one chooses war, nor prepares for war, for war's sake: he would indeed be thought a bloodthirsty villain who should make enemies of his friends to secure the existence of fighting and bloodshed. The working also of the statesman excludes the idea of rest, and, beside the actual work of government, seeks for power and dignities or at least happiness for the man himself and his fellow-citizens: a happiness distinct from the national happiness which we evidently seek as being different and distinct.

If then of all the actions in accordance with the various virtues those of policy and war are pre-eminent in honour and greatness, and these are restless, and aim at some further end, and are not choiceworthy for their own sakes, but the working of the intellect, being apt for contemplation, is thought to excel in earnestness, and to aim at no end beyond itself, and to have pleasure of its own which helps to increase the working; and if the attributes of self-sufficiency, and capacity of rest, and unweariedness (as far as is compatible with the infirmity of human nature), and all other attributes of the highest happiness, plainly belong to this working, this must be perfect happiness, if attaining a complete duration of life; which condition is added because none of the points of happiness is incomplete.

But such a life will be higher than mere human nature, because a man will live thus, not in so far as he is man but in so far as there is in him a divine principle: and in proportion as this principle excels his composite nature so far does the working thereof excel that in accordance with any other kind of excellence: and therefore, if pure intellect, as compared with human nature, is divine, so too will the life in accordance with it be divine compared with man's ordinary life.

Yet must we not give ear to those who bid one as man to mind only man's affairs, or as mortal only mortal things; but, so far as we can, make ourselves like immortals and do all with a view to living in accordance with the highest principle in us; for small as it may be in bulk yet in power and preciousness it far more excels all the others [than they it in bulk].

In fact this principle would seem to constitute each man's 'self', since it is supreme and above all others in goodness: it *would* be absurd then for a man not to choose his own life but that of some other.

And here will apply an observation made before, that whatever is proper to each is naturally best and pleasantest to him: such then is to man the life in accordance with pure intellect (since this principle is most truly man), and if so, then it is also the happiest.

8   And second in degree of happiness will be that life which is in accordance with the other kind of excellence, for the workings in accordance with this are proper to man: I mean, we do actions of justice, courage, and the other virtues, towards one another, in contracts, services of different kinds, and in all kinds of actions and feelings too, by observing what is befitting for each: and all these plainly are proper to man. Further, the excellence of the moral character is thought to result in some points from physical circumstances, and to be, in many, very closely connected with the passions.

Again, practical wisdom and excellence of the moral character are very closely united; since the principles of practical wisdom are in accordance with the moral virtues and these are right when they accord with practical wisdom.

These moreover, as bound up with the passions, must belong to the composite nature, and the excellences or virtues of the composite nature are proper to man: therefore so too will be the life and happiness which is in accordance with them. But that of the pure intellect is separate and distinct: and let this suffice upon the subject, since great exactness is beyond our purpose.

It would seem, moreover, to require supply of external goods to a small degree, or certainly less than the moral happiness: for, as far as necessaries of life are concerned, we will suppose both characters to need them equally (though, in point of fact, the man who lives in society does take more pains about his person and all that kind of thing; there will really be some little difference), but when we come to consider their workings there will be found a great difference.

I mean, the liberal man must have money to do his liberal actions with, and the just man to meet his engagements (for mere intentions are uncertain, and even those who are unjust make a pretence of *wishing* to do justly), and the brave man must have power, if he is to perform any of the actions which appertain to his particular virtue, and the man of perfected self-mastery must have opportunity of temptation, else how shall he or any of the others display his real character?

(By the way, a question is sometimes raised, whether the moral choice or the actions have most to do with virtue, since it consists in both: it is plain that the perfection of virtuous action requires both: but for the actions many things are required, and the greater and more numerous they are the more.) But as for the man engaged in contemplative speculation, not only are such things unnecessary for his working, but, so to speak, they are even hindrances: as regards the contemplation at least; because of course in so far as he is man and lives in society he chooses to do what virtue requires, and so he will need such things for maintaining his character as man though not as a speculative philosopher.

And that the perfect happiness must be a kind of contemplative working may appear also from the following consideration: our conception of the gods is that they are above all blessed and happy: now what kind of moral actions are we to attribute to them? Those of justice? Nay, will they not be set in a ridiculous light if represented as forming contracts, and restoring deposits, and so on? Well then, shall we picture them performing brave actions, withstanding objects of fear and meeting dangers, because it is noble to do so? Or liberal ones? But to whom shall they be giving? And further, it is absurd to think they have money or anything of the kind. And as for actions of perfected self-mastery, what can theirs be? Would it not be a degrading praise that they have no bad desires? In short, if one followed the subject into all details all the circumstances connected with moral actions would appear trivial and unworthy of gods.

Still, everyone believes that they live, and therefore that they work because it is not supposed that they sleep their time away like Endymion: now if from a living being you take away action, still more if creation, what remains but contemplation? So then the working of the gods, eminent in blessedness, will be one apt for contemplative speculation: and of all human workings that will have the greatest capacity for happiness which is nearest akin to this.

A corroboration of which position is the fact that the other animals do not partake of happiness, being completely shut out from any such working.

To the gods then all their life is blessed; and to men in so far as there is in it some copy of such working, but of the other animals none is happy because it in no way shares in contemplative speculation.

Happiness then is co-extensive with this contemplative speculation, and in proportion as people have the act of contemplation so far have they also the being happy, not incidentally, but in the way of contemplative speculation because it is in itself precious.

So happiness must be a kind of contemplative speculation; but since it is man we are speaking of he will need likewise external prosperity, because his nature is not by itself sufficient for speculation, but there must be health of body, and nourishment, and tendance of all kinds.

However, it must not be thought, because without external goods a man cannot enjoy high happiness, that therefore he will require many and great goods in order to be happy; for neither self-sufficiency, nor action, stand in excess, and it is quite possible to act nobly without being ruler of sea and land, since even with moderate means a man may act in accordance with virtue.

And this may be clearly seen in that men in private stations are thought to act justly, not merely no less than men in power but even more: it will be quite enough that just so much should belong to a man as is necessary, for his life will be happy who works in accordance with virtue.

Solon perhaps drew a fair picture of the happy, when he said that they are men moderately supplied with external goods, and who have achieved the most noble deeds, as he thought, and who have lived with perfect self-mastery: for it is quite possible for men of moderate means to act as they ought.

Anaxagoras also seems to have conceived of the happy man not as either rich or powerful, saying that he should not wonder if he were accounted a strange man in the judgment of the multitude: for they judge by outward circumstances of which alone they have any perception.

And thus the opinions of the wise seem to be accordant with our account of the matter: of course such things carry some weight, but truth, in matters of moral action, is judged from facts and from actual life, for herein rests the decision. So what we should do is to examine the preceding statements by referring them to facts and to actual life, and when they harmonise with facts we may accept them, when they are at variance with them conceive of them as mere theories.

Now he that works in accordance with, and pays observance to, pure intellect, and tends this, seems likely to be both in the best frame of mind and dearest to the gods: because if, as is thought, any care is bestowed on human things by the gods then it must be reasonable to think that they take pleasure in what is best and most akin to themselves (and this must be the pure intellect); and that they requite with kindness those who love and honour this most, as paying observance to what is dear to them, and as acting rightly and nobly. And it is quite obvious that the man of science chiefly combines all these: he is therefore dearest to the gods, and it is probable that he is at the same time most happy.

Thus then on this view also the man of science will be most happy.

9 Now then that we have said enough in our sketchy kind of way on these subjects; I mean, on the virtues, and also on friendship and pleasure; are we to suppose that our original purpose is completed? Must we not rather acknowledge, what is commonly said, that in matters of moral action mere speculation and knowledge is not the real end but rather practice: and if so, then neither in respect of virtue is knowledge enough; we must further strive to have and exert it, and take whatever other means there are of becoming good.

Now if talking and writing were of themselves sufficient to make men good, they would justly, as Theognis observes, have reaped numerous and great rewards, and the thing to do would be to provide them: but in point of fact, while they plainly have the power to guide and stimulate the generous among the young and to base upon true virtuous principle any noble and truly high-minded disposition, they as plainly are powerless to guide the mass of men to virtue and goodness; because it is not their nature to be amenable to a sense of shame but only to fear; nor to abstain from what is low and mean because it is disgraceful to do it but because of the punishment attached to it: in fact, as they live at the beck and call of passion, they pursue their own proper pleasures and the means of securing them, and they avoid the contrary pains; but as for what is noble and truly pleasurable they have not an idea of it, inasmuch as they have never tasted of it.

Men such as these then what mere words can transform? No, indeed! It is either actually impossible, or a task of no mean difficulty, to alter by words what has been of old taken into men's very dispositions:

and, it may be, it is a ground for contentment if with all the means and appliances for goodness in our hands we can attain to virtue.

The formation of a virtuous character some ascribe to nature, some to custom, and some to teaching. Now nature's part, be it what it may, obviously does not rest with us; but belongs to those who in the truest sense are fortunate, by reason of certain divine agency.

Then, as for words and precept, they, it is to be feared, will not avail with all; but it may be necessary for the mind of the disciple to have been previously prepared for liking and disliking as he ought; just as the soil must, to nourish the seed sown. For he that lives in obedience to passion cannot hear any advice that would dissuade him, nor, if he heard, understand: now him that is thus how can one reform? In fact, generally, passion is not thought to yield to reason but to brute force. So then there must be, to begin with, a kind of affinity to virtue in the disposition; which must cleave to what is honourable and loathe what is disgraceful. But to get right guidance towards virtue from the earliest youth is not easy unless one is brought up under laws of such kind; because living with self-mastery and endurance is not pleasant to the mass of men, and specially not to the young. For this reason the food, and manner of living generally, ought to be the subject of legal regulation, because things when become habitual will not be disagreeable.

Yet perhaps it is not sufficient that men while young should get right food and tendance, but, inasmuch as they will have to practise and become accustomed to certain things even after they have attained to man's estate, we shall want laws on these points as well, and, in fine, respecting one's whole, life, since the mass of men are amenable to compulsion rather than reason, and to punishment rather than to a sense of honour.

And therefore some men hold that while lawgivers should employ the sense of honour to exhort and guide men to virtue, under the notion that they will then obey who have been well trained in habits; they should impose chastisement and penalties on those who disobey and are of less promising nature; and the incurable expel entirely: because the good man and he who lives under a sense of honour will be obedient to reason; and the baser sort, who grasp at pleasure, will be kept in check, like beasts of burthen by pain. Therefore also they say that the pains should be such as are most contrary to the pleasures which are liked.

As has been said already, he who is to be good must have been brought up and habituated well, and then live accordingly under good institutions, and never do what is low and mean, either against or with his will. Now these objects can be attained, only by men living in accordance with some guiding intellect and right order, with power to back them.

As for the paternal rule, it possesses neither strength nor compulsory power, nor in fact does the rule of any one man, unless he is a king or someone in like case: but the law has power to compel, since it is a declaration emanating from practical wisdom and intellect. And people feel enmity towards their fellow-men who oppose their impulses, however rightly they may do so: the law, on the contrary, is not the object of hatred, though enforcing right rules.

The Lacedaemonian is nearly the only state in which the framer of the constitution has made any provision, it would seem, respecting the food and manner of living of the people: in most states these points are entirely neglected, and each man lives just as he likes, ruling his wife and children Cyclops-fashion.

Of course, the best thing would be that there should be a right public system and that we should be able to carry it out: but, since as a public matter those points are neglected, the duty would seem to devolve upon each individual to contribute to the cause of virtue with his own children and friends, or at least to make this his aim and purpose: and this, it would seem, from what has been said, he will be best able to do by making a legislator of himself: since all public systems, it is plain, are formed by the instrumentality of laws and those are good which are formed by that of good laws: whether they are written or unwritten, whether they are applied to the training of one or many, will not, it seems, make any difference, just as it does not in music, gymnastics, or any other such accomplishments, which are gained by practice.

For just as in communities laws and customs prevail, so too in families the express commands of the head, and customs also: and even more in the latter, because of blood-relationship and the benefits conferred: for there you have, to begin with, people who have affection and are naturally obedient to the authority which controls them.

Then, furthermore, private training has advantages over public, as in the case of the healing art: for instance, as a general rule, a man who is in a fever should keep quiet, and starve; but in a particular case, perhaps, this may not hold good; or, to take a different illustration, the boxer will not use the same way of fighting with all antagonists.

It would seem then that the individual will be most

exactly attended to under private care, because so each will be more likely to obtain what is expedient for him. Of course, whether in the art of healing, or gymnastics, or any other, a man will treat individual cases the better for being acquainted with general rules; as, 'that so and so is good for all, or for men in such and such cases': because general maxims are not only said to be but are the object-matter of sciences: still this is no reason against the possibility of a man's taking excellent care of some *one* case, though he possesses no scientific knowledge but from experience is exactly acquainted with what happens in each point; just as some people are thought to doctor themselves best though they would be wholly unable to administer relief to others. Yet it may seem to be necessary nevertheless, for one who wishes to become a real artist and well acquainted with the theory of his profession, to have recourse to general principles and ascertain all their capacities: for we have already stated that these are the object-matter of sciences.

If then it appears that we may become good through the instrumentality of laws, of course whoso wishes to make men better by a system of care and training must try to make a legislator of himself; for to treat skilfully just anyone who may be put before you is not what any ordinary person can do, but, if anyone, he who has knowledge; as in the healing art, and all others which involve careful practice and skill.

Will not then our next business be to inquire from what sources, or how one may acquire this faculty of legislation; or shall we say, that, as in similar cases, statesmen are the people to learn from, since this faculty was thought to be a part of the social science? Must we not admit that the political science plainly does not stand on a similar footing to that of other sciences and faculties? I mean, that while in all other cases those who impart the faculties and themselves exert them are identical (physicians and painters for instance) matters of statesmanship the sophists profess to teach, but not one of them practises it, that being left to those actually engaged in it: and these might really very well be thought to do it by some singular knack and by mere practice rather than by any intellectual process: for they neither write nor speak on these matters (though it might be more to their credit than composing speeches for the courts or the assembly), nor again have they made statesmen of their own sons or their friends.

One can hardly suppose but that they would have done so if they could, seeing that they could have bequeathed no more precious legacy to their communities, nor would they have preferred, for themselves or their dearest friends, the possession of any faculty rather than this.

Practice, however, seems to contribute no little to its acquisition; merely breathing the atmosphere of politics would never have made statesmen of them, and therefore we may conclude that they who would acquire a knowledge of statesmanship must have in addition practice.

But of the sophists they who profess to teach it are plainly a long way off from doing so: in fact, they have no knowledge at all of its nature and objects; if they had, they would never have put it on the same footing with rhetoric or even on a lower: neither would they have conceived it to be 'an easy matter to legislate by simply collecting such laws as are famous because of course one could select the best', as though the selection were not a matter of skill, and the judging aright a very great matter, as in music; for they alone, who have practical knowledge of a thing, can judge the performances rightly or understand with what means and in what way they are accomplished, and what harmonises with what: the unlearned must be content with being able to discover whether the result is good or bad, as in painting.

Now laws may be called the performances or tangible results of political science; how then can a man acquire from these the faculty of legislation, or choose the best? We do not see men made physicians by compilations: and yet in these treatises men endeavour to give not only the cases but also how they may be cured, and the proper treatment in each case, dividing the various bodily habits. Well, these are thought to be useful to professional men, but to the unprofessional useless. In like manner it may be that collections of laws and constitutions would be exceedingly useful to such as are able to speculate on them, and judge what is well, and what ill, and what kind of things fit in with what others; but they who without this qualification should go through such matters cannot have right judgment, unless they have it by instinct, though they may become more intelligent in such matters.

Since then those who have preceded us have left uninvestigated the subject of legislation, it will be better perhaps for us to investigate it ourselves, and, in fact, the whole subject of polity, that thus what we may call human philosophy may be completed as far as in us lies.

First then, let us endeavour to get whatever fragments of good there may be in the statements of our predecessors; next, from the polities we have collected, ascertain what kind of things preserve or destroy communities, and what, particular constitutions; and the cause why some are well and others ill managed, for after such inquiry, we shall be the better able to take a concentrated view as to what kind of constitution is best, what kind of regulations are best for each, and what laws and customs.

To this let us now proceed.

POLITICS

BOOK ONE

Political community – the household

1   Every state is a community of some kind, and every community is established with a view to some good; for mankind always act in order to obtain that which they think good. But, if all communities aim at some good, the state or political community, which is the highest of all, and which embraces all the rest, aims, and in a greater degree than any other, at the highest good.

Now there is an erroneous opinion that a statesman, king, householder, and master are the same, and that they differ, not in kind, but only in the number of their subjects. For example, the ruler over a few is called a master; over more, the manager of a household; over a still larger number, a statesman or king, as if there were no difference between a great household and a small state. The distinction which is made between the king and the statesman is as follows: When the government is personal, the ruler is a king; when, according to the principles of the political science, the citizens rule and are ruled in turn, then he is called a statesman.

But all this is a mistake; for governments differ in kind, as will be evident to anyone who considers the matter according to the method which has hitherto guided us. As in other departments of science, so in politics, the compound should always be resolved into the simple elements or least parts of the whole. We must therefore look at the elements of which the state is composed, in order that we may see in what they differ from one another, and whether any scientific distinction can be drawn between the different kinds of rule.

2 He who thus considers things in their first growth and origin, whether a state or anything else, will obtain the clearest view of them. In the first place (1) there must be a union of those who cannot exist without each other; for example, of male and female, that the race may continue; and this is a union which is formed, not of deliberate purpose, but because, in common with other animals and with plants, mankind have a natural desire to leave behind them an image of themselves. And (2) there must be a union of natural ruler and subject, that both may be preserved. For he who can foresee with his mind is by nature intended to be lord and master, and he who can work with his body is a subject, and by nature a slave; hence master and slave have the same interest. Nature, however, has distinguished between the female and the slave. For she is not niggardly, like the smith who fashions the Delphian knife for many uses; she makes each thing for a single use, and every instrument is best made when intended for one and not for many uses. But among barbarians no distinction is made between women and slaves, because there is no natural ruler among them: they are a community of slaves, male and female. Wherefore the poets say, –

'It is meet that Hellenes should rule over barbarians;'

as if they thought that the barbarian and the slave were by nature one.

Out of these two relationships between man and

woman, master and slave, the family first arises, and Hesiod is right when he says, –

'First house and wife and an ox for the plough,'

for the ox is the poor man's slave. The family is the association established by nature for the supply of men's every-day wants, and the members of it are called by Charondas 'companions of the cupboard', and by Epimenides the Cretan, 'companions of the manger'. But when several families are united, and the association aims at something more than the supply of daily needs, then comes into existence the village. And the most natural form of the village appears to be that of a colony from the family, composed of the children and grandchildren, who are said to be 'suckled with the same milk'. And this is the reason why Hellenic states were originally governed by kings; because the Hellenes were under royal rule before they came together, as the barbarians still are. Every family is ruled by the eldest, and therefore in the colonies of the family the kingly form of government prevailed because they were of the same blood. As Homer says [of the Cyclopes]: –

'Each one gives law to his children and to his wives.'

For they lived dispersedly, as was the manner in ancient times. Wherefore men say that the gods have a king, because they themselves either are or were in ancient times under the rule of a king. For they imagine, not only the forms of the gods, but their ways of life to be like their own.

When several villages are united in a single community, perfect and large enough to be nearly or quite self-sufficing, the state comes into existence, originating in the bare needs of life, and continuing in existence for the sake of a good life. And therefore, if the earlier forms of society are natural, so is the state, for it is the end of them, and the [completed] nature is the end. For what each thing is when fully developed, we call its nature, whether we are speaking of a man, a horse, or a family. Besides, the final cause and end of a thing is the best, and to be self-sufficing is the end and the best.

Hence it is evident that the state is a creation of nature, and that man is by nature a political animal. And he who by nature and not by mere accident is without a state, is either above humanity, or below it; he is the

'Tribeless, lawless, hearthless one,'

whom Homer denounces – the outcast who is a lover of war; he may be compared to an unprotected piece in the game of draughts.

Now the reason why man is more of a political animal than bees or any other gregarious animals is evident. Nature, as we often say, makes nothing in vain, and man is the only animal whom she has endowed with the gift of speech. And whereas mere sound is but an indication of pleasure or pain, and is therefore found in other animals (for their nature attains to the perception of pleasure and pain and the intimation of them to one another, and no further), the power of speech is intended to set forth the expedient and inexpedient, and likewise the just and the unjust. And it is a characteristic of man that he alone has any sense of good and evil, of just and unjust, and the association of living beings who have this sense makes a family and a state.

Thus the state is by nature clearly prior to the family and to the individual, since the whole is of necessity prior to the part; for example, if the whole body be destroyed, there will be no foot or hand, except in an equivocal sense, as we might speak of a stone hand; for when destroyed the hand will be no better. But things are defined by their working and power; and we ought not to say that they are the same when they are no longer the same, but only that they have the same name. The proof that the state is a creation of nature and prior to the individual is that the individual, when isolated, is not self-sufficing; and therefore he is like a part in relation to the whole. But he who is unable to live in society, or who has no need because he is sufficient for himself, must be either a beast or a god: he is no part of a state. A social instinct is implanted in all men by nature, and yet he who first founded the state was the greatest of benefactors. For man, when perfected, is the best of animals, but, when separated from law and justice, he is the worst of all; since armed injustice is the more dangerous, and he is equipped at birth with the arms of intelligence and with moral qualities which he may use for the worst ends. Wherefore, if he have not virtue, he is the most unholy and the most savage of animals, and the most full of lust and gluttony. But justice is the bond of men in states, and the administration of justice, which is the determination of what is just, is the principle of order in political society.

3   Seeing then that the state is made up of households, before speaking of the state we must speak of the management of the household. The parts of the household are the persons who compose it, and a

complete household consists of slaves and freemen. Now we should begin by examining everything in its least elements; and the first and least parts of a family are master and slave, husband and wife, father and children. We have therefore to consider what each of these three relations is and ought to be – I mean the relation of master and servant, of husband and wife, and thirdly of parent and child. [I say *gamike* and *teknopoietike*, there being no words for the two latter notions which adequately represent them.] And there is another element of a household, the so-called art of money-making, which, according to some, is identical with household management, according to others, a principal part of it; the nature of this art will also have to be considered by us.

Let us first speak of master and slave, looking to the needs of practical life and also seeking to attain some better theory of their relation than exists at present. For some are of opinion that the rule of a master is a science, and that the management of a household, and the mastership of slaves, and the political and royal rule, as I was saying at the outset, are all the same. Others affirm that the rule of a master over slaves is contrary to nature, and that the distinction between slave and freeman exists by law only, and not by nature; and being an interference with nature is therefore unjust.

4 Property is a part of the household, and therefore the art of acquiring property is a part of the art of managing the household; for no man can live well, or indeed live at all, unless he be provided with necessaries. And as in the arts which have a definite sphere the workers must have their own proper instruments

for the accomplishment of their work, so it is in the management of a household. Now, instruments are of various sorts; some are living, others lifeless; in the rudder, the pilot of a ship has a lifeless, in the look-out man, a living instrument; for in the arts the servant is a kind of instrument. Thus, too, a possession is an instrument for maintaining life. And so, in the arrangement of the family, a slave is a living possession, and property a number of such instruments; and the servant is himself an instrument, which takes precedence of all other instruments. For if every instrument could accomplish its own work, obeying or anticipating the will of others, like the statues of Daedalus, or the tripods of Hephaestus, which, says the poet,

> 'of their own accord entered the assembly
> > of the gods';

if, in like manner, the shuttle would weave and the plectrum touch the lyre without a hand to guide them, chief workmen would not want servants, nor masters slaves. Here, however, another distinction must be drawn: the instruments commonly so called are instruments of production, whilst a possession is an instrument of action. The shuttle, for example, is not only of use, but something else is made by it, whereas of a garment or of a bed there is only the use. Further, as production and action are different in kind, and both require instruments, the instruments which they employ must likewise differ in kind. But life is action and not production, and therefore the slave is the minister of action [for he ministers to his master's life]. Again, a possession is spoken of as a part is spoken of; for the part is not only a part of something else, but wholly belongs to it; and this is also true of a possession. The master is only the master of the slave; he does not belong to him, whereas the slave is not only the slave of his master, but wholly belongs to him. Hence we see what is the nature and office of a slave; he who is by nature not his own but another's and yet a man, is by nature a slave; and he may be said to belong to another who, being a human being, is also a possession. And a possession may be defined as an instrument of action, separable from the possessor.

5   But is there anyone thus intended by nature to be a slave, and for whom such a condition is expedient and right, or rather is not all slavery a violation of nature?

There is no difficulty in answering this question, on grounds both of reason and of fact. For that some should rule and others be ruled is a thing, not only necessary, but expedient; from the hour of their birth, some are marked out for subjection, others for rule.

And whereas there are many kinds both of rulers and subjects, that rule is the better which is exercised over better subjects – for example, to rule over men is better than to rule over wild beasts. The work is better which is executed by better workmen; and where one man rules and another is ruled, they may be said to have a work. In all things which form a composite whole and which are made up of parts, whether continuous or discrete, a distinction between the ruling and the subject element comes to light. Such a duality exists in living creatures, but not in them only; it originates in the constitution of the universe; even in things which have no life, there is a ruling principle, as in musical harmony. But we are wandering from the subject. We will, therefore, restrict ourselves to the living creature which, in the first place, consists of soul and body: and of these two, the one is by nature the ruler, and the other the subject. But then we must look for the intentions of nature in things which retain their nature, and not in things which are corrupted. And therefore we must study the man who is in the most perfect state both of body and soul, for in him we shall see the true relation of the two; although in bad or corrupted natures the body will often appear to rule over the soul, because they are in an evil and unnatural condition. First then we may observe in living creatures both a despotical and a constitutional rule; for the soul rules the body with a despotical rule, whereas the intellect rules the appetites with a constitutional and royal rule. And it is clear that the rule of the soul over the body, and of the mind and the rational element over the passionate is natural and expedient; whereas the equality of the two or the rule of the inferior is always hurtful. The same holds good of animals as well as of men; for tame animals have a better nature than wild, and all tame animals are better off when they are ruled by man; for then they are preserved. Again, the male is by nature superior, and the female inferior; and the one rules, and the other is ruled; this principle, of necessity, extends to all mankind. Where then there is such a difference as that between soul and body, or between men and animals (as in the case of those whose business is to use their body, and who can do nothing better), the lower sort are by nature slaves, and it is better for them as for all inferiors that they should be under the rule of a master. For he who can be, and therefore is another's, and he who participates in reason enough to apprehend, but not to have, reason, is a slave by nature. Whereas the lower animals cannot even apprehend reason; they obey their instincts. And indeed the use made of slaves and of tame animals is not very different; for both with their bodies minister to the needs of life. Nature would like to distinguish between the bodies of freemen and slaves, making the one strong for servile labour, the other upright, and although useless for such services, useful for political life in the arts both of war and peace. But this does not hold universally: for some slaves have the souls and others have the bodies of freemen. And doubtless if men differed from one another in the mere forms of their bodies as much as the statues of the gods do from men, all would acknowledge that the inferior class should be slaves of the superior. And if there is a difference in the body, how much more in the soul! But the beauty of the body is seen, whereas the beauty of the soul is not seen. It is clear, then, that some men are by nature free, and others slaves, and that for these latter slavery is both expedient and right.

6   But that those who take the opposite view have in a certain way right on their side, may be easily seen. For the words slavery and slave are used in two senses. There is a slave or slavery by law as well as by nature. The law of which I speak is a sort of convention, according to which whatever is taken in war is supposed to belong to the victors. But this right many jurists impeach, as they would an orator who brought forward an unconstitutional measure: they detest the notion that, because one man has the power of doing violence and is superior in brute strength, another shall be his slave and subject. Even among philosophers there is a difference of opinion. The origin of the dispute, and the reason why the arguments cross, is as follows: virtue,

when furnished with means, may be deemed to have the greatest power of doing violence: and as superior power is only found where there is superior excellence of some kind, power is thought to imply virtue. But does it likewise imply justice? – that is the question. And, in order to make a distinction between them, some assert that justice is benevolence: to which others reply that justice is nothing more than the rule of a superior. If the two views are regarded as antagonistic and exclusive [i.e. if the notion that justice is benevolence excludes the idea of a just rule of a superior], the alternative [viz. that no one should rule over others] has no force or plausibility, because it implies that not even the superior in virtue ought to rule, or be master. Some, clinging, as they think, to a principle of justice (for law and custom are a sort of justice), assume that slavery in war is justified by law, but they are not consistent. For what if the cause of the war be unjust? No one would ever say that he is a slave who is unworthy to be a slave. Were this the case, men of the highest rank would be slaves and the children of slaves if they or their parents chance to have been taken captive and sold. Wherefore Hellenes do not like to call themselves slaves, but confine the term to barbarians. Yet, in using this language, they really mean the natural slave of whom we spoke at first; for it must be admitted that some are slaves everywhere, others nowhere. The same principle applies to nobility. Hellenes regard themselves as noble everywhere, and not only in their own country, but they deem the barbarians noble only when at home, thereby implying that there are two sorts of nobility and freedom, the one absolute, the other relative. The Helen of Theodectes says:

'Who would presume to call me servant who am on
both sides sprung from the stem of the gods?'

What does this mean but that they distinguish
freedom and slavery, noble and humble birth, by the
two principles of good and evil? They think that as
men and animals beget men and animals, so from
good men a good man springs. But this is what nature,
though she may intend it, often fails to accomplish.

We see then that there is some foundation for this
difference of opinion, and that some actual slaves and
freemen are not so by nature, and also that there is in
some cases a marked distinction between the two
classes, rendering it expedient and right for the one to be
slaves and the others to be masters: the one practising
obedience, the others exercising the authority which
nature intended them to have. The abuse of this
authority is injurious to both; for the interests of part
and whole, of body and soul, are the same; and the
slave is a part of the master, a living but separated part
of his bodily frame. Where the relation between them
is natural they are friends and have a common interest,
but where it rests merely on law and force the reverse
is true.

7 The previous remarks are quite enough to show
that the rule of a master is not a constitutional rule,
and therefore that all the different kinds of rule are not,
as some affirm, the same with each other. For there is
one rule exercised over subjects who are by nature
free, another over subjects who are by nature slaves.
The rule of a household is a monarchy, for every house
is under one head: whereas constitutional rule is a
government of freemen and equals. The master is not

called a master because he has science, but because he is of a certain character, and the same remark applies to the slave and the freeman. Still there may be a science for the master and a science for the slave. The science of the slave would be such as the man of Syracuse taught, who made money by instructing slaves in their ordinary duties. And such a knowledge may be carried further, so as to include cookery and similar menial arts. For some duties are of the more necessary, others of the more honourable sort; as the proverb says, 'slave before slave, master before master.' But all such branches of knowledge are servile. There is likewise a science of the master, which teaches the use of slaves; for the master as such is concerned, not with the acquisition, but with the use of them. Yet this so-called science is not anything great or wonderful; for the master need only know how to order that which the slave must know how to execute. Hence those who are in a position which places them above toil, have stewards who attend to their households while they occupy themselves with philosophy or with politics. But the art of acquiring slaves, I mean of justly acquiring them, differs both from the art of the master and the art of the slave, being a species of hunting or war. Enough of the distinction between master and slave.

8 Let us now enquire into property generally, and into the art of money-making, in accordance with our usual method [of resolving a whole into its parts], for a slave has been shown to be a part of property. The first question is whether the art of money-making is the same with the art of managing a household or a part of it, or instrumental to it; and if the last, whether in the

way that the art of making shuttles is instrumental to the art of weaving, or in the way that the casting of bronze is instrumental to the art of the statuary, for they are not instrumental in the same way, but the one provides tools and the other material; and by material I mean the substratum out of which any work is made; thus wool is the material of the weaver, bronze of the statuary. Now it is easy to see that the art of household management is not identical with the art of money-making, for the one uses the material which the other provides. And the art which uses household stores can be no other than the art of household management. There is, however, a doubt whether the art of money-making is a part of household management or a distinct art. [They appear to be connected]; for the money-maker has to consider whence money and property can be procured, but there are many sorts of property and wealth: there is husbandry and the care and provision of food in general; are these parts of the money-making art or distinct arts? Again, there are many sorts of food, and therefore there are many kinds of lives both of animals and men; they must all have food, and the differences in their food have made differences in their ways of life. For of beasts, some are gregarious, others are solitary; they live in the way which is best adapted to sustain them, accordingly as they are carnivorous or herbivorous or omnivorous: and their habits are determined for them by nature in such a manner that they may obtain with greater facility the food of their choice. But, as different individuals have different tastes, the same things are not naturally pleasant to all of them; and therefore the lives of carnivorous or herbivorous animals further differ among themselves. In the lives of men too there is a great difference. The laziest are shepherds, who lead an idle life, and get their subsistence without trouble from tame animals; their flocks having to wander from place to place in search of pasture, they are compelled to follow them, cultivating a sort of living farm. Others support themselves by hunting, which is of different kinds. Some, for example, are pirates, others, who dwell near lakes or marshes or rivers or a sea in which there are fish, are fishermen, and others live by the pursuit of birds or wild beasts. The greater number obtain a living from the fruits of the soil. Such are the modes of subsistence which prevail among those whose industry is employed immediately upon the products of nature, and whose food is not acquired by exchange and retail trade – there is the shepherd, the husbandman, the pirate, the fisherman, the hunter. Some gain a comfortable maintenance out of two employments, eking out the deficiencies of one of them by another: thus the life of a shepherd may be combined with that of a brigand, the life of a farmer with that of a hunter. Other modes of life are similarly combined in any way which the needs of men may require. Property, in the sense of a bare livelihood, seems to be given by nature herself to all, both when they are first born, and when they are grown up. For some animals bring forth, together with their offspring, so much food as will last until they are able to supply themselves; of this the vermiparous or oviparous animals are an instance; and the viviparous animals have up to a certain time a supply of food for their young in themselves, which is called milk. In like manner we may infer that, after the birth of animals, plants exist for their sake, and that the other animals exist for the sake of man, the tame for use and food, the wild, if not all, at least the greater part of them, for food, and for the provision of clothing and various instruments. Now if nature makes nothing incomplete, and nothing in vain, the inference must be that she has made all animals and plants for the sake of man. And so, in one point of view, the art of war is a natural art of acquisition, for it includes hunting, an art which we ought to practise against wild beasts, and against men who, though intended by nature to be governed, will not submit; for war of such a kind is naturally just.

Of the art of acquisition then there is one kind which is natural and is a part of the management of a household. Either we must suppose the necessaries of life to exist previously, or the art of household management must provide a store of them for the common use of the family or state. They are the elements of true wealth; for the amount of property which is needed for a good life is not unlimited, although Solon in one of his poems says that

'No bound to riches has been fixed for man.'

But there is a boundary fixed, just as there is in the arts; for the instruments of any art are never unlimited, either in number or size, and wealth may be defined as a number of instruments to be used in a household or in a state. And so we see that there is a natural art of acquisition which is practised by managers of households and by statesmen, and what is the reason of this.

9 There is another variety of the art of acquisition which is commonly and rightly called the art of making money, and has in fact suggested the notion that wealth and property have no limit. Being nearly

connected with the preceding, it is often identified with it. But though they are not very different, neither are they the same. The kind already described is given by nature, the other is gained by experience and art.

Let us begin our discussion of the question with the following considerations.

Of everything which we possess there are two uses: both belong to the thing as such, but not in the same manner, for one is the proper, and the other the improper or secondary use of it. For example, a shoe is used for wear, and is used for exchange; both are uses of the shoe. He who gives a shoe in exchange for money or food to him who wants one, does indeed use the shoe as a shoe, but this is not its proper or primary purpose, for a shoe is not made to be an object of barter. The same may be said of all possessions, for the art of exchange extends to all of them, and it arises at first in a natural manner from the circumstance that some have too little, others too much. Hence we may infer that retail trade is not a natural part of the art of money-making; had it been so, men would have ceased to exchange when they had enough. And in the first community, which is the family, this art is obviously of no use, but only begins to be useful when the society increases. For the members of the family originally had all things in common; in a more divided state of society they still shared in many things, but they were different things which they had to give in exchange for what they wanted, a kind of barter which is still practised among barbarous nations who exchange with one another the necessaries of life and nothing more; giving and receiving wine, for example, in exchange for corn and the like. This sort of barter is not part of the money-making art and is not contrary to nature, but is needed for the satisfaction of men's natural wants. The other or more complex form of exchange grew out of the simpler. When the inhabitants of one country became more dependent on those of another, and they imported what they needed, and exported the surplus, money necessarily came into use. For the various necessaries of life are not easily carried about, and hence men agreed to employ in their dealings with each other something which was intrinsically useful and easily applicable to the purposes of life, for example, iron, silver, and the like. Of this the value was at first measured by size and weight, but in process of time they put a stamp upon it, to save the trouble of weighing and to mark the value.

When the use of coin had once been discovered, out of the barter of necessary articles arose the other art of money-making, namely, retail trade; which was at first probably a simple matter, but became more complicated as soon as men learned by experience whence and by what exchanges the greatest profit might be made. Originating in the use of coin, the art of money-making is generally thought to be chiefly concerned with it, and to be the art which produces wealth and money; having to consider how they may be accumulated. Indeed, wealth is assumed by many to be only a quantity of coin, because the art of money-making and retail trade are concerned with coin. Others maintain that coined money is a mere sham, a thing not natural, but conventional only, which would have no value or use for any of the purposes of daily life if another commodity were substituted by the users. And, indeed, he who is rich in coin may often be in want of necessary food. But how can that be wealth of which a man may have a great abundance and yet perish with hunger, like Midas in the fable, whose insatiable prayer turned everything that was set before him into gold?

Men seek after a better notion of wealth and of the art of making money than the mere acquisition of coin, and they are right. For natural wealth and the natural art of money-making are a different thing; in their true form they are part of the management of a household; whereas retail trade is the art of producing wealth, not in every way, but by exchange. And it seems to be concerned with coin; for coin is the starting-point and the goal of exchange. And there is no bound to the wealth which springs from this art of money-making. As in the art of medicine there is no limit to the pursuit of health, and as in the other arts there is no limit to the pursuit of their several ends, for they aim at accomplishing their ends to the uttermost (but of the means there is a limit, for the end is always the limit), so, too, in this art of money-making there is no limit of the end, which is wealth of the spurious kind, and the acquisition of money. But the art of household management has a limit; the unlimited acquisition of money is not its business. And, therefore, in one point of view, all wealth must have a limit; nevertheless, as a matter of fact, we find the opposite to be the case; for all money-makers increase their hoard of coin without limit. The source of the confusion is the near connexion between the two kinds of money-making; in either, the instrument [i. e. wealth] is the same, although the use is different, and so they pass into one another; for each is a use of the same property, but with a difference: accumulation is the end in the one case, but there is a further end in the other. Hence some persons are led to believe that making money is the object of household management, and the whole idea of their lives is that they ought either to increase their money without limit, or at any rate not to lose it. The origin of this disposition in men is that they are intent upon living only, and not upon living well; and, as their desires are unlimited, they also desire that the means of gratifying them should be without limit. Even those who aim at a good life seek the means of obtaining bodily pleasures; and, since the enjoyment of these appears to depend on property, they are absorbed in making money: and so there arises the second species of money-making. For, as their enjoyment is in excess, they seek an art which produces the excess of enjoyment; and, if they are not able to supply their pleasures by the art of money-making, they try other arts, using in turn every faculty in a manner contrary to nature. The quality of courage, for example, is not intended to make money, but to inspire confidence; neither is this the aim of the general's or of the physician's art; but the one aims at victory and the other at health. Nevertheless, some men turn every quality or art into a means of making money; this they conceive to be the end, and to the promotion of the end all things must contribute.

Thus, then, we have considered the art of money-making which is unnecessary, and why men want it; and also the necessary art of money-making, which we have seen to be different from the other, and to be a natural part of the art of managing a household, concerned with the provision of food, not, however, like the former kind, unlimited, but having a limit.

10 And we have found the answer to our original question, whether the art of money-making is the

business of the manager of a household and of the statesman or not their business? – viz. that it is an art which is presupposed by them. For political science does not make men, but takes them from nature and uses them; and nature provides them with food from the element of earth, air, or sea. At this stage begins the duty of the manager of a household, who has to order the things which nature supplies; he may be compared to the weaver who has not to make but to use wool, and to know what sort of wool is good and serviceable or bad and unserviceable. Were this otherwise, it would be difficult to see why the art of money-making is a part of the management of a household and the art of medicine not; for surely the members of a household must have health just as they must have life or any other necessary. And as from one point of view the master of the house and the ruler of the state have to consider about health, from another point of view not they but the physician; so in one way the art of household management, in another way the subordinate art, has to consider about money. But, strictly speaking, as I have already said, the means of life must be provided beforehand by nature; for the business of nature is to furnish food to that which is born, and the food of the offspring always remains over in the parent. Wherefore the art of making money out of fruits and animals is always natural.

Of the two sorts of money-making one, as I have just said, is a part of household management, the other is retail trade: the former necessary and honourable, the latter a kind of exchange which is justly censured; for it is unnatural, and a mode by which men gain from one another. The most hated sort, and with the greatest reason, is usury, which makes a gain out of money itself, and not from the natural use of it. For money was intended to be used in exchange, but not to increase at interest. And this term usury [*tokos*], which means the birth of money from money, is applied to the breeding of money because the offspring resembles the parent. Wherefore of all modes of making money this is the most unnatural.

11 Enough has been said about the theory of money-making; we will now proceed to the practical part. The discussion of such matters is not unworthy of philosophy, but to be engaged in them practically is illiberal and irksome. The useful parts of money-making are, first, the knowledge of livestock, – which are most profitable, and where, and how, – as, for example, what sort of horses or sheep or oxen or any other animals are most likely to give a return. A man ought to know which of these pay better than others, and which pay best in particular places, for some do better in one place and some in another. Secondly, husbandry, which may be either tillage or planting, and the keeping of bees and of fish, or fowl, or of any animals which may be useful to man. These are the divisions of the true or proper art of money-making and come first. Of the other, which consists in exchange, the first and most important division is commerce (of which there are three kinds – commerce by sea, commerce by land, selling in shops – these again differing as they are safer or more profitable), the second is usury, the third, service for hire – of this, one kind is employed in the mechanical arts, the other in unskilled and bodily labour. There is still a third sort of money-making intermediate between this and the first or natural

mode which is partly natural, but is also concerned with exchange of the fruits and other products of the earth. Some of these latter, although they bear no fruit, are nevertheless profitable; for example, wood and minerals. The art of mining, by which minerals are obtained, has many branches, for there are various kinds of things dug out of the earth. Of the several divisions of money-making I now speak generally; a minute consideration of them might be useful in practice, but it would be tiresome to dwell upon them at greater length now.

Those occupations are most truly arts in which there is the least element of chance; they are the meanest in which the body is most deteriorated, the most servile in which there is the greatest use of the body, and the illiberal in which there is the least need of excellence.

Works have been written upon these subjects by various persons; for example, by Chares the Parian, and Apollodorus the Lemnian, who have treated of tillage and planting, while others have treated of other branches; anyone who cares for such matters may refer to their writings. It would be well also to collect the scattered stories of the ways in which individuals have succeeded in amassing a fortune; for all this is useful to persons who value the art of making money. There is the anecdote of Thales the Milesian and his financial device, which involves a principle of universal application, but is attributed to him on account of his reputation for wisdom. He was reproached for his poverty, which was supposed to show that philosophy was of no use. According to the story, he knew by his skill in the stars while it was yet winter that there would be a great harvest of olives in the coming year; so, having a little capital, he gave earnest-money for the use of all the olive-presses in Chios and Miletus, which he hired at a low price because no one bid against him. When the harvest-time came, and many wanted them all at once and of a sudden, he let them out at any rate which he pleased, and made a quantity of money. Thus he showed the world that philosophers can easily be rich if they like, but that their ambition is of another sort. He is supposed to have given a striking proof of his wisdom, but, as I was saying, his device for getting money is of universal application, and is nothing but the creation of a monopoly. It is an art often practised by cities when they are in want of money; they make a monopoly of provisions.

There was a man of Sicily, who, having money deposited with him, bought up all the iron from the iron mines; afterwards, when the merchants from their various markets came to buy, he was the only seller, and without much increasing the price he gained 200 per cent. Which when Dionysius heard, he told him that he might take away his money, but that he must not remain at Syracuse, for he thought that the man had discovered a way of making money which was injurious to his own interests. He had the same idea as Thales; they both contrived to create a monopoly for themselves. And statesmen ought to know these things; for a state is often as much in want of money and of such devices for obtaining it as a household, or even more so; hence some public men devote themselves entirely to finance.

12 Of household management we have seen that there are three parts – one is the rule of a master over slaves, which has been discussed already, another of a

father, and the third of a husband. A husband and father rules over wife and children, both free, but the rule differs, the rule over his children being a royal, over his wife a constitutional rule. For although there may be exceptions to the order of nature, the male is by nature fitter for command than the female, just as the elder and full-grown is superior to the younger and more immature. But in most constitutional states the citizens rule and are ruled by turns, for the idea of a constitutional state implies that the natures of the citizens are equal, and do not differ at all. Nevertheless, when one rules and the other is ruled we endeavour to create a difference of outward forms and modes of address and titles of respect, which may be illustrated by the saying of Amasis about his foot-pan. The relation of the male to the female is of this kind, but there the inequality is permanent. The rule of a father over his children is royal, for he receives both love and the respect due to age, exercising a kind of royal power. And therefore Homer has appropriately called Zeus 'father of gods and men', because he is the king of them all. For a king is the natural superior of his subjects, but he should be of the same kin or kind with them, and such is the relation of elder and younger, of father and son.

13 Thus it is clear that household management attends more to men than to the acquisition of inanimate things, and to human excellence more than to the excellence of property which we call wealth, and to the virtue of freemen more than to the virtue of slaves. A question may indeed be raised, whether there is any excellence at all in a slave beyond merely instrumental and ministerial qualities – whether he

can have the virtues of temperance, courage, justice, and the like; or whether slaves possess only bodily and ministerial qualities. And, whichever way we answer the question, a difficulty arises; for, if they have virtue, in what will they differ from freemen? On the other hand, since they are men and share in reason, it seems absurd to say that they have no virtue. A similar question may be raised about women and children, whether they too have virtues: ought a woman to be temperate and brave and just, and is a child to be called temperate, and intemperate, or not? So in general we may ask about the natural ruler, and the natural subject, whether they have the same or different virtues. For a noble nature is equally required in both, but if so, why should one of them always rule, and the other always be ruled? Nor can we say that this is a question of degree, for the difference between ruler and subject is a difference of kind, and therefore not of degree; yet how strange is the supposition that the one ought, and that the other ought not, to have virtue! For if the ruler is intemperate and unjust, how can he rule well? if the subject, how can he obey well? If he be licentious and cowardly, he will certainly not do his duty. It is evident, therefore, that both of them must have a share of virtue, but varying according to their various natures. And this is at once indicated by the soul, in which one part naturally rules, and the other is subject, and the virtue of the ruler we maintain to be different from that of the subject; – the one being the virtue of the rational, and the other of the irrational part. Now, it is obvious that the same principle applies generally, and therefore almost all things rule and are ruled according to nature. But the kind of rule differs; – the freeman rules over the slave after another manner from that in which the male rules over the female, or the man over the child; although the parts of the soul are present in all of them, they are present in different degrees. For the slave has no deliberative faculty at all; the woman has, but it is without authority, and the child has, but it is immature. So it must necessarily be with the moral virtues also; all may be supposed to partake of them, but only in such manner and degree as is required by each for the fulfilment of his duty. Hence the ruler ought to have moral virtue in perfection, for his duty is entirely that of a master artificer, and the master artificer is reason; the subjects, on the other hand, require only that measure of virtue which is proper to each of them. Clearly, then, moral virtue belongs to all of them; but the temperance of a man and of a woman, or the courage and justice of a man and of a woman, are not, as Socrates maintained, the same; the courage of a man is shown in commanding, of a woman in obeying. And this holds of all other virtues, as will be more clearly seen if we look at them in detail, for those who say generally that virtue consists in a good disposition of the soul, or in doing rightly, or the like, only deceive themselves. Far better than such definitions is their mode of speaking, who, like Georgias, enumerate the virtues. All classes must be deemed to have their special attributes; as the poet says of women,

'Silence is a woman's glory,'

but this is not equally the glory of man. The child is imperfect, and therefore obviously his virtue is not relative to himself alone, but to the perfect man and to his teacher, and in like manner the virtue of the slave is relative to a master. Now we determined that a slave is useful for the wants of life, and therefore he will obviously require only so much virtue as will prevent him from failing in his duty through cowardice and intemperance. Someone will ask whether, if what we are saying is true, virtue will not be required also in the artisans, for they often fail in their work through misconduct. But is there not a great difference in the two cases? For the slave shares in his master's life; the artisan is less closely connected with him, and only attains excellence in proportion as he becomes a slave, [i.e. is under the direction of a master]. The meaner sort of mechanic has a special and separate slavery; and whereas the slave exists by nature, not so the shoemaker or other artisan. It is manifest, then, that the master ought to be the source of excellence in the slave; but not merely because he possesses the art which trains him in his duties. Wherefore they are mistaken who forbid us to converse with slaves and say that we should employ command only, for slaves stand even more in need of admonition than children.

The relations of husband and wife, parent and child, their several virtues, what in their intercourse with one another is good, and what is evil, and how we may pursue the good and escape the evil, will have to be discussed when we speak of the different forms of government. For, inasmuch as every family is a part of a state, and these relationships are the parts of a family, the virtue of the part must have regard to the virtue of the whole. And therefore women and children must be trained by education with an eye to the state, if the virtues of either of them are supposed to make any difference in the virtues of the state. And they must make a difference: for the children grow up to be citizens, and half the free persons in a state are women.

Of these matters, enough has been said; of what remains, let us speak at another time. Regarding, then, our present enquiry as complete, we will make a new beginning. And, first, let us examine the various theories of a perfect state.

BOOK TWO

Before outlining our own theories of the ideal constitution for a city we should examine actual cities that have been well governed, as well as the theories of our predecessors.

Among theorists, Plato raised the most fundamental questions. In his Republic, he proposed to abolish private property and the family. But his desire for unity ignores the differentiation of functions, which is a law of nature. In addition, holding wives and children in common would destroy natural affection. Experience has shown that Plato's extreme form of communism is impracticable. The models of Phaleas and Hippodamus are also unsatisfactory.

Cities that are sometimes thought to have come closest to the ideal are Sparta, Crete and Carthage. But the Spartan constitution is based on the subjection of a serf population, which leads to difficulties. Spartan women enjoy too much freedom and influence, property is unfairly distributed, and there are faults in the governing institutions. Crete and Carthage share Sparta's oligarchical nature.

BOOK THREE

Citizenship – the types of constitution

1   He who would enquire into the nature and various kinds of government must first of all determine 'What is a state?' At present this is a disputed question. Some say that the state has done a certain act; others, no, not the state, but the oligarchy or the tyrant. And the legislator or statesman is concerned entirely with the state; a constitution or government being an arrangement of the inhabitants of a state. But a state is composite, and, like any other whole, made up of many parts; – these are the citizens, who compose it. It is evident, therefore, that we must begin by asking, Who is the citizen, and what is the meaning of the term? For here again there may be a difference of opinion. He who is a citizen in a democracy will often not be a citizen in an oligarchy. Leaving out of consideration those who have been made citizens, or who have obtained the name of citizen in any other accidental manner, we may say, first, that a citizen is not a citizen because he lives in a certain place, for resident aliens and slaves share in the place; nor is he a citizen who has no legal right except that of suing and being sued; for this right may be enjoyed under the provisions of a treaty. Even resident aliens in many places possess such rights, although in an imperfect form; for they are obliged to have a patron. Hence they do but imperfectly participate in citizenship, and we call them citizens only in a qualified sense,

as we might apply the term to children who are too young to be on the register, or to old men who have been relieved from state duties. Of these we do not say simply that they are citizens, but add in the one case that they are not of age, and in the other, that they are past the age, or something of that sort; the precise expression is immaterial, for our meaning is clear. Similar difficulties to those which I have mentioned may be raised and answered about deprived citizens and about exiles. But the citizen, whom we are seeking to define, is a citizen in the strictest sense, against whom no such exception can be taken, and his special characteristic is that he shares in the administration of justice, and in offices. Now of offices some have a limit of time, and the same persons are not allowed to hold them twice, or can only hold them after a fixed interval; others have no limit of time – for example, the office of dicast or ecclesiast. It may, indeed, be argued that these are not magistrates at all, and that their functions give them no share in the government. But surely it is ridiculous to say that those who have the supreme power do not govern. Not to dwell further upon this, which is a purely verbal question, what we want is a common term including both dicast and ecclesiast. Let us, for the sake of distinction, call it 'indeterminate office', and we will assume that those who share in such office are citizens. This is the most comprehensive definition of a citizen, and best suits all those who are generally so called.

But we must not forget that things of which the underlying notions differ in kind, one of them being first, another second, another third, have, when regarded in this relation, nothing, or hardly anything, worth mentioning in common. Now we see that governments differ in kind, and that some of them are prior and that others are posterior; those which are faulty or perverted are necessarily posterior to those which are perfect. (What we mean by perversion will be hereafter explained.) The citizen then of necessity differs under each form of government; and our definition is best adapted to the citizen of a democracy; but not necessarily to other states. For in some states the people are not acknowledged, nor have they any regular assembly, but only extraordinary ones; and suits are distributed in turn among the magistrates. At Lacedaemon, for instance, the Ephors determine suits about contracts, which they distribute among themselves, while the elders are judges of homicide, and other causes are decided by other magistrates. A similar principle prevails at Carthage; there certain magistrates decide all causes. We may, indeed, modify our definition of the citizen so as to include these states. [But strictly taken it only applies in democracies.] In other states it is the holder of a determinate, not of an indeterminate, office who legislates and judges, and to some or all such holders of determinate offices is reserved the right of deliberating or judging about some things or about all things. The conception of the citizen now begins to clear up.

He who has the power to take part in the deliberative or judicial administration of any state is said by us to be a citizen of that state; and speaking generally, a state is a body of citizens sufficing for the purposes of life.

2   But in practice a citizen is defined to be one of whom both the parents are citizens; others insist on going further back; say to two or three or more grandparents. This is a short and practical definition;

but there are some who raise the further question: how this third or fourth ancestor came to be a citizen? Gorgias of Leontini, partly because he was in a difficulty, partly in irony, said – 'Mortars are made by the mortar-makers, and the citizens of Larissa are also a manufactured article, made, like the kettles which bear their name [*larisaioi*], by the magistrates.' Yet the question is really simple, for if, according to the definition just given, they shared in the government, they were citizens. [This is a better definition than the other.] For the words, 'born of a father or mother, who is a citizen', cannot possibly apply to the first inhabitants or founders of a state.

There is a greater difficulty in the case of those who have been made citizens after a revolution, as by Cleisthenes at Athens after the expulsion of the tyrants, for he enrolled in tribes a number of strangers and slaves and resident aliens. The doubt in these cases is, not who is, but whether he, who is, ought to be a citizen; and there will still be a further doubt, whether he who ought not to be a citizen is one in fact, for what ought not to be is what is false and is not. Now, there are some who hold office, and yet ought not to hold office, whom we call rulers, although they rule unjustly. And the citizen was defined by the fact of his holding some kind of rule or office – he who holds a judicial or legislative office fulfils our definition of a citizen. It is evident, therefore, that the citizens about whom the doubt has arisen must be called citizens; whether they ought to be so or not is a question which is bound up with the previous enquiry.

3 A parallel question is raised respecting the state whether a certain act is or is not an act of the state; for example, in the transition from an oligarchy or a

tyranny to a democracy. In such cases persons refuse to fulfil their contracts or any other obligations on the ground that the tyrant, and not the state, contracted them; they argue that some constitutions are established by force, and not for the sake of the common good. But this would apply equally to democracies, for they too may be founded on violence, and then the acts of the democracy will be neither more nor less legitimate than those of an oligarchy or of a tyranny. This question runs up into another – When shall we say that the state is the same, and when different? It would be a very superficial view which considered only the place and the inhabitants; for the soil and the population may be separated, and some of the inhabitants may live in one place and some in another. This, however, is not a very serious difficulty; we need only remark that the word 'state' is ambiguous, meaning both state and city.

It is further asked: When are men, living in the same place, to be regarded as a single city – what is the limit? Certainly not the wall of the city, for you might surround all Peloponnesus with a wall. But a city, having such vast circuit, would contain a nation rather than a state, like Babylon, which, as they say, had been taken for three days before some part of the inhabitants became aware of the fact. This difficulty may, however, with advantage be deferred to another occasion; the statesman has to consider the size of the state, and whether it should consist of more than one nation or not.

Again, shall we say that while the race of inhabitants, as well as their place of abode, remain the same, the city is also the same, although the citizens are always dying and being born, as we call rivers and fountains the same, although the water is always flowing away and coming again? Or shall we say that the generations of men, like the rivers, are the same, but that the state changes? For, since the state is a community of citizens united by sharing in one form of government, when the form of the government changes and becomes different, then it may be supposed that the state is no longer the same, just as a tragic differs from a comic chorus, although the members of both may be identical. And in this manner we speak of every union or composition of elements, when the form of their composition alters; for example, harmony of the same sounds is said to be different, accordingly as the Dorian or the Phrygian mode is employed. And if this is true it is evident that the sameness of the state consists chiefly in the sameness of the constitution, and may be called or not called by the same name, whether the inhabitants are the same or entirely different. It is quite another question, whether a state ought or ought not to fulfil engagements when the form of government changes.

4 There is a point nearly allied to the preceding: Whether the virtue of a good man and a good citizen is the same or not. But, before entering on this discussion, we must first obtain some general notion of the virtue of the citizen. Like the sailor, the citizen is a member of a community. Now, sailors have different functions, for one of them is a rower, another a pilot, a third a look-out man, and a fourth is described by some similar term; and while the precise definition of each individual's virtue applies exclusively to him, there is, at the same time, a common definition applicable to them all. For they have all of them a common object,

which is safety in navigation. Similarly, one citizen differs from another, but the salvation of the community is the common business of them all. This community is the state; the virtue of the citizen must therefore be relative to the constitution of which he is a member. If, then, there are many forms of government, it is evident that the virtue of the good citizen cannot be the one perfect virtue. But we say that the good man is he who has perfect virtue. Hence it is evident that the good citizen need not of necessity possess the virtue which makes a good man.

The same question may also be approached by another road, from a consideration of the perfect state. If the state cannot be entirely composed of good men, and each citizen is expected to do his own business well, and must therefore have virtue, inasmuch as all the citizens cannot be alike, the virtue of the citizen and of the good man cannot coincide. All must have the virtue of the good citizen – thus, and thus only, can the state be perfect; but they will not have the virtue of a good man, unless we assume that in the good state all the citizens must be good.

Again, the state may be compared to the living being: as the first elements into which the living being is resolved are soul and body, as the soul is made up of reason and appetite, the family of husband and wife, property of master and slave, so out of all these, as well as other dissimilar elements, the state is composed; and, therefore, the virtue of all the citizens cannot possibly be the same, any more than the excellence of the leader of a chorus is the same as that of the performer who stands by his side. I have said enough to show why the two kinds of virtue cannot be absolutely and always the same.

But will there then be no case in which the virtue of the good citizen and the virtue of the good man coincide? To this we answer [not that the good citizen, but] that the good ruler is a good and wise man, and that he who would be a statesman must be a wise man. And some persons say that even the education of the ruler should be of a special kind; for are not the children of kings instructed in riding and military exercises? As Euripides says:

'No subtle arts for me, but what the state requires.'

As though there were a special education needed by a ruler. If then the virtue of a good ruler is the same as that of a good man, and we assume further that the subject is a citizen as well as the ruler, the virtue of the good citizen and the virtue of the good man cannot be always the same, although in some cases [i.e. in the perfect state] they may; for the virtue of a ruler differs from that of a citizen. It was the sense of this difference which made Jason say that 'he felt hungry when he was not a tyrant', meaning that he could not endure to live in a private station. But, on the other hand, it may be argued that men are praised for knowing both how to rule and how to obey, and he is said to be a citizen of approved virtue who is able to do both. Now if we suppose the virtue of a good man to be that which rules, and the virtue of the citizen to include ruling and obeying, it cannot be said that they are equally worthy of praise. Since, then, it is occasionally held that the ruler and the ruled should learn different things and not the same things, and that the citizen must know and share in both; the inference is obvious. There is, indeed, the rule of a master which is concerned with menial offices, – the master need not know how to perform these, but may employ others in the execution of them: anything else would be degrading; and by anything else I mean the menial duties which vary much in character and are executed by various classes of slaves, such, for example, as handicraftsmen, who, as their name signifies, live by the labour of their hands: – under these the mechanic is included. Hence in ancient times, and among some nations, the working classes had no share in the government – a privilege which they only acquired under the extreme democracy. Certainly the good man and the statesman and the good citizen ought not to learn the crafts of inferiors except for their own occasional use; if they habitually practise them, there will cease to be a distinction between master and slave.

This is not the rule of which we are speaking; but there is a rule of another kind, which is exercised over freemen and equals by birth – a constitutional rule, which the ruler must learn by obeying, as he would learn the duties of a general of cavalry by being under the orders of a general of cavalry, or the duties of a general of infantry by being under the orders of a general of infantry, or by having had the command of a company or brigade. It has been well said that 'he who has never learned to obey cannot be a good commander.' The two are not the same, but the good citizen ought to be capable of both; he should know how to govern like a freeman, and how to obey like a freeman – these are the virtues of a citizen. And, although the temperance and justice of a ruler are distinct from those of a subject, the virtue of a good man will include both; for the good man, who is free and also a subject, will not have one virtue only, say justice, but he will have distinct kinds of virtue, the one qualifying him to rule, the other to obey, and differing as the temperance and courage of men and women differ. For a man would be thought a coward if he had no more courage than a courageous woman, and a woman would be thought loquacious if she imposed no more restraint on her conversation than the good man; and indeed their part in the management of the household is different, for the duty of the one is to acquire, and of the other to preserve. Practical wisdom only is characteristic of the ruler: it would seem that all other virtues must equally belong to ruler and subject. The virtue of the subject is certainly not wisdom, but only true opinion; he may be compared to the maker of the flute, while his master is like the flute-player or user of the flute.

From these considerations may be gathered the answer to the question, whether the virtue of the good man is the same as that of the good citizen, or different, and how far the same, and how far different.

5 There still remains one more question about the citizen: Is he only a true citizen who has a share of office, or is the mechanic to be included? If they who hold no office are to be deemed citizens, not every citizen can have this virtue of ruling and obeying which makes a citizen. And if none of the lower class are citizens, in which part of the state are they to be placed? For they are not resident aliens, and they are not foreigners. To this objection may we not reply, that there is no more absurdity in excluding them than in excluding slaves and freedmen from any of the above-mentioned classes? It must be admitted that we cannot consider all those to be citizens who are necessary to the existence of the state; for example, children are not

citizens equally with grown up men, who are citizens absolutely, but children, not being grown up, are only citizens in a qualified sense. Doubtless in ancient times, and among some nations, the artisan class were slaves or foreigners, and therefore the majority of them are so now. The best form of state will not admit them to citizenship; but if they are admitted, then our definition of the virtue of a citizen will apply to some citizens and freemen only, and not to those who work for their living. The latter class, to whom toil is a necessity, are either slaves who minister to the wants of individuals, or mechanics and labourers who are the servants of the community. These reflections carried a little further will explain their position; and indeed what has been said already is of itself explanation enough.

Since there are many forms of government there must be many varieties of citizens, and especially of citizens who are subjects; so that under some governments the mechanic and the labourer will be citizens, but not in others, as, for example, in aristocracy or the so-called government of the best (if there be such an one), in which honours are given according to virtue and merit; for no man can practise virtue who is living the life of a mechanic or labourer. In oligarchies the qualification for office is high, and therefore no labourer can ever be a citizen; but a mechanic may, for many of them are rich. At Thebes there was a law that no man could hold office who had not retired from business for ten years. In many states the law goes to the length of admitting aliens; for in some democracies a man is a citizen though his mother only be a citizen [and his father an alien]; and a similar principle is applied to illegitimate children;

the law is relaxed when there is a dearth of population. But when the number of citizens increases, first the children of a male or a female slave are excluded; then those whose mothers only are citizens; and at last the right of citizenship is confined to those whose fathers and mothers are both citizens.

Hence, as is evident, there are different kinds of citizens; and he is a citizen in the highest sense who shares in the honours of the state. In the poems of Homer [Achilles complains of Agamemnon treating him] 'like some dishonoured stranger'; for he who is excluded from the honours of the state is no better than an alien. But when this exclusion is concealed, then the object is to deceive one's fellow-countrymen.

As to the question whether the virtue of the good man is the same as that of the good citizen, the considerations already adduced prove that in some states the two are the same, and in others different. When they are the same it is not the virtue of every citizen which is the same as that of the good man, but only the virtue of the statesman and of those who have or may have, alone or in conjunction with others, the conduct of public affairs.

6   Having determined these questions, we have next to consider whether there is only one form of government or many, and if many, what they are, and how many, and what are the differences between them.

A constitution is the arrangement of magistracies in a state, especially of the highest of all. The government is everywhere sovereign in the state, and the constitution is in fact the government. For example, in democracies the people are supreme, but in oligarchies, the few; and, therefore, we say that these two forms of government are different: and so in other cases.

First, let us consider what is the purpose of a state, and how many forms of government there are by which human society is regulated. We have already said, in the former part of this treatise, when drawing a distinction between household-management and the rule of a master, that man is by nature a political animal. And therefore, men, even when they do not require one another's help, desire to live together all the same, and are in fact brought together by their common interests in proportion as they severally attain to any measure of well-being. This is certainly the chief end, both of individuals and of states. And also for the sake of mere life (in which there is possibly some noble element) mankind meet together and maintain the political community, so long as the evils of existence do not greatly overbalance the good. And we all see that men cling to life even in the midst of misfortune, seeming to find in it a natural sweetness and happiness.

There is no difficulty in distinguishing the various kinds of authority; they have been often defined already in popular works. The rule of a master, although the slave by nature and the master by nature have in reality the same interests, is nevertheless exercised primarily with a view to the interest of the master, but accidentally considers the slave, since, if the slave perish, the rule of the master perishes with him. On the other hand, the government of a wife and children and of a household, which we have called household-management, is exercised in the first instance for the good of the governed or for the common good of both parties, but essentially for the good of the governed, as we see to be the case in medicine, gymnastics, and the arts in general, which are only accidentally concerned with the good of the artists themselves. (For there is no reason why the trainer may not sometimes practise gymnastics, and the pilot is always one of the crew.) The trainer or the pilot considers the good of those committed to his care. But, when he is one of the persons taken care of, he accidentally participates in the advantage, for the pilot is also a sailor, and the trainer becomes one of those in training. And so in politics: when the state is framed upon the principle of equality and likeness, the citizens think that they ought to hold office by turns. In the order of nature everyone would take his turn of service; and then again, somebody else would look after his interest, just as he, while in office, had looked after theirs. [That was originally the way.] But nowadays, for the sake of the advantage which is to be gained from the public revenues and from office, men want to be always in office. One might imagine that the rulers, being sickly, were only kept in health while they continued in office; in that case we may be sure that they would be hunting after places. The conclusion is evident: that governments which have a regard to the common interest are constituted in accordance with strict principles of justice, and are therefore true forms; but those which regard only the interest of the rulers are all defective and perverted forms, for they are despotic, whereas a state is a community of freemen.

7 Having determined these points, we have next to consider how many forms of government there are, and what they are; and in the first place what are the true forms, for when they are determined the perversions of them will at once be apparent. The words constitution

and government have the same meaning, and the government, which is the supreme authority in states, must be in the hands of one, or of a few, or of many. The true forms of government, therefore, are those in which the one, or the few, or the many, govern with a view to the common interest; but governments which rule with a view to the private interest, whether of the one, or of the few, or of the many, are perversions. For citizens, if they are truly citizens, ought to participate in the advantages of a state. Of forms of government in which one rules, we call that which regards the common interests, kingship or royalty; that in which more than one, but not many, rule, aristocracy [the rule of the best]; and it is so called, either because the rulers are the best men, or because they have at heart the best interests of the state and of the citizens. But when the citizens at large administer the state for the common interest, the government is called by the generic name – a constitution [*politeia*]. And there is a reason for this use of language. One man or a few may excel in virtue; but of virtue there are many kinds: and as the number increases it becomes more difficult for them to attain perfection in every kind, though they may in military virtue, for this is found in the masses. Hence, in a constitutional government the fighting-men have the supreme power, and those who possess arms are the citizens.

Of the above-mentioned forms, the perversions are as follows: of royalty, tyranny; of aristocracy, oligarchy; of constitutional government, democracy. For tyranny is a kind of monarchy which has in view the interest of the monarch only; oligarchy has in view the interest of the wealthy; democracy, of the needy: none of them the common good of all.

8 But there are difficulties about these forms of government, and it will therefore be necessary to state a little more at length the nature of each of them. For he who would make a philosophical study of the various sciences, and does not regard practice only, ought not to overlook or omit anything, but to set forth the truth in every particular. Tyranny, as I was saying, is monarchy exercising the rule of a master over political society; oligarchy is when men of property have the government in their hands; democracy, the opposite, when the indigent, and not the men of property, are the rulers. And here arises the first of our difficulties, and it relates to the definition just given. For democracy is said to be the government of the many. But what if the many are men of property and have the power in their hands? In like manner oligarchy is said to be the government of the few; but what if the poor are fewer than the rich, and have the power in their hands because they are stronger? In these cases the distinction which we have drawn between these different forms of government would no longer hold good.

Suppose, once more, that we add wealth to the few and poverty to the many, and name the governments accordingly – an oligarchy is said to be that in which the few and the wealthy, and a democracy that in which the many and the poor are the rulers – there will still be a difficulty. For, if the only forms of government are the ones already mentioned, how shall we describe those other governments also just mentioned by us, in which the rich are the more numerous and the poor are the fewer, and both govern in their respective states?

The argument seems to show that, whether in oligarchies or in democracies, the number of the governing body, whether the greater number, as in a democracy, or the smaller number, as in an oligarchy, is an accident due to the fact that the rich everywhere are few, and the poor numerous. But if so, there is a misapprehension of the causes of the difference between them. For the real difference between democracy and oligarchy is poverty and wealth. Wherever men rule by reason of their wealth, whether they be few or many, that is an oligarchy, and where the poor rule, that is a democracy. But as a fact the rich are few and the poor many: for few are well-to-do, whereas freedom is enjoyed by all, and wealth and freedom are the grounds on which the oligarchical and democratical parties respectively claim power in the state.

9 Let us begin by considering the common definitions of oligarchy and democracy, and what is justice oligarchical and democratical. For all men cling to justice of some kind, but their conceptions are imperfect and they do not express the whole idea. For example, justice is thought by them to be, and is, equality, not, however, for all, but only for equals. And inequality is thought to be, and is, justice; neither is this for all, but only for unequals. When the persons are omitted, then men judge erroneously. The reason is that they are passing judgment on themselves, and most people are bad judges in their own case. And whereas justice implies a relation to persons as well as to things, and a just distribution, as I have already said in the *Ethics*, embraces alike persons and things, they acknowledge the equality of the things, but dispute about the merit of the persons, chiefly for the reason which I have just given – because they are bad judges in their own affairs; and secondly, because both the

parties to the argument are speaking of a limited and partial justice, but imagine themselves to be speaking of absolute justice. For those who are unequal in one respect, for example wealth, consider themselves to be unequal in all; and any who are equal in one respect, for example freedom, consider themselves to be equal in all. But they leave out the capital point. For if men met and associated out of regard to wealth only, their share in the state would be proportioned to their property, and the oligarchical doctrine would then seem to carry the day. It would not be just that he who paid one mina should have the same share of a hundred minae, whether of the principal or of the profits, as he who paid the remaining ninety-nine. But a state exists for the sake of a good life, and not for the sake of life only: if life only were the object, slaves and brute animals might form a state, but they cannot, for they have no share in happiness or in a life of free choice. Nor does a state exist for the sake of alliance and security from injustice, nor yet for the sake of exchange and mutual intercourse; for then the Tyrrhenians and the Carthaginians, and all who have commercial treaties with one another, would be the citizens of one state. True, they have agreements about imports, and engagements that they will do no wrong to one another, and written articles of alliance. But there are no magistracies common to the contracting parties who will enforce their engagements; different states have each their own magistracies. Nor does one state take care that the citizens of the other are such as they ought to be, nor see that those who come under the terms of the treaty do no wrong or wickedness at all, but only that they do no injustice to one another. Whereas, those who care for good government take into consideration [the larger question of] virtue and vice in states. Whence it may be further inferred that virtue must be the serious care of a state which truly deserves the name: for [without this ethical end] the community becomes a mere alliance which differs only in place from alliances of which the members live apart; and law is only a convention, 'a surety to one another of justice', as the sophist Lycophron says, and has no real power to make the citizens good and just.

This is obvious; for suppose distinct places, such as Corinth and Megara, to be united by a wall, still they would not be one city, not even if the citizens had the right to intermarry, which is one of the rights peculiarly characteristic of states. Again, if men dwelt at a distance from one another, but not so far off as to have no intercourse, and there were laws among them that they should not wrong each other in their exchanges, neither would this be a state. Let us suppose that one man is a carpenter, another a husbandman, another a shoemaker, and so on, and that their number is ten thousand: nevertheless, if they have nothing in common but exchange, alliance, and the like, that would not constitute a state. Why is this? Surely not because they are at a distance from one another: for even supposing that such a community were to meet in one place, and that each man had a house of his own, which was in a manner his state, and that they made alliance with one another, but only against evil-doers; still an accurate thinker would not deem this to be a state, if their intercourse with one another was of the same character after as before their union. It is clear then that a state is not a mere society, having a common place, established for the prevention of crime and for the sake of exchange. These are conditions without which a state cannot exist; but all of them together do not constitute a state, which is a community of well-being in families and aggregations of families, for the sake of a perfect and self-sufficing life. Such a community can only be established among those who live in the same place and intermarry. Hence arise in cities family connexions, brotherhoods, common sacrifices, amusements which draw men together. They are created by friendship, for friendship is the motive of society. The end is the good life, and these are the means towards it. And the state is the union of families and villages having for an end a perfect and self-sufficing life, by which we mean a happy and honourable life.

Our conclusion, then, is that political society exists for the sake of noble actions, and not of mere companionship. And they who contribute most to such a society have a greater share in it than those who have the same or a greater freedom or nobility of birth but are inferior to them in political virtue; or than those who exceed them in wealth but are surpassed by them in virtue.

From what has been said it will be clearly seen that all the partisans of different forms of government speak of a part of justice only.

10   There is also a doubt as to what is to be the supreme power in the state: Is it the multitude? Or the wealthy? Or the good? Or the one best man? Or a tyrant? Any of these alternatives seems to involve disagreeable consequences. If the poor, for example, because they are more in number, divide among themselves the property of the rich, is not this unjust? No, by heaven (will be the reply), for the lawful authority [i.e. the people] willed it. But if this is not

injustice, pray what is? Again, when [in the first division] all has been taken, and the majority divide anew the property of the minority, is it not evident, if this goes on, that they will ruin the state? Yet surely, virtue is not the ruin of those who possess her, nor is justice destructive of a state; and therefore this law of confiscation clearly cannot be just. If it were, all the acts of a tyrant must of necessity be just; for he only coerces other men by superior power, just as the multitude coerce the rich. But is it just, then, that the few and the wealthy should be the rulers? And what if they, in like manner, rob and plunder the people – is this just? If so, the other case [i.e. the case of the majority plundering the minority] will likewise be just. But there can be no doubt that all these things are wrong and unjust.

Then ought the good to rule and have supreme power? But in that case everybody else, being excluded from power, will be dishonoured. For the offices of a state are posts of honour; and if one set of men always hold them, the rest must be deprived of them. Then will it be well that the one best man should rule? Nay, that is still more oligarchical, for the number of those who are dishonoured is thereby increased. Someone may say that it is bad for a man, subject as he is to all the accidents of human passion, to have the supreme power, rather than the law. But what if the law itself be democratical or oligarchical, how will that help us out of our difficulties? Not at all; the same consequences will follow.

11 Most of these questions may be reserved for another occasion. The principle that the multitude ought to be supreme rather than the few best is capable

of a satisfactory explanation, and, though not free from difficulty, yet seems to contain an element of truth. For the many, of whom each individual is but an ordinary person, when they meet together may very likely be better than the few good, if regarded not individually but collectively, just as a feast to which many contribute is better than a dinner provided out of a single purse. For each individual among the many has a share of virtue and prudence, and when they meet together they become in a manner one man, who has many feet, and hands, and senses; that is a figure of their mind and disposition. Hence the many are better judges than a single man of music and poetry; for some understand one part, and some another, and among them, they understand the whole. There is a similar combination of qualities in good men, who differ from any individual of the many, as the beautiful are said to differ from those who are not beautiful, and works of art from realities, because in them the scattered elements are combined, although, if taken separately, the eye of one person or some other feature in another person would be fairer than in the picture. Whether this principle can apply to every democracy, and to all bodies of men, is not clear. Or rather, by heaven, in some cases it is impossible of application; for the argument would equally hold about brutes; and wherein, it will be asked, do some men differ from brutes? But there may be bodies of men about whom our statement is nevertheless true. And if so, the difficulty which has been already raised, and also another which is akin to it – viz. what power should be assigned to the mass of freemen and citizens, who are not rich and have no personal merit – are both solved. There is still a danger in allowing them to share the great offices of state, for their folly will lead them into error, and their dishonesty into crime. But there is a danger also in not letting them share, for a state in which many poor men are excluded from office will necessarily be full of enemies. The only way of escape is to assign to them some deliberative and judicial functions. For this reason Solon and certain other legislators give them the power of electing to offices, and of calling the magistrates to account, but they do not allow them to hold office singly. When they meet together their perceptions are quite good enough, and combined with the better class they are useful to the state (just as impure food when mixed with what is pure sometimes makes the entire mass more whole-some than a small quantity of the pure would be), but each individual, left to himself, forms an imperfect judgment. On the other hand, the popular form of government involves certain difficulties. In the first place, it might be objected that he who can judge of the healing of a sick man would be one who could himself heal his disease, and make him whole – that is, in other words, the physician; and so in all professions and arts. As, then, the physician ought to be called to account by physicians, so ought men in general to be called to account by their peers. But physicians are of three kinds: there is the apothecary, and there is the physi-cian of the higher class, and thirdly the intelligent man who has studied the art: in all arts there is such a class; and we attribute the power of judging to them quite as much as to professors of the art. Now, does not the same principle apply to elections? For a right election can only be made by those who have knowledge; a geometrician, for example, will choose rightly in mat-ters of geometry, or a pilot in matters of steering; and, even if there be some occupations and arts with which private persons are familiar, they certainly cannot judge better than those who know. So that, according to this argument, neither the election of magistrates, nor the calling of them to account, should be entrusted to the many. Yet possibly these objections are to a great extent met by our old answer, that if the people are not utterly degraded, although individually they may be worse judges than those who have special knowledge – as a body they are as good or better. Moreover, there are some artists whose works are judged of solely, or in the best manner, not by themselves, but by those who do not possess the art; for example, the knowledge of the house is not limited to the builder only; the user, or, in other words, the master, of the house will even be a better judge than the builder, just as the pilot will judge better of a rudder than the carpenter, and the guest will judge better of a feast than the cook.

This difficulty seems now to be sufficiently answered, but there is another akin to it. That inferior persons should have authority in greater matters than the good would appear to be a strange thing, yet the election and calling to account of the magistrates is the greatest of all. And these, as I was saying, are functions which in some states are assigned to the people, for the assembly is supreme in all such matters. Yet persons of any age, and having but a small property qualification, sit in the assembly and deliberate and judge, although for the great officers of state, such as controllers and generals, a high qualification is required. This difficulty may be solved in the same manner as the preceding, and the present practice of democracies may be really defensible. For the power does not reside in the dicast, or senator, or ecclesiast, but in the court and the senate, and the assembly, of which individual senators, or ecclesiasts, or dicasts, are only parts or members. And for this reason the many may claim to have a higher authority than the few; for the people, and the senate, and the courts consist of many persons, and their property collectively is greater than the property of one or of a few individuals holding great offices. But enough of this.

The discussion of the first question shows nothing so clearly as that laws, when good, should be supreme; and that the magistrate or magistrates should regulate those matters only on which the laws are unable to speak with precision owing to the difficulty of any general principle embracing all particulars. But what are good laws has not yet been clearly explained; the old difficulty remains. The goodness or badness, justice or injustice, of laws is of necessity relative to the constitutions of states. But if so, true forms of government will of necessity have just laws, and perverted forms of government will have unjust laws.

12 In all sciences and arts the end is a good, and especially and above all in the highest of all – this is the political science of which the good is justice, in other words, the common interest. All men think justice to be a sort of equality; and to a certain extent they agree in the philosophical distinctions which have been laid down by us about Ethics. For they admit that justice is a thing having relation to persons, and that equals ought to have equality. But there still remains a question – equality or inequality of what? Here is a difficulty which the political philosopher has to resolve. For very likely some persons will say that offices of state ought to be unequally distributed according to superior excellence,

in whatever respect, of the citizen, although there is no other difference between him and the rest of the community; for that those who differ in any one respect have different rights and claims. But, surely, if this is true, the complexion or height of a man, or any other advantage, will be a reason for his obtaining a greater share of political rights. The error here lies upon the surface, and may be illustrated from the other arts and sciences. When a number of flute-players are equal in their art, there is no reason why those of them who are better born should have better flutes given to them; for they will not play any better on the flute, and the superior instrument should be reserved for him who is the superior artist. If what I am saying is still obscure, it will be made clearer as we proceed. For if there were a superior flute-player who was far inferior in birth and beauty, although either of these may be a greater good than the art of flute-playing, and persons gifted with these qualities may excel the flute-player in a greater ratio than he excels them in his art, still he ought to have the best flutes given to him, unless the advantages of wealth and birth contribute to excellence in flute-playing, which they do not. Moreover upon this principle any good may be compared with any other. For if a given height, then height in general may be measured either against height or against freedom. Thus if A excels in height more than B in virtue, and height in general is more excellent than virtue, all things will be commensurable [which is absurd]; for if a certain magnitude is greater than some other, it is clear that some other will be equal. But since no such comparison can be made, it is evident that there is good reason why in politics men do not ground their claim to office on every sort of inequality any more than in the arts. For if some be slow, and others swift, that is no reason why the one should have little and the others much; it is in gymnastic contests that such excellence is rewarded. Whereas the rival claims of candidates for office can only be based on the possession of elements which enter into the composition of a state, [such as wealth, virtue, etc.]. And therefore the noble, or freeborn, or rich, may with good reason claim office; for holders of offices must be freemen and tax-payers: a state can be no more composed entirely of poor men than entirely of slaves. But if wealth and freedom are necessary elements, justice and valour are equally so; for without the former a state cannot exist at all, without the latter not well.

13 If the existence of the state is alone to be considered, then it would seem that all, or some at least, of these claims are just; but, if we take into account a good life, as I have already said, education and virtue have superior claims. As, however, those who are equal in one thing ought not to be equal in all, nor those who are unequal in one thing to be unequal in all, it is certain that all forms of government which rest on either of these principles are perversions. All men have a claim in a certain sense, as I have already admitted, but they have not an absolute claim. The rich claim because they have a greater share in the land, and land is the common element of the state; also they are generally more trustworthy in contracts. The free claim under the same title as the noble; for they are nearly akin. And the noble are citizens in a truer sense than the ignoble, since good birth is always valued in a man's own home and country. Another

reason is, that those who are sprung from better ancestors are likely to be better men, for nobility is excellence of race. Virtue, too, may be truly said to have a claim, for justice has been acknowledged by us to be a social virtue, and it implies all others. Again, the many may urge their claim against the few; for, when taken collectively, and compared with the few, they are stronger and richer and better. But, what if the good, the rich, the noble, and the other classes who make up a state, are all living together in the same city; will there, or will there not, be any doubt who shall rule? – No doubt at all in determining who ought to rule in each of the above-mentioned forms of government. For states are characterized by differences in their governing bodies – one of them has a government of the rich, another of the virtuous, and so on. But a difficulty arises when all these elements coexist. How are we to decide? Suppose the virtuous to be very few in number: may we consider their numbers in relation to their duties, and ask whether they are enough to administer the state, or must they be so many as will make up a state? Objections may be urged against all the aspirants to political power. For those who found their claims on wealth or family have no basis of justice; on this principle, if any one person were richer than all the rest, it is clear that he ought to be the ruler of them. In like manner he who is very distinguished by his birth ought to have the superiority over all those who claim on the ground that they are freeborn. In an aristocracy, or government of the best, a like difficulty occurs about virtue; for if one citizen be better than the other members of the government, however good they may be, he too, upon the same principle of justice, should rule over them. And if the people are to be supreme because they are stronger than the few, then if one man, or more than one, but not a majority, is stronger than the many, they ought to rule, and not the many.

All these considerations appear to show that none of the principles on which men claim to rule, and hold all other men in subjection to them, are strictly right. To those who claim to be the masters of state on the ground of their virtue or their wealth, the many might fairly answer that they themselves are often better and richer than the few – I do not say individually, but collectively. And another ingenious objection which is sometimes put forward may be met in a similar manner. Some persons doubt whether the legislator who desires to make the justest laws ought to legislate with a view to the good of the higher classes or of the many, when the case which we have mentioned occurs [i. e. when all the elements coexist]. Now what is just or right is to be interpreted in the sense of 'what is equal'; and that which is right in the sense of being equal is to be considered with reference to the advantage of the state, and the common good of the citizens. And a citizen is one who shares in governing and being governed. He differs under different forms of government, but in the best state he is one who is able and willing to be governed and to govern with a view to the life of virtue.

If, however, there be some one person, or more than one, although not enough to make up the full complement of a state, whose virtue is so pre-eminent that the virtues or the political capacity of all the rest admit of no comparison with his or theirs, he or they can be no longer regarded as part of a state; for justice will not be done to the superior, if he is reckoned only as the equal of those who are so far inferior to him in virtue and in political capacity. Such an one may truly be deemed a god among men. Hence we see that legislation is necessarily concerned only with those who are equal in birth and in power; and that for men of pre-eminent virtue there is no law – they are themselves a law. Anyone would be ridiculous who attempted to make laws for them: they would probably retort what, in the fable of Antisthenes, the lions said to the hares ['where are your claws?'], when in the council of the beasts the latter began haranguing and claiming equality for all. And for this reason democratic states have instituted ostracism; equality is above all things their aim, and therefore they ostracise and banish from the city for a time those who seem to predominate too much through their wealth, or the number of their friends, or through any other political influence. Mythology tells us that the Argonauts left Heracles behind for a similar reason; the ship Argo would not take him because she feared that he would have been too much for the rest of the crew. Wherefore those who denounce tyranny and blame the counsel which Periander gave to Thrasybulus cannot be held altogether just in their censure. The story is that Periander, when the herald was sent to ask counsel of him, said nothing, but only cut off the tallest ears of corn till he had brought the field to a level. The herald did not know the meaning of the action, but came and reported what he had seen to Thrasybulus, who understood that he was to cut off the principal men in the state; and this is a policy not only expedient for tyrants or in practice confined to them, but equally necessary in oligarchies and democracies. Ostracism is a measure of the same kind, which acts by disabling and banishing the most prominent citizens. Great powers do the same to whole cities and nations, as the Athenians did to the Samians, Chians, and Lesbians; no sooner had they obtained a firm grasp of the empire, than they humbled their allies contrary to treaty; and the Persian king has repeatedly crushed the Medes, Babylonians, and other nations, when their spirit has been stirred by the recollection of their former greatness.

The problem is a universal one, and equally concerns all forms of government, true as well as false; for, although perverted forms with a view to their own interests may adopt this policy, those which seek the common interest do so likewise. The same thing may be observed in the arts and sciences; for the painter will not allow the figure to have a foot which, however beautiful, is not in proportion, nor will the ship-builder allow the stern or any other part of the vessel to be unduly large, any more than the chorusmaster will allow anyone who sings louder or better than all the rest to sing in the choir. Monarchs, too, may practise compulsion and still live in harmony with their cities, if their government is for the interest of the state. Hence where there is an acknowledged superiority the argument in favour of ostracism is based upon a kind of political justice. It would certainly be better that the legislator should from the first so order his state as to have no need of such a remedy. But if the need arises, the next best thing is that he should endeavour to correct the evil by this or some similar measure. The principle, however, has not been fairly applied in states; for, instead of looking to the public good, they have used ostracism for factious purposes. It is true that under perverted forms of government, and from their special point of view, such a measure is just and expedient, but it is also clear that it is not absolutely just. In the perfect state there would be great doubts about the use of it, not when applied to excess in strength, wealth, popularity, or the like, but when used against someone who is pre-eminent in virtue – what is to be done with him? Mankind will not say that such an one is to be expelled and exiled: on the other hand, he ought not to be a subject – that would be as if men should claim to rule over Zeus on the principle of rotation of office. The only alternative is that all should joyfully obey such a ruler, according to what seems to be the order of nature, and that men like him should be kings in their state for life.

14   The preceding discussion, by a natural transition, leads to the consideration of royalty, which we admit to be one of the true forms of government. Let us see whether in order to be well governed a state or country should be under the rule of a king or under some other form of government; and whether monarchy, although good for some, may not be bad for others. But first we must determine whether there is one species of royalty or many. It is not easy to see that there are many, and that the manner of government is not the same in all of them.

(1) Of royalties according to law, the Lacedaemonian is thought to answer best to the true pattern; but there the royal power is not absolute, except when the kings go on an expedition, and then they take the command. Matters of religion are likewise committed to them. The kingly office is in truth a kind of generalship, irresponsible and perpetual. The king has not the power of life and death, except when upon a campaign and in the field; after the manner of the ancients which

is described in Homer. For Agamemnon is patient when he is attacked in the assembly, but when the army goes out to battle he has the power even of life and death. Does he not say? –

'When I find a man skulking apart from the battle, nothing shall save him from the dogs and vultures, for in my hands is death.'

This, then, is one form of royalty – a generalship for life: and of such royalties some are hereditary and others elective.

(2) There is another sort of monarchy not uncommon among the barbarians, which nearly resembles tyranny. But even this is legal and hereditary. For barbarians, being more servile in character than Hellenes, and Asiatics than Europeans, do not rebel against a despotic government. Such royalties have the nature of tyrannies because the people are by nature slaves; but there is no danger of their being overthrown, for they are hereditary and legal. Wherefore also their guards are such as a king and not such as a tyrant would employ, that is to say, they are composed of citizens, whereas the guards of tyrants are mercenaries. For kings rule according to law over voluntary subjects, but tyrants over involuntary; and the one are guarded by their fellow-citizens, the others are guarded against them.

These are two forms of monarchy, and there was a third (3) which existed in ancient Hellas, called an *aesymnetia* or dictatorship. This may be defined generally as an elective tyranny, which, like the barbarian monarchy, is legal, but differs from it in not being hereditary. Sometimes the office is held for life, sometimes for a term of years, or until certain duties have been performed. For example, the Mitylenaeans elected Pittacus leader against the exiles, who were headed by Antimenides and Alcaeus the poet. And Alcaeus himself says in one of his irregular songs, 'They chose Pittacus tyrant,' and he reproaches his fellow-citizens for

'having made the low-born Pittacus tyrant of the spiritless and ill-fated city, with one voice shouting his praises.'

These forms of government have always had the character of despotism, because they possess tyrannical power; but inasmuch as they are elective and acquiesced in by their subjects, they are kingly.

(4) There is a fourth species of kingly rule – that of the heroic times – which was hereditary and legal, and was exercised over willing subjects. For the first chiefs were benefactors of the people in arts or arms; they either gathered them into a community, or procured land for them; and thus they became kings of voluntary subjects, and their power was inherited by their descendants. They took the command in war and presided over the sacrifices, except those which required a priest. They also decided causes either with or without an oath; and when they swore, the form of the oath was the stretching out of their sceptre. In ancient times their power extended to all things whatsoever, in city and country, as well as in foreign parts; but at a later date they relinquished several of these privileges, and others the people took from them, until in some states nothing was left to them but the sacrifices; and where they retained more of the reality they had only the right of leadership in war beyond the border.

These, then, are the four kinds of royalty. First the monarchy of the heroic ages; this was exercised over voluntary subjects, but limited to certain functions; the king was a general and a judge, and had the control of religion. The second is that of the barbarians, which is an hereditary despotic government in accordance with law. A third is the power of the so-called aesymnete or dictator; this is an elective tyranny. The fourth is the Lacedaemonian, which is in fact a generalship, hereditary and perpetual. These four forms differ from one another in the manner which I have described.

There is a fifth form of kingly rule in which one has the disposal of all, just as each tribe or each state has the disposal of the public property; this form corresponds to the control of a household. For as household management is the kingly rule of a house, so kingly rule is the household management of a city, or of a nation, or of many nations.

15 Of these forms we need only consider two, the Lacedaemonian and the absolute royalty; for most of the others lie in a region between them, having less power than the last, and more than the first. Thus the enquiry is reduced to two points: first, is it advantageous to the state that there should be a perpetual general, and if so, should the office be confined to one family, or open to the citizens in turn? Secondly, is it well that a single man should have the supreme power in all things? The first question falls under the head of laws rather than of constitutions; for perpetual generalship might equally exist under any form of government, so that this matter may be dismissed for the present. The other kind of royalty

is a sort of constitution; this we have now to consider, and briefly to run over the difficulties involved in it. We will begin by enquiring whether it is more advantageous to be ruled by the best man or by the best laws.

The advocates of royalty maintain that the laws speak only in general terms, and cannot provide for circumstances; and that for any science to abide by written rules is absurd. Even in Egypt the physician is allowed to alter his treatment after the fourth day, but if sooner, he takes the risk. Hence it is argued that a government acting according to written laws is plainly not the best. Yet surely the ruler cannot dispense with the general principle which exists in law; and he is a better ruler who is free from passion than he who is passionate. Whereas the law is passionless, passion must ever sway the heart of man.

Yes, someone will answer, but then on the other hand an individual will be better able to advise in particular cases. [To whom we in turn make reply:] A king must legislate, and laws must be passed, but these laws will have no authority when they miss the mark, though in all other cases retaining their authority. [Yet a further question remains behind:] When the law cannot determine a point at all, or not well, should the one best man or should all decide? According to our present practice assemblies meet, sit in judgment, deliberate and decide, and their judgments all relate to individual cases. Now any member of the assembly, taken separately, is certainly inferior to the wise man. But the state is made up of many individuals. And as a feast to which all the guests contribute is better than a banquet furnished by a single man, so a multitude is a better judge of many things than any individual.

Again, the many are more incorruptible than the few;

they are like the greater quantity of water which is less easily corrupted than a little. The individual is liable to be overcome by anger or by some other passion, and then his judgment is necessarily perverted; but it is hardly to be supposed that a great number of persons would all get into a passion and go wrong at the same moment. Let us assume that they are freemen, never acting in violation of the law, but filling up the gaps which the law is obliged to leave. Or, if such virtue is scarcely attainable by the multitude, we need only suppose that the majority are good men and good citizens, and ask which will be the more incorruptible, the one good ruler, or the many who are all good? Will not the many? But, you will say, there may be parties among them, whereas the one man is not divided against himself. To which we may answer that their character is as good as his. If we call the rule of many men, who are all of them good, aristocracy, and the rule of one man royalty, then aristocracy will be better for states than royalty, whether the government is supported by force or not, provided only that a number of men equal in virtue can be found.

The first governments were kingships, probably for this reason, because of old, when cities were small, men of eminent virtue were few. They were made kings because they were benefactors, and benefits can only be bestowed by good men. But when many persons equal in merit arose, no longer enduring the pre-eminence of one, they desired to have a commonwealth, and set up a constitution. The ruling class soon deteriorated and enriched themselves out of the public treasury; riches became the path to honour, and so oligarchies naturally grew up. These passed into tyrannies and tyrannies into democracies; for love of gain in the ruling classes was always tending to diminish their number, and so to strengthen the masses, who in the end set upon their masters and established democracies. Since cities have increased in size, no other form of government appears to be any longer possible.

Even supposing the principle to be maintained that kingly power is the best thing for states, how about the family of the king? Are his children to succeed him? If they are no better than anybody else, that will be mischievous. But [says the lover of royalty] the king, though he might, will not hand on his power to his children. That, however, is hardly to be expected, and is too much to ask of human nature. There is also a difficulty about the force which he is to employ; should a king have guards about him by whose aid he may be able to coerce the refractory? But if not, how will he administer his kingdom? Even if he be the lawful sovereign who does nothing arbitrarily or contrary to law, still he must have some force wherewith to maintain the law. In the case of a limited monarchy there is not much difficulty in answering this question; the king must have such force as will be more than a match for one or more individuals, but not so great as that of the people. The ancients observed this principle when they gave the guards to anyone whom they appointed dictator or tyrant. Thus, when Dionysius asked the Syracusans to allow him guards, somebody advised that they should give him only a certain number.

16   At this place in the discussion naturally follows the enquiry respecting the king who acts solely according to his own will; he has now to be considered. The so-

called limited monarchy, or kingship according to law, as I have already remarked, is not a distinct form of government, for under all governments, as, for example, in a democracy or aristocracy, there may be a general holding office for life, and one person is often made supreme over the internal administration of a state. A magistracy of this kind exists at Epidamnus, and also at Opus, but in the latter city has a more limited power. Now, absolute monarchy, or the arbitrary rule of a sovereign over all the citizens, in a city which consists of equals, is thought by some to be quite contrary to nature; it is argued that those who are by nature equals must have the same natural right and worth, and that for unequals to have an equal share, or for equals to have an unequal share, in the offices of state, is as bad as for different bodily constitutions to have the same food and clothing or the same different. Wherefore it is thought to be just that among equals everyone be ruled as well as rule, and that all should have their turn. We thus arrive at law; for an order of succession implies law. And the rule of the law is preferable to that of any individual. On the same principle, even if it be better for certain individuals to govern, they should be made only guardians and ministers of the law. For magistrates there must be – this is admitted; but then men say that to give authority to any one man when all are equal is unjust. There may indeed be cases which the law seems unable to determine, but in such cases can a man? Nay, it will be replied, the law trains officers for this express purpose, and appoints them to determine matters which are left undecided by it to the best of their judgment. Further it permits them to make any amendment of the existing laws which experience suggests. [But still they are only the ministers of the law.] He who bids the law rule, may be deemed to bid god and reason alone rule, but he who bids man rule adds an element of the beast; for desire is a wild beast, and passion perverts the minds of rulers, even when they are the best of men. The law is reason unaffected by desire. We are told that a patient should call in a physician; he will not get better if he is doctored out of a book. But the parallel of the arts is clearly not in point; for the physician does nothing contrary to reason from motives of friendship; he only cures a patient and takes a fee; whereas magistrates do many things from spite and partiality. And, indeed, if a man suspected the physician of being in league with his enemies to destroy him for a bribe, he would rather have recourse to the book. Even physicians when they are sick, call in other physicians, and training-masters when they are in training, other training-masters, as if they could not judge truly about their own case and might be influenced by their feelings. Hence it is evident that in seeking for justice men seek for the mean or neutral, and the law is the mean. Again, customary laws have more weight, and relate to more important matters, than written laws, and a man may be a safer ruler than the written law, but not safer than the customary law.

Again, it is by no means easy for one man to superintend many things; he will have to appoint a number of subordinates; and what difference does it make whether these subordinates always existed or were appointed by him because he needed them? If, as I said before, the good man has a right to rule because he is better, then two good men are better than one: this is the old saying, –

'two going together;'

and the prayer of Agamemnon, –

'would that I had ten such counsellors!'

And at this day there are some magistrates, for example judges, who have authority to decide matters which the law is unable to determine, since no one doubts that the law would command and decide in the best manner whatever it could. But some things can, and other things cannot, be comprehended under the law, and this is the origin of the vexed question whether the best law or the best man should rule. For matters of detail about which men deliberate cannot be included in legislation. Nor does anyone deny that the decision of such matters must be left to man, but it is argued that there should be many judges, and not one only. For every ruler who has been trained by the law judges well; and it would surely seem strange that a person should see better with two eyes, or hear better with two ears, or act better with two hands or feet, than many with many; indeed, it is already the practice of kings to make to themselves many eyes and ears and hands and feet. For they make colleagues of those who are the friends of themselves and their governments. They must be friends of the monarch and of his government; if not his friends, they will not do what he wants; but friendship implies likeness and equality; and, therefore, if he thinks that friends ought to rule, he must think that those who are equal to himself and like himself ought to rule. These are the principal controversies relating to monarchy.

17 But may not all this be true in some cases and not in others? For there is a natural justice and expediency in the relation of a master to his servants, or, again, of a king to his subjects, as also in the relation of free citizens to one another; whereas there is no such justice or expediency in a tyranny, or in any other perverted form of government, which comes into being contrary to nature. Now, from what has been said, it is manifest that, where men are alike and equal, it is neither expedient nor just that one man should be lord of all, whether there are laws, or whether there are no laws, but he himself is in the place of law. Neither should a good man be lord over good men, or a bad man over bad; nor, even if he excels in virtue, should he have a right to rule, unless in a particular case, which I have already mentioned, and to which I will once more recur. But first of all, I must determine what natures are suited for royalties, and what for an aristocracy, and what for a constitutional government.

A people who are by nature capable of producing a race superior in virtue and political talent are fitted for kingly government; and a people submitting to be ruled as freemen by men whose virtue renders them capable of political command are adapted for an aristocracy: while the people who are suited for constitutional freedom are those among whom there naturally exists a warlike multitude able to rule and to obey in turn by a law which gives office to the well-to-do according to their desert. But when a whole family, or some individual, happens to be so pre-eminent in virtue as to surpass all others, then it is just that they should be the royal family and supreme over all, or that this one citizen should be king of the whole nation. For, as I said before, to give them authority is not only agreeable to that ground of right which the founders of all states, whether aristocratical, or oligarchical, or again democratical, are accustomed to put forward (for these all recognize the claim of excellence, although not the same excellence), but accords with the principle already laid down. For it would not be right to kill, or ostracize, or exile such a person, or require that he should take his turn in being governed. The whole is naturally superior to the part, and he who has this pre-eminence is in the relation of a whole to a part. But if so, the only alternative is that he should have the supreme power, and that mankind should obey him, not in turn, but always. These are the conclusions at which we arrive respecting royalty and its various forms, and this is the answer to the question, whether it is or is not advantageous to states, and to whom, and how.

18   We maintain that the true forms of government are three, and that the best must be that which is administered by the best, and in which there is one man, or a whole family, or many persons, excelling in virtue, and both rulers and subjects are fitted, the one to rule, the others to be ruled, in such a manner as to attain the most eligible life. We showed at the commencement of our enquiry that the virtue of the good man is necessarily the same as the virtue of the citizen of the perfect state. Clearly then in the same manner, and by the same means through which a man becomes truly good, he will frame a state [which will be truly good] whether aristocratical, or under kingly rule, and the same education and the same habits will be found to make a good man and a good statesman and king.

Having arrived at these conclusions, we must proceed to speak of the perfect state, and describe how it comes into being and is established. He who would proceed with the enquiry in due manner . . .

BOOK FOUR

Different constitutions compared

1 In all arts and sciences which embrace the whole of any subject, and are not restricted to a part only, it is the province of a single art or science to consider all that appertains to a single subject. For example, the art of gymnastic considers not only the suitableness of different modes of training to different bodies, but what sort is absolutely the best (for the absolutely best must suit that which is by nature best and best furnished with the means of life), and also what common form of training is adapted to the great majority of men. And if a man does not desire the best habit of body or the greatest skill in gymnastics, which might be attained by him, still the trainer or the teacher of gymnastic should be able to impart any lower degree of either. The same principle equally holds in medicine and ship-building, and the making of clothes, and in the arts generally.

Hence it is obvious that government too is the subject of a single science, which has to consider what kind of government would be best and most in accordance with our aspirations, if there were no external impediment, and also what kind of government is adapted to particular states. For the best is often unattainable, and therefore the true legislator and statesman ought to be acquainted, not only with that which is best in the abstract, but also with that which is best relatively to circumstances. We should be able further to say how a state may be constituted under any given conditions; both how it is originally formed and, when formed, how it may be longest preserved; the supposed state being so far from the very best that it is unprovided even with the conditions necessary for the very best; neither is it the best under the circumstances, but of an inferior type.

He ought, moreover, to know the form of government which is best suited to states in general; for political writers, although they have excellent ideas, are often unpractical. We should consider, not only what form of government is best, but also what is possible and what is easily attainable by all. There are some who would have none but the most perfect; for this many natural advantages are required. Others, again, speak of a more attainable form, and, although they reject the constitution under which they are living, they extol some one in particular, for example the Lacedaemonian. Any change of government which has to be introduced should be one which men will be both willing and able to adopt, since there is quite as much trouble in the reformation of an old constitution as in the establishment of a new one, just as to unlearn is as hard as to learn. And therefore, in addition to the qualifications of the statesman already mentioned, he should be able to find remedies for the defects of existing constitutions. This he cannot do unless he knows how many forms of government there are. It is often supposed that there is only one kind of democracy and one of oligarchy. But this is a mistake; and, in order to avoid such mistakes, we must ascertain what differences there are in the constitutions of states, and in how many ways they are combined. The same political insight will enable a man to know which laws are the best, and which are suited to different constitutions; for the laws are, and ought to be, relative to the constitution, and not the constitution to the laws. A constitution is the organization of offices in a state, and determines what is to be the governing body, and what is the end of each community. But laws are not to be confounded with the principles of the constitution: they are the rules according to which the magistrates should administer the state, and proceed against offenders. So that we must know the number and varieties of the several forms of government, if only with a view to making laws. For the same laws cannot be equally suited to all oligarchies and to all democracies, and there is certainly more than one form both of democracy and of oligarchy.

2   In our original discussion about governments we divided them into three true forms: kingly rule, aristocracy, and constitutional government, and three corresponding perversions – tyranny, oligarchy, and democracy. Of kingly rule and of aristocracy we have already spoken, for the enquiry into the perfect state is the same thing with the discussion of the two forms thus named, since both imply a principle of virtue provided with external means. We have already determined in what aristocracy and kingly rule differ from one another, and when the latter should be established. In what follows we have to describe the so-called constitutional government, which bears the common name of all constitutions, and the other forms, tyranny, oligarchy, and democracy.

It is obvious which of the three perversions is the worst, and which is the next in badness. That which is the perversion of the first and most divine is necessarily the worst. And just as a royal rule, if not a mere name, must exist by virtue of some great personal superiority in the king, so tyranny, which is the worst of governments, is necessarily the farthest removed from a well-constituted form; oligarchy is a little better, but a long way from aristocracy, and democracy is the most tolerable of the three.

A writer who preceded me has already made these distinctions, but his point of view is not the same as mine. For he lays down the principle that of all good constitutions (under which he would include a virtuous oligarchy and the like) democracy is the worst, but the best of bad ones. Whereas we maintain that they are all defective, and that one oligarchy is not to be accounted better than another, but only less bad.

Not to pursue this question further at present, let us begin by determining (1) how many varieties of states there are (since of democracy and oligarchy there are several); (2) what constitution is the most generally acceptable, and what is eligible in the next degree after the perfect or any other aristocratical and well-constituted form of government – if any other there be – which is at the same time adapted to states in general; (3) of the other forms of government to whom each is suited. For democracy may meet the needs of some better than oligarchy, and conversely. In the next place (4) we have to consider in what manner a man ought to proceed who desires to establish some one among these various forms, whether of democracy or of oligarchy; and lastly, (5) having briefly discussed these subjects to the best of our power, we will endeavour to ascertain whence arise the ruin and preservation of states, both generally and in individual cases, and to what causes they are to be attributed.

3 The reason why there are many forms of government is that every state contains many elements. In the first place we see that all states are made up of families, and in the multitude of citizens there must be some rich and some poor, and some in a middle condition; the rich are heavy-armed, and the poor not. Of the common people, some are husbandmen, and some traders, and some artisans. There are also among the notables differences of wealth and property – for example, in the number of horses which they keep, for they cannot afford to keep them unless they are rich. And therefore in old times the cities whose strength lay in the cavalry were oligarchies, and they used cavalry in wars against their neighbours; as was the practice of the Eretrians and Chalcidians, and also of the Magnesians on the river Maeander, and of other peoples in Asia. Besides differences of wealth there are differences of rank and merit, and there are some other elements which were mentioned by us when in treating of aristocracy we enumerated the essentials of a state. Of these elements, sometimes all, sometimes the lesser and sometimes the greater number, have a share in the government. It is evident then that there must be many forms of government, differing in kind, since the parts of which they are composed differ from each other in kind. For a constitution is an organization of offices which all the citizens distribute among themselves, according to the power which different classes possess, for example the rich or the poor, or according to some common equality subsisting among them or some power common to both. There must

therefore be as many forms of government as there are modes of arranging the offices, according to the superiorities and other inequalities of the different parts of the state.

There are generally thought to be two principal forms: as men say of the winds that there are but two – north and south – and that the rest of them are only variations of these, so of governments there are said to be only two forms – democracy and oligarchy. For aristocracy is considered to be a kind of oligarchy, as being the rule of a few, and the so-called constitutional government to be really a democracy, just as among the winds we make the west a variation of the north, and the east of the south wind. Similarly of harmonies there are said to be two kinds, the Dorian and the Phrygian; the other arrangements of the scale are comprehended under one of these two. About forms of government this is a very favourite notion. But in either case the better and more exact way is to distinguish, as I have done, the one or two which are true forms, and to regard the others as perversions, whether of the most perfectly attempered harmony or of the best form of government; we may compare the oligarchical forms to the severer and more over-powering modes, and the democratic to the more relaxed and gentler ones.

4 It must not be assumed, as some are fond of saying, that democracy is simply that form of government in which the greater number are sovereign, for in oligarchies, and indeed in every government, the majority rules; nor again is oligarchy that form of government in which a few are sovereign. Suppose the whole population of a city to be 1300, and that of these

1000 are rich, and do not allow the remaining 300 who are poor, but free, and in all other respects their equals, a share of the government – no one will say that this is a democracy. In like manner, if the poor were few and the masters of the rich, who outnumber them, no one would ever call such a government, in which the rich majority have no share of office, an oligarchy. Therefore we should rather say that democracy is the form of government in which the free are rulers, and oligarchy in which the rich; it is only an accident that the free are the many and the rich are the few. Otherwise a government in which the offices were given according to stature, as is said to be the case in Ethiopia, or according to beauty, would be an oligarchy; for the number of tall or good-looking men is small. And yet oligarchy and democracy are not sufficiently distinguished merely by these two characteristics of wealth and freedom. Both of them contain many other elements, and therefore we must carry our analysis further, and say that the government is not a democracy in which the freemen, being few in number, rule over the many who art not free, as at Apollonia, on the Ionian Gulf, and at Thera (for in each of these states the nobles, who were also the earliest settlers, were held in chief honour, although they were but a few out of many). Neither is it a democracy when the rich have the government, because they exceed in number; as was the case formerly at Colophon, where the bulk of the inhabitants were possessed of large property before the Lydian War. But the form of government is a democracy when the free, who are also poor and the majority, govern, and oligarchy when the rich and the noble govern, they being at the same time few in number.

I have said that there are many forms of government, and have explained to what causes the variety is due. Why there are more than those already mentioned, and what they are, and whence they arise, I will now proceed to consider, starting from the principle already admitted, which is that every state consists, not of one, but of many parts. If we were going to speak of the different species of animals, we should first of all determine the organs which are indispensable to every animal, as for example some organs of sense and instruments of receiving and digesting food, such as the mouth and the stomach, besides organs of locomotion. Assuming now that there are only so many kinds of organs, but that there may be differences in them – I mean different kinds of mouths, and stomachs, and perceptive and locomotive organs – the possible combinations of these differences will necessarily furnish many varieties of animals. (For animals cannot be the same which have different kinds of mouths or of ears.) And when all the combinations are exhausted, there will be as many sorts of animals as there are combinations of the necessary organs. In like manner the forms of government which have been described, as I have repeatedly said, are composed, not of one, but of many elements. One element is the food-producing class, who are called husbandmen; a second, a class of mechanics, who practise the arts without which a city cannot exist – of these arts some are absolutely necessary, others contribute to luxury or to the grace of life. The third class is that of traders, and by traders I mean those who are engaged in buying and selling, whether in commerce or in retail trade. A fourth class is that of the serfs or labourers. The warriors make up the fifth class, and they are as necessary as any of the others, if the country is not to be the slave of every invader. For how can a state which has any title to the name be of a slavish nature? The state is independent and self-sufficing, but a slave is the reverse of independent. Hence we see that this subject, though ingeniously, has not been satis-factorily treated in the *Republic*. Socrates says that a state is made up of four sorts of people who are absolutely necessary; these are a weaver, a husband-man, a shoemaker, and a builder; afterwards, finding that they are not enough, he adds a smith, and again a herdsman, to look after the necessary animals; then a merchant, and then a retail trader. All these together form the complement of the first state, as if a state were established merely to supply the necessaries of life, rather than for the sake of the good, or stood equally in need of shoemakers and of husbandmen. But he does not admit into the state a military class until the country has increased in size, and is beginning to encroach on its neighbour's land, whereupon they go to war. Yet even amongst his four original citizens, or whatever be the number of those whom he associates in the state, there must be someone who will dispense justice and determine what is just. And as the soul may be said to be more truly part of an animal than the body, so the higher parts of states, that is to say, the warrior class, the class engaged in the administration of justice, and in deliberation, which is the special business of political common sense, – these are more essential to the state than the parts which minister to the necessaries of life. Whether their several functions are the functions of different citizens, or of the same – for it may often happen that the same persons are both warriors and husbandmen – is immaterial to the argument. The higher as well as the lower elements are to be equally considered parts of the state, and if so, the military element must be included. There are also the wealthy who minister to the state with their property; these form the seventh class. The eighth class is that of magistrates and of officers; for the state cannot exist without rulers. And therefore some must be able to take office and to serve the state, either always or in turn. There only remains the class of those who deliberate and who judge between disputants; we were just now distinguishing them. If the fair and equitable organization of all these elements is necessary to states, then there must also be persons who have the ability of statesmen. Many are of opinion that different functions can be combined in the same individual; for example, the warrior may be a husbandman, or an artisan; or again, the counsellor a judge. And all claim to possess political ability, and think that they are quite competent to fill most offices. But the same persons cannot be rich and poor at the same time. For this reason the rich and the poor are regarded in an especial sense as parts of a state. Again, because the rich are generally few in number, while the poor are many, they appear to be antagonistic, and as the one or the other prevails they form the government. Hence arises the common opinion that there are two kinds of government – democracy and oligarchy.

I have already explained that there are many differences of constitutions, and to what causes the variety is due. Let me now show that there are different forms both of democracy and oligarchy, as will indeed be evident from what has preceded. For both in the common people and in the notables various classes are included; of the common people, one class are husbandmen, another artisans; another traders, who are employed in buying and selling; another are the seafaring class, whether engaged in war or in trade, as ferrymen or as fishermen. (In many places any one of these classes forms quite a large population; for example, fishermen at Tarentum and Byzantium, crews of triremes at Athens, merchant seamen at Aegina and Chios, ferrymen at Tenedos.) To the classes already mentioned may be added day-labourers, and those who, owing to their needy circumstances, have no leisure, or those who are not free of birth on both sides; and there may be other classes as well. The notables again may be divided according to their wealth, birth, virtue, education, and similar differences.

Of forms of democracy first comes that which is said to be based strictly on equality. In such a democracy the law says that it is just for nobody to be poor, and for nobody to be rich; and that neither should be masters, but both equal. For if liberty and equality, as is thought by some, are chiefly to be found in democracy, they will be best attained when all persons alike share in the government to the utmost. And since the people are the majority, and the opinion of the majority is decisive, such a government must necessarily be a democracy. Here then is one sort of democracy. There is another in which the magistrates are elected according to a certain property qualification, but a low one; he who has the required amount of property has a share in the government, but he who loses his property loses his rights. Another kind is that in which all the citizens who are under no disqualification share in the government, but still the law is supreme. In another, everybody, if he be only a citizen, is admitted to the government, but the law is supreme as before. A fifth form of democracy, in other respects the same, is that in which, not the law, but the multitude, have the supreme power, and supersede the law by their decrees. This is a state of affairs brought about by the demagogues. For in democracies which are subject to the law the best citizens hold the first place, and there are no demagogues; but where the laws are not supreme, there demagogues spring up. For the people becomes a monarch, and is many in one; and the many have the power in their hands, not as individuals, but collectively. Homer says that, 'it is not good to have a rule of many', but whether he means this corporate rule, or the rule of many individuals, is uncertain. And the people, who is now a monarch, and no longer under the control of law, seeks to exercise monarchical sway, and grows into a despot; the flatterer is held in honour; this sort of democracy being relatively to other democracies what tyranny is to other forms of monarchy. The spirit of both is the same, and they alike exercise a despotic rule over the better citizens. The decrees of the demos correspond to the edicts of the tyrant; and the demagogue is to the one what the flatterer is to the other. Both have great power – the flatterer with the tyrant, the demagogue with democracies of the kind which we are describing. The demagogues make the decrees of the people override the laws, and refer all things to the popular assembly. And therefore they grow great, because the people have all things in their hands, and they hold in their hands the votes of the people, who are too ready to listen to them. Further, those who have any complaint to bring against the magistrates say, 'let the people be judges'; the people are too happy to accept the invitation; and so the authority of every office is undermined. Such a democracy is fairly open to the objection that it is not a constitution at all; for where the laws have no authority, there is no constitution. The law ought to be supreme over all, and the magistracies and the government should judge only of particulars. So that if democracy be a real form of government, the sort of constitution in which all things are regulated by decrees is clearly not a democracy in the true sense of the word, for decrees relate only to particulars.

5 These then are the different kinds of democracies. Of oligarchies, too, there are different kinds – one where the property qualification for office is so high that the poor, although they form the majority, have no share in the government, yet he who acquires a qualification may obtain a share. Another sort is when there is a qualification for office, but a high one, and the vacancies in the governing body are filled by co-optation. If the election is made out of all the qualified persons, a constitution of this kind inclines to an aristocracy, if out of a privileged class, to an oligarchy. Another sort of oligarchy is when the son succeeds the father. There is a fourth form, likewise hereditary, in which the magistrates are supreme and not the law. Among oligarchies this is what tyranny is among monarchies, and the last-mentioned form of democracy among democracies; and in fact this sort of oligarchy receives the name of a dynasty (or rule of powerful families).

These are the different sorts of oligarchies and democracies. It should however be remembered that in many states the constitution which is established by law, although not democratic, owing to the character

and habits of the people, may be administered demo-
cratically, and conversely in other states the established
constitution may incline to democracy, but may be
administered in an oligarchical spirit. This most often
happens after a revolution: for governments do not
change at once; at first the dominant party are content
with encroaching a little upon their opponents. The
laws which existed previously continue in force, but the
authors of the revolution have the power in their hands.

6   From what has been already said we may safely
infer that there are so many different kinds of democracies and of oligarchies. For it is evident that either
all the classes whom we mentioned must share in the
government, or some only and not others. When the
class of husbandmen and of those who possess
moderate fortunes have the supreme power, the
government is administered according to law. For
the citizens being compelled to live by their labour
have no leisure; and so they set up the authority of the
law, and attend assemblies only when necessary.
Since they all obtain a share in the government when
they have acquired the qualification which is fixed by
the law, nobody is excluded – the absolute exclusion
of any class would be a step towards oligarchy. But
leisure cannot be provided for them unless there are
revenues to support them. This is one sort of democracy, and these are the causes which give birth to it.
Another kind is based on the mode of election, which
naturally comes next in order; in this, everyone to
whose birth there is no objection is eligible, and may
share in the government if he can find leisure. And in
such a democracy the supreme power is vested in the
laws, because the state has no means of paying the

citizens. A third kind is when all freemen have a right to share in the government, but do not actually share, for the reason which has been already given; so that in this form again the law must rule. A fourth kind of democracy is that which comes latest in the history of states. In our own day, when cities have far outgrown their original size, and their revenues have increased, all the citizens have a place in the government, through the great preponderance of their numbers; and they all, including the poor who receive pay, and therefore have leisure to exercise their rights, share in the administration. Indeed, when they are paid, the common people have the most leisure, for they are not hindered by the care of their property, which often fetters the rich, who are thereby prevented from taking part in the assembly or in the courts, and so the state is governed by the poor, who are a majority, and not by the laws. So many kinds of democracies there are, and they grow out of these necessary causes.

Of oligarchies, one form is that in which the majority of the citizens have some property, but not very much; and this is the first form, which allows to anyone who obtains the required amount the right of sharing in the government. The sharers in the government being a numerous body, it follows that the law must govern, and not individuals. For in proportion as they are further removed from a monarchical form of government, and in respect of property have neither so much as to be able to live without attending to business, nor so little as to need state support, they must admit the rule of law and not claim to rule themselves. But if the men of property in the state are fewer than in the former case, and own more property, there arises a second form of oligarchy. For the stronger they are, the more power they claim, and having this object in view, they themselves select those of the other classes who are to be admitted to the government; but, not being as yet strong enough to rule without the law, they make the law represent their wishes. When this power is intensified by a further diminution of their numbers and increase of their property, there arises a third and further stage of oligarchy, in which the governing class keep the offices in their own hands, and the law ordains that the son shall succeed the father. When, again, the rulers have great wealth and numerous friends, this sort of dynastia or family despotism approaches a monarchy; individuals rule and not the law. This is the fourth sort of oligarchy, and is analogous to the last sort of democracy.

7 There are still two forms besides democracy and oligarchy; one of them is universally recognized and included among the four principal forms of government, which are said to be (1) monarchy, (2) oligarchy, (3) democracy, and (4) the so-called aristocracy or government of the best. But there is also a fifth, which retains the generic name of polity or constitutional government; this is not common, and therefore has not been noticed by writers who attempt to enumerate the different kinds of government; like Plato in his books about the state, they recognize four only. The term 'aristocracy' is rightly applied to the form of government which is described in the first part of our treatise: for that only can be rightly called aristocracy [the government of the best] which is a government formed of the best men absolutely, and not merely of men who are good when tried by any given standard. In the perfect state the good man is absolutely the same as the

good citizen; whereas in other states the good citizen is only good relatively to his own form of government. But there are some states differing from oligarchies and also differing from the so-called polity or constitutional government; these are termed aristocracies, and in them magistrates are certainly chosen, both according to their wealth and according to their merit. Such a form of government is not the same with the two just now mentioned, and is termed an aristocracy. For indeed in states which do not make virtue the aim of the community, men of merit and reputation for virtue may be found. And so where a government has regard to wealth, virtue, and numbers, as at Carthage, that is aristocracy; and also where it has regard only to two out of the three, as at Lacedaemon, to virtue and numbers, and the two principles of democracy and virtue temper each other. There are these two forms of aristocracy in addition to the first and perfect state, and there is a third form, viz. the polities which incline towards oligarchy.

8　I have yet to speak of the so-called polity and of tyranny. I put them in this order, not because a polity or constitutional government is to be regarded as a perversion any more than the above-mentioned aristocracies. The truth is, that they all fall short of the most perfect form of government, and so they are reckoned among perversions, and other forms (sc. the really perverted forms) are perversions of these, as I said before. Last of all I will speak of tyranny, which I place last in the series because I am enquiring into the constitutions of states, and this is the very reverse of a constitution.

Having explained why I have adopted this order, I

will proceed to consider constitutional government; of which the nature will be clearer now that oligarchy and democracy have been defined. For polity or constitutional government may be described generally as a fusion of oligarchy and democracy; but the term is usually applied to those forms of government which incline towards democracy, and the term aristocracy to those which incline towards oligarchy, because birth and education are commonly the accompaniments of wealth. Moreover, the rich already possess the external advantages the want of which is a temptation to crime, and hence they are called noblemen and gentlemen. And inasmuch as aristocracy seeks to give predominance to the best of the citizens, people say also of oligarchies that they are composed of noblemen and gentlemen. Now it appears to be an impossible thing that the state which is governed by the best citizens should be ill-governed, and equally impossible that the state which is ill-governed should be governed by the best. But we must remember that good laws, if they are not obeyed, do not constitute good government. For there are two parts of good government; one is the actual obedience of citizens to the laws, the other part is the goodness of the laws which they obey; they may obey bad laws as well as good. And there may be a further subdivision; they may obey either the best laws which are attainable to them, or the best absolutely.

The distribution of offices according to merit is a special characteristic of aristocracy, for the principle of an aristocracy is virtue, as wealth is of an oligarchy, and freedom of a democracy. In all of them there of course exists the right of the majority, and whatever seems good to the majority of those who share in the government has authority. Generally, however, a state of this kind is called a constitutional government [not an aristocracy], for the fusion goes no further than the attempt to unite the freedom of the poor and the wealth of the rich, who commonly take the place of the noble. And as there are three grounds on which men claim an equal share in the government – freedom, wealth, and virtue (for the fourth or good birth is the result of the two last, being only ancient wealth and virtue) – it is clear that the admixture of the two elements, that is to say, of the rich and poor, is to be called a polity or constitutional government: and the union of the three is to be called aristocracy or the government of the best, and more than any other form of government, except the true and ideal, has a right to this name.

Thus far I have described the different forms of states which exist besides monarchy, democracy, and oligarchy, and what they are, and in what aristocracies differ from one another, and polities from aristocracies – that the two latter are not very unlike is obvious.

9 Next we have to consider how by the side of oligarchy and democracy the so-called polity or constitutional government springs up, and how it should be organized. The nature of it will be at once understood from a comparison of oligarchy and democracy; we must ascertain their different characteristics, and taking a portion from each, put the two together, like the parts of an indenture. Now there are three modes in which fusions of government may be effected. The nature of the fusion will be made intelligible by an example of the manner in

which different governments legislate, say concerning the administration of justice. In oligarchies they impose a fine on the rich if they do not serve as judges, and to the poor they give no pay; but in democracies they give pay to the poor and do not fine the rich. Now (1) the union of these two modes is a common or middle term between them, and is therefore characteristic of a constitutional government, for it is a combination of both. This is one mode of uniting the two elements. Or (2) a mean may be taken between the enactments of the two: thus democracies require no property qualification, or only a small one, from members of the assembly, oligarchies a high one; here neither of these is the common term, but a mean between them. (3) There is a third mode, in which something is borrowed from the oligarchical and something from the democratical principle. For example, the appointment of magistrates by lot is democratical, and the election of them oligarchical; democratical again when there is no property qualification, oligarchical when there is. In the aristocratical or constitutional state, one element will be taken from each – from oligarchy the mode of electing to offices, from democracy the disregard of qualification. Such are the various modes of combination.

There is a true union of oligarchy and democracy when the same state may be termed either a democracy or an oligarchy; those who use both names evidently feel that the fusion is complete. Such a fusion there is also in the mean; for both extremes appear in it. The Lacedaemonian constitution, for example, is often described as a democracy, because it has many democratical features. In the first place the youth receive a democratical education. For the sons of the poor are brought up with the sons of the rich, who are educated in such a manner as to make it possible for the sons of the poor to be educated like them. A similar equality prevails in the following period of life, and when the citizens are grown up to manhood the same rule is observed; there is no distinction between the rich and poor. In like manner they all have the same food at their public tables, and the rich wear only such clothing as any poor man can afford. Again, the people elect to one of the two greatest offices of states, and in the other they share; for they elect the Senators and share in the Ephoralty. By others the Spartan constitution is said to be an oligarchy, because it has many oligarchical elements. That all offices are filled by election and none by lot, is one of these oligarchical characteristics; that the power of inflicting death or banishment rests with a few persons is another; and there are others. In a well attempered polity there should appear to be both elements and yet neither; also the government should rely on itself, and not on foreign aid, nor on the good will of a majority of foreign states – they might be equally well-disposed when there is a vicious form of government – but on the general willingness of all classes in the state to maintain the constitution.

Enough of the manner in which a constitutional government, and in which the so-called aristocracies ought to be framed.

10   Of the nature of tyranny I have still to speak, in order that it may have its place in our enquiry, since even tyranny is reckoned by us to be a form of government, although there is not much to be said about it. I have already in the former part of this

treatise discussed royalty or kingship according to the most usual meaning of the term, and considered whether it is or is not advantageous to states, and what kind of royalty should be established, and whence, and how it arises.

When speaking of royalty we also spoke of two forms of tyranny, which are both according to law, and therefore easily pass into royalty. Among Barbarians there are elected monarchs who exercise a despotic power; despotic rulers were also elected in ancient Hellas, called *aesymnetes* or dictators. These monarchies, when compared with one another, exhibit certain differences. And they are, as I said before, royal, in so far as the monarch rules according to law and over willing subjects; but they are tyrannical in so far as he is despotic and rules according to his own fancy. There is also a third kind of tyranny, which is the most typical form, and is the counterpart of the perfect monarchy. This tyranny is just that arbitrary power of an individual which is responsible to no one, and governs all alike, whether equals or betters, with a view to its own advantage, not to that of its subjects, and therefore against their will. No freeman, if he can escape from it, will endure such a government.

The kinds of tyranny are such and so many, and for the reasons which I have given.

11 We have now to enquire what is the best constitution for most states, and the best life for most men, neither assuming a standard of virtue which is above ordinary persons, nor an education which is exceptionally favoured by nature and circumstances, nor yet an ideal state which is an aspiration only, but having regard to the life in which the majority are able to

share, and to the form of government which states in general can attain. As to those aristocracies, as they are called, of which we were just now speaking, they either lie beyond the possibilities of the greater number of states, or they approximate to the so-called constitutional government, and therefore need no separate discussion. And in fact the conclusion at which we arrive respecting all these forms rests upon the same grounds. For if it has been truly said in the *Ethics* that the happy life is the life according to unimpeded virtue, and that virtue is a mean, then the life which is in a mean, and in a mean attainable by everyone, must be the best. And the same criteria of virtue and vice apply both to cities and to constitutions; for the constitution is in a figure the life of the city.

Now in all states there are three elements; one class is very rich, another very poor, and a third in a mean. It is admitted that moderation and the mean are best, and therefore it will clearly be best to possess the gifts of fortune in moderation; for in that condition of life men are most ready to listen to reason. But he who greatly excels in beauty, strength, birth or wealth, or on the other hand who is very poor, or very weak, or very much disgraced, finds it difficult to follow reason. Of these two the one sort grow into violent and great criminals, the others into rogues and petty rascals. And two sorts of offences correspond to them, the one committed from violence, the other from roguery. The petty rogues are disinclined to hold office, whether military or civil, and their aversion to these two duties is as great an injury to the state as their tendency to crime. Again, those who have too much of the goods of fortune, strength, wealth, friends, and the like, are neither willing nor able to submit to authority.

The evil begins at home: for when they are boys, by reason of the luxury in which they are brought up, they never learn, even at school, the habit of obedience. On the other hand, the very poor, who are in the opposite extreme, are too degraded. So that the one class cannot obey, and can only rule despotically; the other knows not how to command and must be ruled like slaves. Thus arises a city, not of freemen, but of masters and slaves, the one despising, the other envying; and nothing can be more fatal to friendship and good fellowship in states than this: for good fellowship tends to friendship; when men are at enmity with one another, they would rather not even share the same path. But a city ought to be composed, as far as possible, of equals and similars; and these are generally the middle classes. Wherefore the city which is composed of middle-class citizens is necessarily best governed; they are, as we say, the natural elements of a state. And this is the class of citizens which is most secure in a state, for they do not, like the poor, covet their neighbours' goods; nor do others covet theirs, as the poor covet the goods of the rich; and as they neither plot against others, nor are themselves plotted against, they pass through life safely. Wisely then did Phocylides pray –

'Many things are best in the mean; I desire to be of a middle condition in my city.'

Thus it is manifest that the best political community is formed by citizens of the middle class, and that those states are likely to be well-administered, in which the middle class is large, and larger if possible than both the other classes, or at any rate than either singly; for the addition of the middle class turns the scale, and prevents either of the extremes from being dominant. Great then is the good fortune of a state in which the citizens have a moderate and sufficient property; for where some possess much, and the others nothing, there may arise an extreme democracy, or a pure oligarchy; or a tyranny may grow out of either extreme – either out of the most rampant democracy, or out of an oligarchy; but it is not so likely to arise out of a middle and nearly equal condition. I will explain the reason of this hereafter, when I speak of the revolutions of states. The mean condition of states is clearly best, for no other is free from faction; and where the middle class is large, there are least likely to be factions and dissensions. For a similar reason large states are less liable to faction than small ones, because in them the middle class is large; whereas in small states it is easy to divide all the citizens into two classes who are either rich or poor, and to leave nothing in the middle. And democracies are safer and more permanent than oligarchies, because they have a middle class which is more numerous and has a greater share in the government; for when there is no middle class, and the poor greatly exceed in number, troubles arise, and the state soon comes to an end. A proof of the superiority of the middle class is that the best legislators have been of a middle condition; for example, Solon, as his own verses testify; and Lycurgus, for he was not a king; and Charondas, and almost all legislators.

These considerations will help us to understand why most governments are either democratical or oligarchical. The reason is that the middle class is seldom numerous in them, and whichever party, whether the rich or the common people, transgresses the mean and predominates, draws the government to itself, and thus arises either oligarchy or democracy. There is another reason – the poor and the rich quarrel with one another, and whichever side gets the better, instead of establishing a just or popular government, regards political supremacy as the prize of victory, and the one party sets up a democracy and the other an oligarchy. Both the parties which had the supremacy in Hellas looked only to the interest of their own form of government, and established in states, the one, democracies, and the other, oligarchies; they thought of their own advantage, of the public not at all. For these reasons the middle form of government has rarely, if ever, existed, and among a very few only. One man alone of all who ever ruled in Hellas was induced to give this middle constitution to states. But it has now become a habit among the citizens of states, not even to care about equality; all men are seeking for dominion, or, if conquered, are willing to submit.

What then is the best form of government, and what makes it the best, is evident; and of other states, since we say that there are many kinds of democracy and many of oligarchy, it is not difficult to see which has the first and which the second or any other place in the order of excellence, now that we have determined which is the best. For that which is nearest to the best must of necessity be better, and that which is furthest from it worse, if we are judging absolutely and not relatively to given conditions: I say 'relatively to given conditions', since a particular government may be preferable for some, but another form may be better for others.

Section 12 to end

Any constitution must have the support of the strongest class in the state – the poor in a democracy, the rich in an oligarchy. The middle class must be included as partners in any constitution. A variety of devices are used to exclude one class or another from power. In framing a constitution, the legislator must consider three elements: the deliberative, the executive and the judicial.

BOOK FIVE

Revolutionary changes and their causes

Democracy and oligarchy are both prone to factional conflict between parties holding incompatible views on equality. In democracies revolutions can occur when demagogues attack the rich and compete for the favour of the people. In oligarchies the people may rebel against oppression, or sections of the ruling class may feud amongst themselves. Aristocracies and constitutional governments are liable to collapse when the different elements of the society are not properly balanced.

Precautions to be taken against sedition. Certain qualities required for those who hold office. Maintaining stability in monarchies.

BOOK SIX

The organisation of democracies and oligarchies

In a democracy the underlying principle is liberty. Each citizen should be in a position of equality, and therefore the poor hold more power than the rich since they are in the majority. Officers are elected and their tenure of office is short: thus all take a share in ruling by turns. The best kind of democracy is where a population of farmers, too busy to take part actively in government themselves, are content to elect to office the most notable citizens, who can be held to account and therefore prevented from governing unjustly.

Of oligarchies, the best form is that which most resembles an agricultural democracy, with a higher property qualification for the most important offices.

BOOK SEVEN

Nature of the ideal political state – its educational system

1   He who would duly enquire about the best form of a state ought first to determine which is the most eligible life; while this remains uncertain the best form of the state must also be uncertain; for, in the natural order of things, those may be expected to lead the best life who are governed in the best manner of which their circumstances admit. We ought therefore to ascertain, first of all, which is the most generally eligible life, and then whether the same life is or is not best for the state and for individuals.

Assuming that enough has been already said in exoteric discourses concerning the best life, we will now only repeat the statements contained in them. Certainly no one will dispute the propriety of that partition of goods which separates them into three classes, viz. external goods, goods of the body, and goods of the soul, or deny that the happy man must have all three. For no one would maintain that he is happy who has not in him a particle of courage or temperance or justice or prudence, who is afraid of every insect which flutters past him, and will commit any crime, however great, in order to gratify his lust of meat or drink, who will sacrifice his dearest friend for the sake of half a farthing, and is as feeble and false in mind as a child or a madman. These propositions are universally acknowledged as soon as they are uttered, but men differ about the quantity which is desirable or the relative superiority of this or that good. Some think that a very moderate amount of virtue is enough, but set no limit to their desires of wealth, property, power, reputation, and the like. To whom we reply by an appeal to facts, which easily prove that mankind do not acquire or preserve virtue by the help of external goods, but external goods by the help of virtue, and that happiness, whether consisting in pleasure or virtue, or both, is more often found with those who are most highly cultivated in their mind and in their character, and have only a moderate share of external goods, than among those who possess external goods to a useless extent but are deficient in higher qualities; and this is not only matter of experience, but, if reflected upon, will easily appear to be in accordance with reason. For, whereas external goods have a limit, like any other instrument, and all things useful are of such a nature that where there is too much of them they must either do harm, or at any rate be of no use, to their possessors, every good of the soul, the greater it is, is also of greater use, if the epithet 'useful' as well as 'noble' is appropriate to such subjects. No proof is required to show that the best state of one thing in relation to another is proportioned to the degree of excellence by which the natures corresponding to those states are separated from each other: so that, if the soul is more noble than our possessions or our bodies, both absolutely and in relation to us, it must be admitted that the best state of either has a similar ratio to the other. Again, it is for the sake of the soul that goods external and goods of the body are eligible at all, and all wise men ought to choose them for the sake of the soul, and not the soul for the sake of them.

Let us acknowledge then that each one has just so much of happiness as he has of virtue and wisdom, and of virtuous and wise action. God is a witness to us of this truth; for he is happy and blessed, not by reason of any external good, but in himself and by reason of his own nature. And herein of necessity lies the difference between good fortune and happiness; for external goods come of themselves, and chance is the author of them, but no one is just or temperate by or through chance. In like manner, and by a similar train of argument, the happy state may be shown to be that which is [morally] best and which acts rightly; and rightly it cannot act without doing right actions, and neither individual nor state can do right actions without virtue and wisdom. Thus the courage, justice, and wisdom of a state have the same form and nature as the qualities which give the individual who possesses them the name of just, wise, or temperate.

Thus much may suffice by way of preface: for I could not avoid touching upon these questions, neither could I go through all the arguments affecting them; these must be reserved for another discussion.

Let us assume then that the best life, both for individuals and states, is the life of virtue, having external goods enough for the performance of good actions. If there are any who controvert our assertion, we will in this treatise pass them over, and consider their objections hereafter.

2 There remains to be discussed the question, Whether the happiness of the individual is the same as that of the state, or different? Here again there can be

no doubt – no one denies that they are the same. For those who hold that the well-being of the individual consists in his wealth, also think that riches make the happiness of the whole state, and those who value most highly the life of a tyrant deem that city the happiest which rules over the greatest number; while they who approve an individual for his virtue say that the more virtuous a city is, the happier it is. Two points here present themselves for consideration: first (1), which is the more eligible life, that of a citizen who is a member of a state, or that of an alien who has no political ties; and again (2), which is the best form of constitution or the best condition of a state, either on the supposition that political privileges are given to all, or that they are given to a majority only? Since the good of the state and not of the individual is the proper subject of political thought and speculation, and we are engaged in a political discussion, while the first of these two points has a secondary interest for us, the latter will be the main subject of our enquiry.

Now it is evident that the form of government is best in which every man, whoever he is, can act for the best and live happily. But even those who agree in thinking that the life of virtue is the most eligible raise a question, whether the life of business and politics is or is not more eligible than one which is wholly independent of external goods, I mean than a contemplative life, which by some is maintained to be the only one worthy of a philosopher. For these two lives – the life of the philosopher and the life of the statesman – appear to have been preferred by those who have been most keen in the pursuit of virtue, both in our own and in other ages. Which is the better is a question of no small moment; for the wise man, like the wise state, will necessarily regulate his life according to the best end. There are some who think that while a despotic rule over others is the greatest injustice, to exercise a constitutional rule over them, even though not unjust, is a great impediment to a man's individual well-being. Others take an opposite view; they maintain that the true life of man is the practical and political, and that every virtue admits of being practised, quite as much by statesmen and rulers as by private individuals. Others, again, are of opinion that arbitrary and tyrannical rule alone consists with happiness; indeed, in some states the entire aim of the laws is to give men despotic power over their neighbours. And, therefore, although in most cities the laws may be said generally to be in a chaotic state, still, if they aim at anything, they aim at the maintenance of power: thus in Lacedaemon and Crete the system of education and the greater part of the laws are framed with a view to war. And in all nations which are able to gratify their ambition military power is held in esteem, for example among the Scythians and Persians and Thracians and Celts. In some nations there are even laws tending to stimulate the warlike virtues, as at Carthage, where we are told that men obtain the honour of wearing as many armlets as they have served campaigns. There was once a law in Macedonia that he who had not killed an enemy should wear a halter, and among the Scythians no one who had not slain his man was allowed to drink out of the cup which was handed round at a certain feast. Among the Iberians, a warlike nation, the number of enemies whom a man has slain is indicated by the number of spits which are fixed in the earth round his tomb; and there are numerous practices among other nations of a like kind, some of them established by law and others by custom. Yet to a reflecting mind it must appear very strange that the statesman should be always considering how he can dominate and tyrannize over others, whether they will or not. How can that which is not even lawful be the business of the statesman or the legislator? Unlawful it certainly is to rule without regard to justice, for there may be might where there is no right. The other arts and sciences offer no parallel; a physician is not expected to persuade or coerce his patients, nor a pilot the passengers in his ship. Yet many appear to think that a despotic government is a true political form, and what men affirm to be unjust and inexpedient in their own case they are not ashamed of practising towards others; they demand justice for themselves, but where other men are concerned they care nothing about it. Such behaviour is irrational; unless the one party is born to command, and the other born to serve, in which case men have a right to command, not indeed all their fellows, but only those who are intended to be subjects; just as we ought not to hunt mankind, whether for food or sacrifice, but only the animals which are intended for food or sacrifice, that is to say, such wild animals as are eatable. And surely there may be a city happy in isolation, which we will assume to be well-governed (for it is quite possible that a city thus isolated might be well-administered and have good laws); but such a city would not be constituted with any view to war or the conquest of enemies – all that sort of thing must be excluded. Hence we see very plainly that warlike pursuits, although generally to be deemed honourable, are not the supreme end of all things, but only means. And the good lawgiver should enquire how states and races of men and communities may participate in a good life, and in the happiness which is attainable by them. His enactments will not be always the same; and where there are neighbours he will have to deal with them according to their characters, and to see what duties are to be performed towards each. The end at which the best form of government should aim may be properly made a matter of future consideration.

3   Let us now address those who, while they agree that the life of virtue is the most eligible, differ about the manner of practising it. For some renounce political power, and think that the life of the freeman is different from the life of the statesman and the best of all; but others think the life of the statesman best. The argument of the latter is that he who does nothing cannot do well, and that virtuous activity is identical with happiness. To both we say: 'you are partly right and partly wrong.' The first class are right in affirming that the life of the freeman is better than the life of the despot; for there is nothing grand or noble in having the use of a slave, in so far as he is a slave; or in issuing commands about necessary things. But it is an error to suppose that every sort of rule is despotic like that of a master over slaves, for there is as great a difference between the rule over freemen and the rule over slaves as there is between slavery by nature and freedom by nature, about which I have said enough at the commencement of this treatise. And it is equally a mistake to place inactivity above action, for happiness is activity, and the actions of the just and wise are the realization of much that is noble.

But perhaps someone, accepting these premises, may still maintain that supreme power is the best of all things, because the possessors of it are able to perform the greatest number of noble actions. If so, the man who is able to rule, instead of giving up anything to his neighbour, ought rather to take away his power; and the father should make no account of his son, nor the son of his father, nor friend of friend; they should not bestow a thought on one another in comparison with this higher object, for the best is the most eligible and 'doing well' is the best. There might be some truth in such a view if we assume that robbers and plunderers attain the chief good. But this can never be; and hence we infer the view to be false. For the actions of a ruler cannot really be honourable, unless he is as much superior to other men as a husband is to a wife, or a father to his children, or a master to his slaves. And therefore he who violates the law can never recover by any success, however great, what he has already lost in departing from virtue. For equals share alike in the honourable and the just, as is just and equal. But that the unequal should be given to equals, and the unlike to those who are like, is contrary to nature, and nothing which is contrary to nature is good. If, therefore, there is anyone superior in virtue and in the power of performing the best actions, him we ought to follow and obey, but he must have the capacity for action as well as virtue.

If we are right in our view, and happiness is assumed to be virtuous activity, the active life will be the best, both for the city collectively, and for individuals. Not that a life of action must necessarily have relations to others, as some persons think, nor are those ideas only to be regarded as practical which are pursued for the sake of practical results, but much more the thoughts and contemplations which are independent and complete in themselves; since virtuous activity, and therefore action, is an end, and even in the case of external actions the directing mind is most truly said to act. Neither, again, is it necessary that states which are cut off from others and choose to live alone should be inactive; for there may be activity also in the parts; there are many ways in which the members of a state act upon one another. The same thing is equally true of every individual. If this were otherwise, god and the universe, who have no external actions over and above their own energies, would be far enough from perfection. Hence it is evident that the same life is best for each individual, and for states, and for mankind collectively.

4   Thus far by way of introduction. In what has preceded I have discussed other forms of government; in what remains, the first point to be considered is what should be the conditions of the ideal or perfect state; for the perfect state cannot exist without a due supply of the means of life. And therefore we must presuppose many purely imaginary conditions, but nothing impossible. There will be a certain number of citizens, a country in which to place them, and the like. As the weaver or shipbuilder or any other artisan must have the material proper for his work (and in proportion as this is better prepared, so will the result of his art be nobler), so the statesman or legislator must also have the materials suited to him.

First among the materials required by the statesman is population: he will consider what should be the number and character of the citizens, and then what should be the size and character of the country. Most persons think that a state in order to be happy ought to be large; but even if they are right, they have no idea what is a large and what a small state. For they judge of the size of the city by the number of the inhabitants; whereas they ought to regard, not their number, but their power. A city too, like an individual, has a work to do; and that city which is best adapted to the fulfilment of its work is to be deemed greatest, in the same sense of the word great in which Hippocrates might be called greater, not as a man, but as a physician, than someone else who was taller. And even if we reckon greatness by numbers, we ought not to include everybody, for there must always be in cities a multitude of slaves and sojourners and foreigners; but we should include those only who are members of the state, and who form an essential part of it. The number of the latter is a proof of the greatness of a city; but a city which produces numerous artisans and comparatively few soldiers cannot be great, for a great city is not to be confounded with a populous one. Moreover, experience shows that a very populous city can rarely, if ever, be well governed; since all cities which have a reputation for good government have a limit of population. We may argue on grounds of reason, and the same result will follow. For law is order, and good law is good order; but a very great multitude cannot be orderly: to introduce order into the unlimited is the work of a divine power – of such a power as holds together the universe. Beauty is realized in number and magnitude, and the state which combines magnitude with good order must necessarily be the most beautiful. To the size of states there is a limit, as there is to other things, plants, animals, implements; for none of these retain their natural power when they are too large or too small, but they either wholly lose their nature, or are spoiled. For example, a ship which is only a span long will not be a ship at all, nor a ship a quarter of a mile long; yet there may be a ship of a certain size, either too large or too small, which will still be a ship, but bad for sailing. In like manner a state when composed of too few is not as a state ought to be, self-sufficing; when of too many, though self-sufficing in all mere necessaries, it is a nation and not a state, being almost incapable of constitutional government. For who can be the general of such a vast multitude, or who the herald, unless he have the voice of a Stentor?

A state then only begins to exist when it has attained a population sufficient for a good life in the political community: it may indeed somewhat exceed this number. But, as I was saying, there must be a limit. What should be the limit will be easily ascertained by experience. For both governors and governed have duties to perform; the special functions of a governor are to command and to judge. But if the citizens of a state are to judge and to distribute offices according to merit, then they must know each other's characters; where they do not possess this knowledge, both the election to offices and the decision of lawsuits will go wrong. When the population is very large they are manifestly settled at haphazard, which clearly ought not to be. Besides, in an overpopulous state foreigners and metics will readily acquire the rights of citizens, for who will find them out? Clearly, then, the best limit of the population of a state is the largest number which suffices for the purposes of life, and can be taken in at a single view. Enough concerning the size of a city.

5 Much the same principle will apply to the territory of the state: everyone would agree in praising the state which is most entirely self-sufficing; and that must be

the state which is all-producing, for to have all things and to want nothing is sufficiency. In size and extent it should be such as may enable the inhabitants to live temperately and liberally in the enjoyment of leisure. Whether we are right or wrong in laying down this limit we will enquire more precisely hereafter, when we have occasion to consider what is the right use of property and wealth: a matter which is much disputed, because men are inclined to rush into one of two extremes, some into meanness, others into luxury.

It is not difficult to determine the general character of the territory which is required; there are, however, some points on which military authorities should be heard; they tell us that it should be difficult of access to the enemy, and easy of egress to the inhabitants. Further, we require that the land as well as the inhabitants of whom we were just now speaking should be taken in at a single view, for a country which is easily seen can be easily protected. As to the position of the city, if we could have what we wish, it should be well situated in regard both to sea or land. This then is one principle, that it should be a convenient centre for the protection of the whole country: the other is, that it should be suitable for receiving the fruits of the soil, and also for the bringing in of timber and any other products.

6 Whether a communication with the sea is beneficial to a well-ordered state or not is a question which has often been asked. It is argued that the introduction of strangers brought up under other laws, and the increase of population, will be adverse to good order (for a maritime people will always have a crowd of merchants coming and going), and that intercourse by sea is

inimical to good government. Apart from these considerations, it would be undoubtedly better, both with a view to safety and to the provision of necessaries, that the city and territory should be connected with the sea; the defenders of a country, if they are to maintain themselves against an enemy, should be easily relieved both by land and by sea; and even if they are not able to attack by sea and land at once, they will have less difficulty in doing mischief to their assailants on one element, if they themselves can use both. Moreover, it is necessary that they should import from abroad what is not found in their own country, and that they should export what they have in excess; for a city ought to be a market, not indeed for others, but for herself.

Those who make themselves a market for the world only do so for the sake of revenue, and if a state ought not to desire profit of this kind it ought not to have such an emporium. Nowadays we often see in countries and cities dockyards and harbours very conveniently placed outside the city, but not too far off; and they are kept in dependence by walls and similar fortifications. Cities thus situated manifestly reap the benefit of intercourse with their ports; and any harm which is likely to accrue may be easily guarded against by the laws, which will pronounce and determine who may hold communication with one another, and who may not.

There can be no doubt that the possession of a moderate naval force is advantageous to a city; the citizens require such a force for their own needs, and they should also be formidable to their neighbours in certain cases, or, if necessary, able to assist them by sea as well as by land. The proper number or magnitude of this naval force is relative to the character of the state;

for if her function is to take a leading part in politics, her naval power should be commensurate with the scale of her enterprises. The population of the state need not be much increased, since there is no necessity that the sailors should be citizens: the marines who have the control and command will be freemen, and belong also to the infantry; and wherever there is a dense population of *perioeci* and husbandmen, there will always be sailors more than enough. Of this we see instances at the present day. The city of Heraclea, for example, although small in comparison with many others, can man a considerable fleet. Such are our conclusions respecting the territory of the state, its harbour, its towns, its relations to the sea, and its maritime power.

7   Having spoken of the number of the citizens, we will proceed to speak of what should be their character. This is a subject which can be easily understood by anyone who casts his eye on the more celebrated states of Hellas, and generally on the distribution of races in the habitable world. Those who live in a cold climate and in [northern] Europe are full of spirit, but wanting in intelligence and skill; and therefore they keep their freedom, but have no political organization, and are incapable of ruling over others. Whereas the natives of Asia are intelligent and inventive, but they are wanting in spirit, and therefore they are always in a state of subjection and slavery. But the Hellenic race, which is situated between them, is likewise intermediate in character, being high-spirited and also intelligent. Hence it continues free, and is the best governed of any nation, and, if it could be formed into one state, would be able to rule the world. There are also similar

differences in the different tribes of Hellas; for some of them are of a one-sided nature, and are intelligent or courageous only, while in others there is a happy combination of both qualities. And clearly those whom the legislator will most easily lead to virtue may be expected to be both intelligent and courageous. Some [like Plato] say that the guardians should be friendly towards those whom they know, fierce towards those whom they do not know. Now, passion is the quality of the soul which begets friendship and inspires affection; notably the spirit within us is more stirred against our friends and acquaintances than against those who are unknown to us, when we think that we are despised by them; for which reason Archilochus, complaining of his friends, very naturally addresses his soul in these words,

'For wert thou not plagued on account of friends?'

The power of command and the love of freedom are in all men based upon this quality, for passion is commanding and invincible. Nor is it right to say that the guardians should be fierce towards those whom they do not know, for we ought not to be out of temper with anyone; and a lofty spirit is not fierce by nature, but only when excited against evil-doers. And this, as I was saying before, is a feeling which men show most strongly towards their friends if they think they have received a wrong at their hands: as indeed is reasonable; for, besides the actual injury, they seem to be deprived of a benefit by those who owe them one. Hence the saying,

'Cruel is the strife of brethren;'

and again,

'They who love in excess also hate in excess.'

Thus we have nearly determined the number and character of the citizens of our state, and also the size and nature of their territory. I say 'nearly', for we ought not to require the same minuteness in theory as in fact.

8 As in other natural compounds the conditions of a composite whole are not necessarily organic parts of it, so in a state or in any other combination forming a unity not everything is a part, which is a necessary condition. The members of an association have necessarily some one thing the same and common to all, in which they share equally or unequally; for example, food or land or any other thing. But where there are two things of which one is a means and the other an end, they have nothing in common except that the one receives what the other produces. Such, for example, is the relation in which workmen and tools stand to their work; the house and the builder have nothing in common, but the art of the builder is for the sake of the house. And so states require property, but property, even though living beings are included in it, is no part of a state; for a state is not a community of living beings only, but a community of equals, aiming at the best life possible. Now, whereas happiness is the highest good, being a realization and perfect practice of virtue, which some attain, while others have little or none of it, the various qualities of men are clearly the reason why there are various kinds of states and many forms of government; for different men seek after happiness in different ways and by different means, and so make for themselves different modes of life and forms of government. We

must see also how many things are indispensable to the existence of a state, for what we call the parts of a state will be found among them. Let us then enumerate the functions of a state, and we shall easily elicit what we want.

First, there must be food; secondly, arts, for life requires many instruments; thirdly, there must be arms, for the members of a community have need of them in order to maintain authority both against disobedient subjects and against external assailants; fourthly, there must be a certain amount of revenue, both for internal needs and for the purposes of war; fifthly, or rather first, there must be a care of religion, which is commonly called worship; sixthly, and most necessary of all, there must be a power of deciding what is for the public interest, and what is just in men's dealings with one another.

These are the things which every state may be said to need. For a state is not a mere aggregate of persons, but a union of them sufficing for the purposes of life; and if any of these things be wanting, it is simply impossible that the community can be self-sufficing. A state then should be framed with a view to the fulfilment of these functions. There must be husbandmen to procure food, and artisans, and a warlike and a wealthy class, and priests, and judges to decide what is just and expedient.

9 Having determined these points, we have in the next place to consider whether all ought to share in every sort of occupation. Shall every man be at once husbandman, artisan, councillor, judge, or shall we suppose the several occupations just mentioned assigned to different persons? Or, thirdly, shall some

employments be assigned to individuals and others common to all? The question, however, does not occur in every state; as we were saying, all may be shared by all, or not all by all, but only some by some; and hence arise the differences of states, for in democracies all share in all, in oligarchies the opposite practice prevails. Now, since we are here speaking of the best form of government, and that under which the state will be most happy (and happiness, as has been already said, cannot exist without virtue), it clearly follows that in the state which is best governed the citizens who are absolutely and not merely relatively just men must not lead the life of mechanics or tradesmen, for such a life is ignoble and inimical to virtue. Neither must they be husbandmen, since leisure is necessary both for the development of virtue and the performance of political duties.

Again, there is in a state a class of warriors, and another of councillors, who advise about the expedient and determine matters of law, and these seem in an especial manner parts of a state. Now, should these two classes be distinguished, or are both functions to be assigned to the same persons? Here again there is no difficulty in seeing that both functions will in one way belong to the same, in another, to different persons. To different persons in so far as their employments are suited to different ages of life, for the one requires wisdom, and the other strength. But on the other hand, since it is an impossible thing that those who are able to use or to resist force should be willing to remain always in subjection, from this point of view the persons are the same; for those who carry arms can always determine the fate of the constitution. It remains therefore that both functions of government should be entrusted to the same persons, not, however, at the same time, but in the order prescribed by nature, who has given to young men strength and to older men wisdom. Such a distribution of duties will be expedient and also just, for it is in accordance with desert. Besides, the ruling class should be the owners of property, for they are citizens, and the citizens of a state should be in good circumstances; whereas mechanics or any other class whose art excludes the art of virtue have no share in the state. This follows from our first principle, for happiness cannot exist without virtue, and a city is not to be termed happy in regard to a portion of the citizens, but in regard to them all. And clearly property should be in their hands, since the husbandmen will of necessity be slaves or barbarians or *perioeci*.

Of the classes enumerated there remain only the priests, and the manner in which their office is to be regulated is obvious. No husbandman or mechanic should be appointed to it; for the gods should receive honour from the citizens only. Now since the body of the citizens is divided into two classes, the warriors and the councillors; and it is beseeming that the worship of the gods should be duly performed, and also a rest provided in their service for those who from age have given up active life – to the old men of these two classes should be assigned the duties of the priesthood.

We have shown what are the necessary conditions, and what the parts of a state: husbandmen, craftsmen, and labourers of all kinds are necessary to the existence of states, but the parts of the state are the warriors and councillors. And these are distinguished severally from one another, the distinction being in some cases permanent, in others not.

Sections 10–13

Historical digression on the separation of the military class from the agricultural class. Land should be distributed amongst those who share in the constitution, but farmed by slaves or foreign serfs. When choosing the site for a city, account must be taken of public health, general convenience and military security. Certain arrangements may be made for having common meals.

General theory of happiness. For a city, this is to be achieved through creating good citizens.

14 Since every political society is composed of rulers and subjects, let us consider whether the relations of one to the other should interchange or be permanent. For the education of the citizens will necessarily vary with the answer given to this question. Now, if some men excelled others in the same degree in which gods and heroes are supposed to excel mankind in general, having in the first place a great advantage even in their bodies, and secondly in their minds, so that the superiority of the governors over their subjects was patent and undisputed, it would clearly be better that once for all the one class should rule and the others serve. But since this is unattainable, and kings have no marked superiority over their subjects, such as Scylax affirms to be found among the Indians, it is obviously necessary on many grounds that all the citizens alike should take their turn of governing and being governed. Equality consists in the same treatment of similar persons, and no government can stand which is not founded upon justice. For [if the government

be unjust] everyone in the country unites with the governed in the desire to have a revolution, and it is an impossibility that the members of the government can be so numerous as to be stronger than all their enemies put together. Yet that governors should excel their subjects is undeniable. How all this is to be effected, and in what way they will respectively share in the government, the legislator has to consider. The subject has been already mentioned. Nature herself has given the principle of choice when she made a difference between old and young (though they are really the same in kind), of whom she fitted the one to govern and the others to be governed. No one takes offence at being governed when he is young, nor does he think himself better than his governors, especially if he will enjoy the same privilege when he reaches the required age.

We conclude that from one point of view governors and governed are identical, and from another different. And therefore their education must be the same and also different. For he who would learn to command well must, as men say, first of all learn to obey. As I observed in the first part of this treatise, there is one rule which is for the sake of the rulers and another rule which is for the sake of the ruled; the former is a despotic, the latter a free government. Some commands differ not in the thing commanded, but in the intention with which they are imposed. Wherefore, many apparently menial offices are an honour to the free youth by whom they are performed; for actions do not differ as honourable or dishonourable in themselves so much as in the end and intention of them. But since we say that the virtue of the citizen and ruler is the same as that of the good man, and that the same person must first be a subject and then a ruler, the legislator has to see that they become good men, and by what means this may be accomplished, and what is the end of the perfect life.

Now the soul of man is divided into two parts, one of which has reason in itself, and the other, not having reason in itself, is able to obey reason. And we call a man good because he has the virtues of these two parts. In which of them the end is more likely to be found is no matter of doubt to those who adopt our division; for in the world both of nature and of art the inferior always exists for the sake of the better or superior, and the better or superior is that which has reason. The reason too, in our ordinary way of speaking, is divided into two parts, for there is a practical and a speculative reason, and there must be a corresponding division of actions; the actions of the naturally better principle are to be preferred by those who have it in their power to attain to both or to all, for that is always to everyone the most eligible which is the highest attainable by him. The whole of life is further divided into two parts, business and leisure, war and peace, and all actions into those which are necessary and useful, and those which are honourable. And the preference given to one or the other class of actions must necessarily be like the preference given to one or other part of the soul and its actions over the other; there must be war for the sake of peace, business for the sake of leisure, things useful and necessary for the sake of things honourable. All these points the statesman should keep in view when he frames his laws; he should consider the parts of the soul and their functions, and above all the better and the end; he should also remember the diversities of human lives and actions. For men must engage in business and go to war, but leisure and peace are better; they must do what is necessary and useful, but what is honourable is better. In such principles children and persons of every age which requires education should be trained. Whereas even the Hellenes of the present day, who are reputed to be best governed, and the legislators who gave them their constitutions, do not appear to have framed their governments with a regard to the best end, or to have given them laws and education with a view to all the virtues, but in a vulgar spirit have fallen back on those which promised to be more useful and profitable. Many modern writers have taken a similar view: they commend the Lacedaemonian constitution, and praise the legislator for making conquest and war his sole aim, a doctrine which may be refuted by argument and has long ago been refuted by facts. For most men desire empire in the hope of accumulating the goods of fortune; and on this ground Thibron and all those who have written about the Lacedaemonian constitution have praised their legislator, because the Lacedaemonians, by a training in hardships, gained great power. But surely they are not a happy people now that their empire has passed away, nor was their legislator right. How ridiculous is the result, if, while they are continuing in the observances of his laws and no one interferes with them they have lost the better part of life. These writers further err about the sort of government which the legislator should approve, for the government of freemen is noble, and implies more virtue than despotic government. Neither is a city to be deemed happy or a legislator to be praised because he trains his citizens to conquer and obtain dominion over their neighbours, for there is great evil in this. On a similar principle any citizen who could, would obviously try to obtain the power in his own state – the crime which the Lacedaemonians accused king Pausanias of attempting, although he had so great honour already. No such principle and no law having this object is either statesmanlike or useful or right. For the same things are best both for individuals and for states, and these are the things which the legislator ought to implant in the minds of his citizens. Neither should men study war with a view to the enslavement of those who do not deserve to be enslaved; but first of all they should provide against their own enslavement, and in the second place obtain empire for the good of the governed, and not for the sake of exercising a general despotism, and in the third place they should seek to be masters only over those who deserve to be slaves. Facts, as well as arguments, prove that the legislator should direct all his military and other measures to the provision of leisure and the establishment of peace. For most of these military states are safe only while they are at war, but fall when they have acquired their empire; like unused iron they lose their edge in time of peace. And for this the legislator is to blame, he never having taught them how to lead the life of peace.

15 Since the end of individuals and of states is the same, the end of the best man and of the best state must also be the same; it is therefore evident that there ought to exist in both of them the virtues of leisure; for peace, as has been often repeated, is the end of war, and leisure of toil. But leisure and cultivation may be promoted, not only by those virtues which are practised in leisure, but also by some of those which are useful to business. For many necessaries of life have to

be supplied before we can have leisure. Therefore a city must be temperate and brave, and able to endure: for truly, as the proverb says, 'There is no leisure for slaves', and those who cannot face danger like men are the slaves of any invader. Courage and endurance are required for business and intellectual virtue for leisure, temperance and justice for both, more especially in times of peace and leisure, for war compels men to be just and temperate, whereas the enjoyment of good fortune and the leisure which comes with peace tends to make them insolent. Those, then, who seem to be the best off and to be in the possession of every good, have special need of justice and temperance – for example, those (if such there be, as the poets say) who dwell in the Islands of the Blest; they above all will need philosophy and temperance and justice, and all the more the more leisure they have, living in the midst of abundance. There is no difficulty in seeing why the state that would be happy and good ought to have these virtues. If it be disgraceful in men not to be able to use the goods of life, it is peculiarly disgraceful not to be able to use them in time of peace – to show excellent qualities in action and war, and when they have peace and leisure to be no better than slaves. Wherefore we should not practise virtue after the manner of the Lacedaemonians. For they, while agreeing with other men in their conception of the highest goods, differ from the rest of mankind in thinking that they are to be obtained by the practice of a single virtue. And since these goods and the enjoyment of them are clearly greater than the enjoyment derived from the virtues of which they are the end, we must now consider how and by what means they are to be attained.

We have already determined that nature and habit and reason are required, and what should be the character of the citizens has also been defined by us. But we have still to consider whether the training of early life is to be that of reason or habit, for these two must accord, and when in accord they will then form the best of harmonies. Reason may make mistakes and fail in attaining the highest ideal of life, and there may be a like evil influence of habit. Thus much is clear in the first place, that, as in all other things, generation starts from a beginning, and that the ends of some beginnings are related to another end. Now, in men reason and mind are the end towards which nature strives, so that the generation and moral discipline of the citizens ought to be ordered with a view to them. In the second place, as the soul and body are two, we see also that there are two parts of the soul, the rational and the irrational, and two corresponding states – reason and appetite. And as the body is prior in order of generation to the soul, so the irrational is prior to the rational. The proof is that anger and will and desire are implanted in children from their very birth, but reason and understanding are developed as they grow older. Wherefore, the care of the body ought to precede that of the soul, and the training of the appetitive part should follow: none the less our care of it must be for the sake of the reason, and our care of the body for the sake of the soul.

16 Since the legislator should begin by considering how the frames of the children whom he is rearing may be as good as possible, his first care will be about marriage – at what age should his citizens marry, and who are fit to marry? In legislating on this subject he

ought to consider the persons and their relative ages, that there may be no disproportion in them, and that they may not differ in their bodily powers, as will be the case if the man is still able to beget children while the woman is unable to bear them, or the woman able to bear while the man is unable to beget, for from these causes arise quarrels and differences between married persons. Secondly, he must consider the time at which the children will succeed to their parents; there ought not to be too great an interval of age, for then the parents will be too old to derive any pleasure from their affection, or to be of any use of them. Nor ought they to be too nearly of an age; to youthful marriages there are many objections – the children will be wanting in respect to their parents, who will seem to be their contemporaries, and disputes will arise in the management of the household. Thirdly, and this is the point from which we digressed, the legislator must mould to his will the frames of newly-born children. Almost all these objects may be secured by attention to one point. Since the time of generation is commonly limited within the age of seventy years in the case of a man, and of fifty in the case of a woman, the commencement of the union should conform to these periods. The union of male and female when too young is bad for the procreation of children; in all other animals the offspring of the young are small and ill-developed, and generally of the female sex, and therefore also in man, as is proved by the fact that in those cities in which men and women are accustomed to marry young, the people are small and weak; in childbirth also younger women suffer more, and more of them die; some persons say that this was the meaning of the response once given to the Troezenians – ['Shear not the young field'] – the oracle really meant that many died because they married too young; it had nothing to do with the ingathering of the harvest. It also conduces to temperance not to marry too soon; for women who marry early are apt to be wanton; and in men too the bodily frame is stunted if they marry while they are growing (for there is a time when the growth of the body ceases). Women should marry when they are about eighteen years of age, and men at seven-and-thirty; then they are in the prime of life, and the decline in the powers of both will coincide. Further, the children, if their birth takes place at the time that may reasonably be expected, will succeed in their prime, when the fathers are already in the decline of life, and have nearly reached their term of three-score years and ten.

Thus much of the age proper for marriage: the season of the year should also be considered; according to our present custom, people generally limit marriage to the season of winter, and they are right. The precepts of physicians and natural philosophers about generation should also be studied by the parents themselves; the physicians give good advice about the right age of the body, and the natural philosophers about the winds; of which they prefer the north to the south.

What constitution in the parent is most advantageous to the offspring is a subject which we will hereafter consider when we speak of the education of children, and we will only make a few general remarks at present. The temperament of an athlete is not suited to the life of a citizen, or to health, or to the procreation of children, any more than the valetudinarian or exhausted constitution, but one which is in a mean between them. A man's constitution should be inured to labour, but not to labour which is excessive or of one sort only, such as is practised by athletes; he should be capable of all the actions of a freeman. These remarks apply equally to both parents.

Women who are with child should be careful of themselves; they should take exercise and have a nourishing diet. The first of these prescriptions the legislator will easily carry into effect by requiring that they shall take a walk daily to some temple, where they can worship the gods who preside over birth. Their minds, however, unlike their bodies, they ought to keep unexercised, for the offspring derive their natures from their mothers as plants do from the earth.

As to the exposure and rearing of children, let there be a law that no deformed child shall live, but where there are too many (for in our state population has a limit), when couples have children in excess, and the state of feeling is averse to the exposure of offspring, let abortion be procured before sense and life have begun; what may or may not be lawfully done in these cases depends on the question of life and sensation.

And now, having determined at what ages men and women are to begin their union, let us also determine how long they shall continue to beget and bear offspring for the state; men who are too old, like men who are too young, produce children who are defective in body and mind; the children of very old men are weakly. The limit, then, should be the age which is the prime of their intelligence, and this in most persons, according to the notion of some poets who measure life by periods of seven years, is about fifty; at four or five years later, they should cease from having families; and from that time forward only cohabit with one another for the sake of health, or for some similar reason.

As to adultery, let it be held disgraceful for any man or woman to be unfaithful when they are married, and called husband and wife. If during the time of bearing children anything of the sort occur, let the guilty person be punished with a loss of privileges in proportion to the offence.

17 After the children have been born, the manner of rearing them may be supposed to have a great effect on their bodily strength. It would appear from the example of animals, and of those nations who desire to create the military habit, that the food which has most milk in it is best suited to human beings; but the less wine the better, if they would escape disease. Also all the motions to which children can be subjected at their early age are very useful. But in order to preserve their tender limbs from distortion, some nations have had recourse to mechanical appliances which straighten their bodies. To accustom children to the cold from their earliest years is also an excellent practice, which greatly conduces to health, and hardens them for military service. Hence many barbarians have a custom of plunging their children at birth into a cold stream; others, like the Celts, clothe them in a light wrapper only. For human nature should be early habituated to endure all which by habit it can be made to endure; but the process must be gradual. And children, from their natural warmth, may be easily trained to bear cold. Such care should attend them in the first stage of life.

The next period lasts to the age of five; during this no demand should be made upon the child for study or labour, lest its growth be impeded; and there should be sufficient motion to prevent the limbs from being inactive. This can be secured, among other ways, by amusement, but the amusement should not be vulgar or tiring or riotous. The Directors of Education, as they are termed, should be careful what tales or stories the children hear, for the sports of children are designed to prepare the way for the business of later life, and should be for the most part imitations of the occupations which they will hereafter pursue in earnest. Those are wrong who [like Plato] in the *Laws* attempt to check the loud crying and screaming of children, for these contribute towards their growth, and, in a manner, exercise their bodies. Straining the voice has an effect similar to that produced by the retention of the breath in violent exertions. Besides other duties, the Directors of Education should have an eye to their bringing up, and should take care that they are left as little as possible with slaves. For until they are seven years old they must live at home; and therefore, even at this early age, all that is mean and low should be banished from their sight and hearing. Indeed, there is nothing which the legislator should be more careful to drive away than indecency of speech; for the light utterance of shameful words is akin to shameful actions. The young especially should never be allowed to repeat or hear anything of the sort. A freeman who is found saying or doing what is forbidden, if he be too young as yet to have the privilege of a place at the public table, should be disgraced and beaten, and an elder person degraded as his slavish conduct deserves. And since we do not allow improper language, clearly we should also banish pictures or tales which are indecent. Let the rulers take care that there be no image or picture representing unseemly actions, except in the temples of those gods at whose festivals the law permits even ribaldry, and whom the law also permits to be worshipped by persons of mature age on behalf of themselves, their children, and their wives. But the legislator should not allow youth to be hearers of satirical iambic verses or spectators of comedy until they are of an age to sit at the public tables and to drink strong wine; by that time education will have armed them against the evil influences of such representations.

We have made these remarks in a cursory manner – they are enough for the present occasion; but hereafter we will return to the subject and after a fuller discussion determine whether such liberty should or should not be granted, and in what way granted, if at all. Theodorus, the tragic actor, was quite right in saying that he would not allow any other actor, not even if he were quite second-rate, to enter before himself, because the spectators grew fond of the voices which they first heard. And the same principle of association applies universally to things as well as persons, for we always like best whatever comes first. And therefore youth should be kept strangers to all that is bad, and especially to things which suggest vice or hate. When the five years have passed away, during the two following years they must look on at the pursuits which they are hereafter to learn. There are two periods of life into which education has to be divided – from seven to the age of puberty, and onwards to the age of one-and-twenty. [The poets] who divide ages by sevens are not always right: we should rather adhere to the divisions actually made by nature; for the deficiencies of nature are what art and education seek to fill up.

Let us then first enquire if any regulations are to be laid down about children, and secondly, whether the care of them should be the concern of the state or of private individuals – which latter is in our own day the common custom – and in the third place, what these regulations should be.

BOOK EIGHT

Education (continued)

1 No one will doubt that the legislator should direct his attention above all to the education of youth, or that the neglect of education does harm to states. The citizen should be moulded to suit the form of government under which he lives. For each government has a peculiar character which originally formed and which continues to preserve it. The character of democracy creates democracy, and the character of oligarchy creates oligarchy; and always the better the character, the better the government.

Now for the exercise of any faculty or art a previous training and habituation are required; clearly therefore for the practice of virtue. And since the whole city has one end, it is manifest that education should be one and the same for all, and that it should be public, and not private – not as at present, when everyone looks after his own children separately, and gives them separate instruction of the sort which he thinks best; the training in things which are of common interest should be the same for all. Neither must we suppose that any one of the citizens belongs to himself, for they all belong to the state, and are each of them a part of the state, and the care of each part is inseparable from the care of the whole. In this particular the Lacedaemonians are to be praised, for they take the greatest pains about their children, and make education the business of the state.

2   That education should be regulated by law and
should be an affair of state is not to be denied, but what
should be the character of this public education, and
how young persons should be educated, are questions
which remain to be considered. For mankind are by
no means agreed about the things to be taught,
whether we look to virtue or the best life. Neither is
it clear whether education is more concerned with
intellectual or with moral virtue. The existing practice
is perplexing; no one knows on what principle we
should proceed – should the useful in life, or should
virtue, or should the higher knowledge, be the aim of
our training; all three opinions have been entertained.
Again, about the means there is no agreement; for
different persons, starting with different ideas about
the nature of virtue, naturally disagree about the
practice of it. There can be no doubt that children
should be taught those useful things which are really
necessary, but not all things; for occupations are
divided into liberal and illiberal; and to young children
should be imparted only such kinds of knowledge as
will be useful to them without vulgarizing them. And
any occupation, art, or science, which makes the body
or soul or mind of the freeman less fit for the practice
or exercise of virtue, is vulgar; wherefore we call those
arts vulgar which tend to deform the body, and
likewise all paid employments, for they absorb and
degrade the mind. There are also some liberal arts
quite proper for a freeman to acquire, but only in a
certain degree, and if he attend to them too closely, in
order to attain perfection in them, the same evil effects
will follow. The object also which a man sets before
him makes a great difference; if he does or learns
anything for his own sake or for the sake of his friends,

or with a view to excellence, the action will not appear illiberal; but if done for the sake of others, the very same action will be thought menial and servile. The received subjects of instruction, as I have already remarked, are partly of a liberal and partly of an illiberal character.

3   The customary branches of education are in number four; they are – (1) reading and writing, (2) gymnastic exercises, (3) music, to which is sometimes added (4) drawing. Of these, reading and writing and drawing are regarded as useful for the purposes of life in a variety of ways, and gymnastic exercises are thought to infuse courage. Concerning music a doubt may be raised – in our own day most men cultivate it for the sake of pleasure, but originally it was included in education, because nature herself, as has been often said, requires that we should be able not only to work well, but to use leisure well; for, as I must repeat once and again, the first principle of all action is leisure. Both are required, but leisure is better than occupation; and therefore the question must be asked in good earnest, what ought we to do when at leisure? Clearly we ought not to be amusing ourselves, for then amusement would be the end of life. But if this is inconceivable, and yet amid serious occupations amusement is needed more than at other times (for he who is hard at work has need of relaxation, and amusement gives relaxation, whereas occupation is always accompanied with exertion and effort), at suitable times we should introduce amusements, and they should be our medicines, for the emotion which they create in the soul is a relaxation, and from the pleasure we obtain rest.

Leisure of itself gives pleasure and happiness and enjoyment of life, which are experienced, not by the busy man, but by those who have leisure. For he who is occupied has in view some end which he has not attained; but happiness is an end which all men deem to be accompanied with pleasure and not with pain. This pleasure, however, is regarded differently by different persons, and varies according to the habit of individuals; the pleasure of the best man is the best, and springs from the noblest sources. It is clear, then, that there are branches of learning and education which we must study with a view to the enjoyment of leisure, and these are to be valued for their own sake; whereas those kinds of knowledge which are useful in business are to be deemed necessary, and exist for the sake of other things. And therefore our fathers admitted music into education, not on the ground either of its necessity or utility, for it is not necessary, nor indeed useful in the same manner as reading and writing, which are useful in money-making, in the management of a household, in the acquisition of knowledge and in political life, nor like drawing, useful for a more correct judgment of the works of artists, nor again like gymnastic, which gives health and strength; for neither of these is to be gained from music. There remains, then, the use of music for intellectual enjoyment in leisure; which appears to have been the reason of its introduction, this being one of the ways in which it is thought that a freeman should pass his leisure; as Homer says –

'How good is it to invite men to the pleasant feast,'

and afterwards he speaks of others whom he describes as inviting

'The bard who would delight them all.'

And in another place Odysseus says there is no better way of passing life than when

'Men's hearts are merry and the banqueters in the hall, sitting in order, hear the voice of the minstrel.'

It is evident, then, that there is a sort of education in which parents should train their sons, not as being useful or necessary, but because it is liberal or noble. Whether this is of one kind only, or of more than one, and if so, what they are, and how they are to be imparted, must hereafter be determined. Thus much we are now in a position to say that the ancients witness to us; for their opinion may be gathered from the fact that music is one of the received and traditional branches of education. Further, it is clear that children should be instructed in some useful things – for example, in reading and writing – not only for their usefulness, but also because many other sorts of knowledge are acquired through them. With a like view they may be taught drawing, not to prevent their making mistakes in their own purchases, or in order that they may not be imposed upon in the buying or selling of articles, but rather because it makes them judges of the beauty of the human form. To be always seeking after the useful does not become free and exalted souls. Now it is clear that in education habit must go before reason, and the body before the mind; and therefore boys should be handed over to the trainer, who creates in them the proper habit of body, and to the wrestling-master, who teaches them their exercises.

4   Of those states which in our own day seem to take the greatest care of children, some aim at producing in them an athletic habit, but they only injure their forms and stunt their growth. Although the Lacedaemonians have not fallen into this mistake, yet they brutalize their children by laborious exercises which they think will make them courageous. But in truth, as we have often repeated, education should not be exclusively directed to this or to any other single end. And even if we suppose the Lacedaemonians to be right in their end, they do not attain it. For among barbarians and among animals courage is found associated, not with the greatest ferocity, but with a gentle and lion-like temper. There are many races who are ready enough to kill and eat men, such as the Achaeans and Heniochi, who both live about the Black Sea; and there are other inland tribes, as bad or worse, who all live by plunder, but have no courage. It is notorious that the Lacedaemonians, while they were themselves assiduous in their laborious drill, were superior to others, but now they are beaten both in war and gymnastic exercises. For their ancient superiority did not depend on their mode of training their youth, but only on the circumstance that they trained them at a time when others did not. Hence we may infer that what is noble, not what is brutal, should have the first place; no wolf or other wild animal will face a really noble danger; such dangers are for the brave man. And parents who devote their children to gymnastics while they neglect their necessary education, in reality vulgarize them; for they make them useful to the state in one quality only, and even in this the argument proves them to be inferior to others. We should judge the Lacedaemonians not from what they have been,

but from what they are; for now they have rivals who compete with their education; formerly they had none.

It is an admitted principle that gymnastic exercises should be employed in education, and that for children they should be of a lighter kind, avoiding severe regimen or painful toil, lest the growth of the body be impaired. The evil of excessive training in early years is strikingly proved by the example of the Olympic victors; for not more than two or three of them have gained a prize both as boys and as men; their early training and severe gymnastic exercises exhausted their constitutions. When boyhood is over, three years should be spent in other studies; the period of life which follows may then be devoted to hard exercise and strict regimen. Men ought not to labour at the same time with their minds and with their bodies; for the two kinds of labour are opposed to one another – the labour of the body impedes the mind, and the labour of the mind the body.

5   Concerning music there are some questions which we have already raised; these we may now resume and carry further; and our remarks will serve as a prelude to this or any other discussion of the subject. It is not easy to determine the nature of music, or why anyone should have a knowledge of it. Shall we say, for the sake of amusement and relaxation, like sleep or drinking, which are not good in themselves, but are pleasant, and at the same time 'make care to cease', as Euripides says? And therefore men rank them with music, and make use of all three – sleep, drinking, music – to which some add dancing. Or shall we argue that music conduces to virtue, on the ground that it can form our

minds and habituate us to true pleasures as our bodies are made by gymnastic to be of a certain character? Or shall we say that it contributes to the enjoyment of leisure and mental cultivation, which is a third alternative? Now obviously youth are not to be instructed with a view to their amusement, for learning is no pleasure, but is accompanied with pain. Neither is intellectual enjoyment suitable to boys of that age, for it is the end, and that which is imperfect cannot attain the perfect or end. But perhaps it may be said that boys learn music for the sake of the amusement which they will have when they are grown up. If so, why should they learn themselves, and not, like the Persian and Median kings, enjoy the pleasure and instruction which is derived from hearing others? (for surely skilled persons who have made music the business and profession of their lives will be better performers than those who practise only to learn). If they must learn music, on the same principle they should learn cookery, which is absurd. And even granting that music may form the character, the objection still holds: why should we learn ourselves? Why cannot we attain true pleasure and form a correct judgment from hearing others, like the Lacedaemonians? – for they, without learning music, nevertheless can correctly judge, as they say, of good and bad melodies. Or again, if music should be used to promote cheerfulness and refined intellectual enjoyment, the objection still remains – why should we learn ourselves instead of enjoying the performances of others? We may illustrate what we are saying by our conception of the gods; for in the poets Zeus does not himself sing or play on the lyre. Nay, we call professional performers vulgar; no freeman would play or sing unless he were intoxicated or in jest. But these matters may be left for the present.

The first question is whether music is or is not to be a part of education. Of the three things mentioned in our discussion, which is it? – education or amusement or intellectual enjoyment, for it may be reckoned under all three, and seems to share in the nature of all of them. Amusement is for the sake of relaxation, and relaxation is of necessity sweet, for it is the remedy of pain caused by toil, and intellectual enjoyment is universally acknowledged to contain an element not only of the noble but of the pleasant, for happiness is made up of both. All men agree that music is one of the pleasantest things, whether with or without song; as Musaeus says,

'Song is to mortals of all things the sweetest.'

Hence and with good reason it is introduced into social gatherings and entertainments, because it makes the hearts of men glad: so that on this ground alone we may assume that the young ought to be trained in it. For innocent pleasures are not only in harmony with the perfect end of life, but they also provide relaxation. And whereas men rarely attain the end, but often rest by the way and amuse themselves, not only with a view to some good, but also for the pleasure's sake, it may be well for them at times to find a refreshment in music. It sometimes happens that men make amusement the end, for the end probably contains some element of pleasure, though not any ordinary or lower pleasure; but they mistake the lower for the higher, and in seeking for the one find the other, since every pleasure has a likeness to the end of action. For the end is not eligible, nor do the pleasures which we have described exist for the sake of any future good but of the past, that is to say, they are the alleviation of past toils and pains. And we may infer this to be the reason why men seek happiness from common pleasures. But music is pursued, not only as an alleviation of past toil, but also as providing recreation. And who can say whether, having this use, it may not also have a nobler one? In addition to this common pleasure, felt and shared in by all (for the pleasure given by music is natural, and therefore adapted to all ages and characters), may it not have also some influence over the character and the soul? It must have such an influence if characters are affected by it. And that they are so affected is proved by the power which the songs of Olympus and of many others exercise; for beyond question they inspire enthusiasm, and enthusiasm is an emotion of the ethical part of the soul. Besides, when men hear imitations, even unaccompanied by melody or rhythm, their feelings move in sympathy. Since, then, music is a pleasure, and virtue consists in rejoicing and loving and hating aright, there is clearly nothing which we are so much concerned to acquire and to cultivate as the power of forming right judgments, and of taking delight in good dispositions and noble actions. Rhythm and melody supply imitations of anger and gentleness, and also of courage and temperance and of virtues and vices in general, which hardly fall short of the actual affections, as we know from our own experience, for in listening to such strains our souls undergo a change. The habit of feeling pleasure or pain at mere representations is not far removed from the same feeling about realities; for example, if anyone delights in the sight of a statue for its beauty only, it necessarily follows that the sight of the original will be pleasant to him. No other sense, such as taste or touch, has any resemblance to moral qualities; in sight only there is a little, for figures are to some extent of a moral character, and [so far] all participate in the feeling about them. Again, figures and colours are not imitations, but signs of moral habits, and these signs occur only when the body is under the influence of emotions. The connexion of them with morals is slight, but in so far as there is any, young men should be taught to look, not at the works of Pauson, but at those of Polygnotus, or any other painter or statuary who expresses moral ideas. On the other hand, even in mere melodies there is an imitation of character, for the musical modes differ essentially from one another, and those who hear them are differently affected by each. Some of them make men sad and grave, like the so-called Mixolydian, others enfeeble the mind, like the relaxed harmonies, others, again, produce a moderate and settled temper, which appears to be the peculiar effect of the Dorian; the Phrygian inspires enthusiasm. The whole subject has been well treated by philosophical writers on this branch of education, and they confirm their arguments by facts. The same principles apply to rhythms: some have a character of rest, others of motion, and of these latter again, some have a more vulgar, others a nobler movement. Enough has been said to show that music has a power of forming the character, and should therefore be introduced into the education of the young. The study is suited to the stage of youth, for young persons will not, if they can help, endure anything which is not sweetened by pleasure, and music has a natural sweetness. There seems to be in us a sort of affinity to harmonies and rhythms, which makes some philosophers say that the soul is a harmony, others, that she possesses harmony.

Section 6 to end

A musical education should include learning to sing and play. But pupils should not be encouraged to aim at a professional level, for that would make them like hired workers.

The melodies and modes suitable for training of the young.